Library of
Davidson College

THE MAKING OF SYMBOLIC INTERACTIONISM

The Making of Symbolic Interactionism

Paul Rock

Rowman and Littlefield
Totowa, New Jersey

© Paul Rock 1979
All rights reserved. No part of this publication may be reproduced or transmitted, in any form or by any means, without permission

Library of Congress Cataloging in Publication Data
Rock, Paul Elliott.
   The making of symbolic interactionism.
   Includes bibliographical references and index.
   1. Symbolic interactionism. 2. Sociology--Great Britain. I. Title.
HM24.R64   301   78-23337
ISBN 0-8476-6130-X

First published in the United States 1979 by
Rowman and Littlefield, Totowa, New Jersey

Printed in Great Britain

For Peter Manning and Robert Scott

Contents

Preface	ix
1 Symbolic Interactionism as an Understated Sociology	1
2 The Roots of Symbolic Interactionism	24
3 Pragmatism and Symbolic Interactionism	59
4 The Self	102
5 Problematic Aspects of the Interactionist Idea of the Self	147
6 Participant Observation	178
7 Conclusion	217
Notes	239
Index	265

Preface

There was a perverse strain in much of the sociology which I learned as an undergraduate. My education introduced me to a number of simple principles. Like many others, I was encouraged to distrust ideas that stemmed from my own experience and reason. Sociology was presented as a science whose precepts necessarily contradicted lay thought and common sense. Its competence was emphasised by the scale of contradiction. Ideas which seemed plausible and sensible were most liable to be in error. Those which were extraordinary and incredible became candidates for serious attention. I was led to recognise distinctions between manifest and latent functions, ideology and science, false consciousness and truth. If assertions were not amazing or confusing, they were likely to be either trivial or false. In a sense, then, the world was turned on its head. All appearances became deceptive, and descriptions which deferred to them were defined as 'journalistic' or superficial.

Sociology thus became a form of high mystery. The initiate was required to shed worldly knowledge and take on the trappings of intellectual innocence and naïvety. Learning revealed the hidden order of things, an order which was immeasurably complex, profound and subtle. Simple analyses were redefined as simplistic; focused studies were held to lack context and breadth; and interest in meaning indicated an improper fascination with the epiphenomenal. For a while I was almost made to believe in a nightmare realm in which all was strange and unexpected. Sociology being a mystery, abstruseness became a guarantee of authentic knowledge. The more opaque the analysis, the more arcane the thought, the greater was the possibility of an argument being profound and illuminating. My fellow students toyed with Talcott Parsons, the graver Marxists and the weighty debates of grand sociology. They dismissed sociology which was literate and lucid because it smacked of insubstantial and frivolous thought.

It took me some time to discover that there were other sociological possibilities. Anyone who studied symbolic interactionism in the

England of the early 1960s had to be an autodidact. Sociology students had to build up a working knowledge of the approach in a solitary and faltering fashion. They had to assemble bibliographies and intellectual histories without any assistance from those who had been formally trained in the sociology. After all, there was no older generation of British interactionists. Moreover a Ph.D. from a British university hinges on an examination by thesis alone. It is acquired without the organised co-operation and preparation that prevail in North American centres of graduate education. Instead of the joint work that is imposed by mandatory courses, the British student proceeds in an environment of structured neglect. Intellectual innovation is encouraged, but so is solitude. There are real bars to the development of a network of peers and patrons. There is no orderly arrangement of meetings between those who think alike. On the contrary, all such encounters are either fortuitous or calculated to be staged at a relatively late period in an intellectual career. It is only when ideas are published and gossip emerges that academic anonymity wanes.

Those who explored interactionism in the 1960s were then isolated for some time. Many produced personal syntheses which fused the orthodox and the heterodox together. Some even created genuinely novel observations and comparisons.[1] Lacking a common tradition which might have suppressed distinction, they formed an array of moderately independent thinkers. In time they were to emulate their American counterparts by building a social world for themselves.[2] It was a fairly cohesive world which celebrated shared interests and a shared marginality. Britain is small enough to permit the development of a close association between the few who were concerned with symbolic interactionism.

The thought of that world was curiously intertwined with the original American sociology. At one level it was little more than a reflection and refraction of American ideas. There was a borrowing, sifting and redrafting which formed part of an unacknowledged division of labour. Much work was performed on American arguments; there was copious exegesis; controversies arose and declined; and revisions were adopted and discarded. In the main the American interactionists were unaware of those echoing debates in Britain. Those who came to Britain were bemused by the extent of the interest which they excited. That unawareness still persists. There is very little reference in American writing to what transpired outside the American universities during that period. British ideas did not feed back into thinking in the United States.

At another level the British version of interactionism possessed deviant qualities. It was frail and unstable because it was not anchored in an enduring tradition. Borne by a small number of identifiable and changing people, it was itself volatile. Estrangement from the parent tradition also made the subtler and more incommunicable contents of interactionism inaccessible in Britain. The British adaptation was compounded out of diverse ideas which are only infrequently discussed in the United States. There were strands of Marxism and existentialism which are quite foreign to American writing. More important, that adaptation was the property of a distinct group which acquired its own history, authority and intellectual autonomy. The transformations undergone by British interactionism depended, in part, on the comparatively contained and peculiar nature of its context.

A few of the eccentric characteristics of this book must be explained by my own initial experience of isolation and subsequent exposure to the people working in Britain. Mine is a personal construction of interactionism which was modified as I came to know various members of the group who had flirted with the sociology. I have never had an orthodox education in the approach. Yet it is that education which has conferred many of the special qualities of interactionism. As I shall argue in Chapter 1, the sociology is lodged in something of an oral culture which has been carried by three generations of American scholars. Those scholars have tended to treat the sociology as a version of normal science, refraining from the analysis which might expose its philosophical basis and supports. Their abstention from philosophy is itself a philosophical stance, but it is a stance that is covert and largely unexamined. My own intellectual marginality is perhaps best illustrated by this book's concentration on the historical and epistemological roots of interactionism. I have described the sociology in a way that is probably uncongenial to those who are more centrally placed.

In brief, I have attempted to expound interactionism as a particular kind of answer to the dilemmas which confront all sociologists. The fundamental problems which first produced sociology remain unsettled, and interactionism is one significant strategy for contending with them. Those problems revolve around the basic nature of social life, the observer's relations with that life, and the sorts of question which can properly be asked of it. Symbolic interactionism is a working amalgam of two rather discrete solutions: the formalism of Simmel which stressed the partial, evolving and synthetic *a priori* character of social knowledge; and the pragmatism of Mead, Dewey and James which emphasised how valid knowledge must be grounded, practical and experiential. Both strains abjured systematic *a priori* expositions of sociology. Both denied the legitimacy of proceeding as if society were a tangible entity whose innermost essence could be understood. Both advanced an interpretation of society as a shifting combination of forms which were variously in conflict, harmony and contradiction. They refused to describe the social as unambiguously or obviously organised. Rather they maintained that it can be understood only through a detailed process of enquiry whose conclusions are destined to be provisional and partial. It was held that enquiry, in turn, must be embedded in an active investigation of observable social phenomena. It cannot be deductive, speculative or contemplative. It cannot establish truths about the unobservable. Neither can it prepare the way for substantial generalisation.

Those conceptions of society, sociology and scientific work mirror one another. A sociology which portrays society as fluid and often unknowable cannot itself be highly structured. It tends to shun abstract reasoning and theorising, being justified by works. An appropriate motto for the sociology might be *facta non verba*. Indeed the principal member of the sociology department which founded symbolic interactionism announced in the first volume of the *American Journal of Sociology*, 'the most impressive lesson which I have learned in the vast sociological laboratory which the city of Chicago constitutes is that action, not speculation, is the supreme teacher.'[3] And Charles Peirce, the man who framed the pragmatism that animated interactionism, declared 'modern students of science have been successful because they have spent their lives not in their libraries and museums but in their laboratories and in the field.'[4]

Interactionism is significant and it ought to be part of the range of alternatives which all sociologists should consider. But it clearly produces paradox. Sociology is an academic pursuit which, like all such pursuits, is conveyed and refined in writing and talk. A form of sociology which devalues theory and metaphysics will tend to silence itself. It becomes a mute whose influence is reduced and whose exposition is a contradictory enterprise. My own discussion is accordingly a wayward undertaking for an interactionist. It expounds what wilts with description. Its task is therefore a little absurd. I have tried to accomplish it by relegating a discussion of contemporary symbolic interactionism to later passages in the book. Chapters 2 and 3 will dwell on the more articulate ideas which were to become recognised as symbolic interactionism. By working as if I were writing a history of ideas, I have systematically reconstituted a relatively unsystematic sociology. It is those mute and unschematic properties which I address in Chapter 1. They are significant not only because they have led to a radical misrepresentation of interactionism, but also because they are the very core of the sociology. I am not unaware of the irony that arises as a result. Plummer has argued 'is not the core issue the inherent ambiguity of interactionism, which permits talk, but works against reificatory, systematizing writing?'[5] If this book should fail, it will be partly because that core issue presents insoluble dilemmas.

Most of the book was written whilst I was an academic visitor at Princeton University. I am grateful to the Sociology Department, and especially to Marvin Bressler and Robert Scott, for allowing me to spend such a pleasant and profitable year. My interest in interactionism was first stimulated by Philip Hughes. It is to him that I owe a great deal, for without him I might never have left the nightmare realm. I would also like to thank Howard Becker, Peter Manning, Kenneth Plummer and Robert Scott for their kindness, advice and support. They gave me invaluable guidance which corrected many of the mistakes which I might otherwise have made.

Paul Rock

London School of Economics

1 Symbolic Interactionism as an Understated Sociology

Symbolic interactionism is an unusual sociology whose vision, style, methods and accompanying social organisation display common qualities. It is unusual because it suppresses those arguments and conventions which would make it systematic and readily communicable. Instead of clearly announcing its principles and techniques, it resorts to understatement and covert argument. By orthodox sociological standards it lacks many of the features which characterise a substantial and serious approach. It is commonly regarded as a disordered and incoherent posture. Such understatement and incoherence are assumed to signify a want of discipline and rigour. The general theme of this book will be that interactionism is the outcome of a scholarly rejection of ordinary scholarly pursuits. There is a reasoned refusal to entertain certain forms of intellectual practice. The particular theme of this chapter is the nature and effects of the peculiar social organisation which promotes that rejection. Attention will be directed at the integrated world which engendered the sociology and at the culture which that world supported. It will be argued that there has been an interplay between the community of interactionists and the ideas of interactionism itself. Flowing from an intimate association between sociologists, interactionism is framed by an unstated context of meanings and intentions. In its turn, that unstated context requires an intimate association for its survival.

Introduction

Sociology tends to be the academic hydra. Although attempts have been made to portray it as a monolithic enterprise, it is riven with disparate visions of social life. There is neither a single conception of society nor a uniform understanding of the intellectual possibilities of analysis. The discipline has become fused with too many competing philosophies and methodologies for any concerted work to materialise. At most, sociologists share a common ancestry in the social thinkers of nineteenth-century France, Germany and England. They inhabit a joint world of books, journals, universities and research institutions. But they do not always turn to the same language, imagery or strategies when they embark on research or commentary.

In the main the evolution of sociology has been guided by an oligopolistic cluster of schools which have overshadowed their rivals.[1] Marxism, functionalism, applied statistics and structuralism have established the major ways in which conceptions of social order can be phrased. Their particular prominence has emerged out of a very real struggle for intellectual sovereignty. Each has sought to control the definition of analytic problems, methods and answers. Each has advertised its capacity to furnish comprehensive explanations of human conduct. A conviction of certainty and an appreciable ambition must have characterised any of the sociologies which participated in that struggle.

Yet only a very small rump of schools have not come forward to proclaim themselves vessels of truth. At one time the precursor of symbolic interactionism was itself lauded as a substantial scheme which could properly compete for the right to dominate thinking. It was then presented as a particular philosophy of action which displaced all previous epistemologies.[2] However, interactionism has been a member of the non-combatant rump for some decades. Its own complex logic has prevented it from appearing as a champion of sure knowledge. It pretends neither to absolute truth nor to an exhaustive interpretation of society. It is unusual in its acceptance of uncertainty and a modest scope. Instead of constructing great edifices of formal thought, it has produced a mosaic of minor ethnographic studies. Instead of treating the world as a resource for theory, theory has been made subordinate to particular and concrete problems. Interactionism does not offer a definitive ontology, but merely stresses the difficulties which are involved in describing human affairs. Its very reticence has transformed it into a significant alternative to the vast architectonic schemes of sociology. Its emphasis on the opaque quality of social life makes it an important source of contrasts with more exalted analytic systems. Symbolic interactionism has performed a valuable service in contradicting the claims of orthodox sociology. In a sense, it may be the one sociology which still continues to acknowledge the puzzling and open nature of intellectual enquiry.

But its role has not only been taken up with overt and tacit criticism. It has also fashioned a distinct perspective on the social world. It celebrates a discrete imagery and a special vision which are too little appreciated. The sociology has tended to become so eccentric and understated that it has receded into an unproblematic background for most outsiders.

This book will be primarily devoted to an examination of the intellectual bases of doubt in interactionism. It will attempt to resurrect some of the themes and contentions which are commonly ignored when the sociology is discussed. In so doing, I shall review problems and positions which the interactionists have themselves occasionally suppressed. Vital to symbolic interactionism is a denial of the philosophical tradition which gave birth to the sociology. Interactionism revolves around a rejection of certain forms of intellectuality. It does not rest on an explicitly intellectual vocabulary of explanation and justification. In part, that posture derives from an extolling of practice. As Becker has argued, 'the position . . . doesn't think theoretical explication is the way to justify itself, but that it justifies itself through research results.'[3] Understanding and knowledge are held to flow from praxis, not from contemplation and abstract exposition. Of course every sociology is lent form by theory. Symbolic interactionism itself rests on a version of theorising which directs and clarifies research. Yet the interactionists take theory to be secondary to ethnography. They also regard theory as parasitic on research. Theory is a prop and an aid, but it cannot stand alone.

It is clear, then, that this book is a paradoxical enterprise. It seeks to accomplish a task which cannot be achieved solely by analytic writing. Yet paradox must be endured because interactionism is important enough to warrant systematic exposition. Exposition will betray it, but it cannot be appreciated without exposition. My argument must also depend on terms and ideas which are often foreign to interactionism. It must initially resort to an explanatory language which simultaneously produces enlightenment and distortion. I shall advance from an external to an internal perspective, at first seeming to criticise the perspective. My final chapter will attempt to vindicate the sociology. If interactionism is absurd, it is probably less absurd than most of its rivals. The contradictions which plague it tend to stem from a confrontation with issues which are conventionally obscured elsewhere. They are manifest in interactionism, but they are latent in many other sociologies. Their suppression is no sure defence.

It is both illuminating and convenient to take such a course. As I have argued, the interactionists themselves have not prepared much of a foundation for expounding their most fundamental ideas. They have abandoned metatheoretical problems and turned to the solving of puzzles and the making of discoveries as if the philosophy and methodology were relatively unprofitable and distracting activities. The structure of their work resembles that of 'normal science'.[4] It appears to be shaped by minor issues of practical enquiry, not by portentous arguments which explore the very legitimacy and meaning of sociology. Interactionists do not generally tax themselves with perplexing and probably insoluble questions about the nature of research and speculation.

I, too, find that stance useful and sensible, but it does not encourage the development of broad descriptions of thought and technique. At bottom, the sociology is built around an appreciation of man which is simultaneously simple and complex. Thus Howard Becker has observed, 'it is not an easy position to understand . . . partly, I think, because (like Zen) it's so simple.'[5] A sophisticated and analytically active mind is not always prepared to court the possibility of simplicity. There is an expectation of abundant irony, subtlety and complexity which is sometimes frustrated by interactionism. Sociologists are trained to unearth contradictions, anomalies and affronts to common sense. Their reading of interactionism is correspondingly fraught by imputations and questions which are somewhat misplaced. Interactionism requires an innocence of the mind which has often been schooled out of the sociologist. Perversely, that innocence is itself a highly cultured state. Its origins are to be found in a long history of philosophical reasoning which culminated in the shedding of philosophy. It did not arise full-blown, but evolved out of complexity. It can be reproduced only by re-creating that complexity and the analytic structures which sustained it.

It follows that I must turn to the criteria and arguments of conventional sociology in order to reconstruct an unconventional sociology. I shall borrow an alien vocabulary until its job is done. A kind of simulated understanding may emerge despite the interactionist emphasis on justification by practice. The use of foreign concepts will enable me to underscore the contrasts between interactionism and other styles of sociology. My intention is to place the approach in the context of sociology at large. It is only by demonstrating the links and discontinuities between the approach and its setting that the unique character of interactionism can appear. If I seem to belittle interactionism initially, it is only to reveal how distinctive it is. Such disparagement stems from an opening use of the conventional sociological stance. As my argument unfolds, so I hope to show that much of that stance is ill-founded. The apparent failures of interactionism may become its strengths. The critical position of its opponents may become seen as analytic infirmity. The position is founded in an insecure belief in the promise of sociology. If interactionism does not satisfy that promise, it is because sociology itself is a victim of excessive ambition. Accordingly I shall employ terms like 'inadequate' and 'incomplete' when I describe interactionism in Chapter 1, but they should not be taken with full seriousness.

The Oral Tradition

Contemporary interactionism must be understood as the culmination of prolonged thought. Its hostility to detailed explanation reflects a reasoned aversion to certain forms of rationality. Structurally, the community of interactionists has itself been marked by the ideas which it bears. It has tended to turn in on itself, lodging the sociology in an oral tradition which teaches by example and practice as well as by formal exposition. The content and form of the tradition have worked on one another to suppress some of the rationally-describable and reproducible features of the sociology. They have changed interactionism into an approach which is peculiarly resistant to summary.

The interactionist perspective was first given its distinctive structure by a community of psychologists, philosophers and sociologists who were centred on the new University of Chicago at the beginning of the century. There was an unusually intense collaboration between such people as Edward Sapir, John Dewey, W. I. Thomas, Robert Park and George Herbert Mead which gave definition to the emerging sociology.[6] The University of Chicago, and a few other institutions, continued for a long while to serve as the instrument for propagating and modifying interactionism. The position took form in a distinct intellectual community. Indeed one sociologist who confronted the task of defining it preferred not to allude to its structure or substance but to its anchorage in the world of Chicago. Its location and history represented its most tangible and identifiable facets.[7] From the very first, an oral tradition dwarfed the formal and articulate processes of disseminating ideas. There was something of a systematic reluctance to organise thought or publicly review what passed for sociological knowledge at Chicago. Instead, the members of the community were forced to become the personal bearers of clarifying information about interactionism. As Broom observed:

> '... the Chicago tradition was to a great extent an oral tradition whose crystallization in expository works is still being written by second and third generations of student descendants. Even today sociologists who depend on the *publications* of the Chicago school are instructed that corrective qualifications have long since been made by Robert E. Park and Ernest W. Burgess — in lectures. One should also bear in mind that we are dependent on a posthumous salvage operation for much of our knowledge of the thinking of George Herbert Mead. How much must have escaped the notes of his faithful students....'[8]

The community which was established then appears significant still. The interdependence between the perspective and the social management of its revision and transmission persists. Interactionists remain a world for one another, relying as much upon intimate association as upon mediated exchanges.[9] The character of that association has been traced by Reynolds and his colleagues. They assert that the organised perspectives of interactionism reflect a companion organisation of relationships which is exceptionally integrated, enduring and well-defined.[10]

Howard Becker provides an excellent example of sponsored induction into the informal world of interactionism. As a student at the University of Chicago, he was taught by interactionists of the first and second generations: Herbert Blumer, Ernest Burgess, Lloyd Warner and William Ogburn. He received especial patronage from Everett Hughes. Having completed the compiling of field notes on a tavern, he was directed by Burgess to speak to Hughes: 'Everett read them and when I came back to see him he treated me very royally. It was great ... It turned out that he had had a lot of students who had studied various professions, medicine and law in particular, but he found it very difficult to get people to study lowly kinds of occupations. Here was somebody doing it without being urged.'[11] Becker was encouraged by Hughes to pursue sociology, he was guided towards research projects and aided in obtaining research fellowships and posts. The students, too, were largely composed of embryo interactionists who collaborated to build up a community of knowledge: 'I can't even begin to tell you all the people who were in my class — Erving Goffman, David Gold, Bill Kornhauser, Eliot Freidson, Jim Short — I could go on half a day naming them. We were all very excited about sociology, and we talked very seriously about it so there was a lot of education going on among the students themselves.'[12] Becker's intellectual training centred on such themes as process, change, ecology, symbolic interactionism and the like. Much of it was taken for granted as a simple, common-sense view of the world: 'although we fought a lot with one another, without quite knowing it we all shared that basic point of view and became more aware of it as we got out into the world and met people from Columbia, Harvard and other places who didn't seem to understand things the right way.'[13]

It would be misleading to interpret the oral tradition as no more than an outgrowth of a segregated and cohesive social world. As I shall argue, symbolic interactionism is a synthesis of ideas which can independently explain why articulate public discussion has been muted. But it is instructive to examine the interplay between styles of discourse and their accompanying forms of communication. It is possible to assert that interactionism was always so organised that it did not lend itself to conventional exposition. In turn, oral reproduction has emphasised aspects of its peculiar doctrine. I shall accordingly proceed as if it were feasible to distinguish between the special phrasing of the sociology and its mode of teaching, pretending that the one gave rise to the other. That distinction allows particular qualities of the sociology to become usefully pronounced.

The Unformulated Nature of Symbolic Interactionism

Since its very beginnings interactionism has never been concisely formulated. Much has been left unstated or left to implication. Interactionists themselves have generally shunned the major etiquette of academic writing. They do not normally list the problems that encouraged their analysis; acknowledge or review all preceding work; offer a coherent and schematic conclusion; and end with a bridging passage which would link an argument with its anticipated successors. On the contrary, the formal procedures of scholarship and, occasionally, the *persona* of the sociologist himself are dimmed and blurred. The work would seem to be offered as a direct emanation of the scenes described, appearing without the intervention of strategy or strategist. The interactionist distrust of the observing, contemplating intellect has impelled writers to diminish the distance between subject and object. They censor away the obvious trappings of analysis, the analysing mind and analytic technique. Much of their work is thus characterised by a certain amorphousness, ambiguity and apparent aimlessness. Its productions resemble those of a *camera obscura* – a mirroring of the world whose sense of illusion would be destroyed by the presence of obtrusive equipment and technicians. More particularly that sense of illusion is enhanced by a special style which some interactionists practise. As I shall argue, the symbolic interactionists portray knowledge as an active process rather than as a state. Understanding is an emergent property of focused enquiry. That conception is often built into the fabric of interactionist writing itself. Enlightenment is expected to gradually appear as the reader proceeds. It is not conferred immediately. Neither is it prepared in a systematic manner. It arises out of the reader's sympathetic response to his materials. Thus Plummer observes, 'the writings of most major interactionists . . . have an "emergent" style which makes them *very* difficult to read.'[14]

The shapeless and elusive qualities of the interactionist vision have had palpable effects. They have fed into the production and distribution of the approach so that those processes have themselves borrowed something of its inchoate nature. Above all, restraints have been placed on the dissemination of interactionist ideas and methodology. The sociology cannot be easily conveyed by the normal procedures of academic instruction. Its successful transmission depends on peculiar forms of teaching and some exposure to the network of corresponding sociologists whose work is identified as interactionist. That mode of transmission cannot or would not be provided by most universities.

It is clear that sociology is critically moulded by the institutions in which it is reproduced. In some senses it can be analysed as an entity which becomes the object of standardised work practices. The practices impose their stamp on it, defining its structure and its intellectual possibilities. What is processed and presented as sociology must lend itself in some measure to the routine business of teaching and enquiry. The most serviceable form of sociology is one that is neatly and lucidly organised into a series of schematic statements about topics, each topic being constructed out of an articulate logic. Much industry has been devoted to the preparation of readily-diffused knowledge. 'Readers', text-books, articles and other kinds of ordered thinking have been designed to meet such purposes.

The unmanageable and the unusual tend to be rejected or distorted, and the main stock of sociology is correspondingly affected. Symbolic interactionism has not been assembled in a manner which allows it to be smoothly absorbed by conventional work practices. As a partially unassimilable vision, it has been translated into a segment of sociology which is either misconstrued or thrust to the margins of interest. 'Readers' in interactionism abound, but there are almost no comprehensive and programmatic expositions. Most of the works which can be taken up in teaching or research convey the impression that they rely upon a hidden agenda and a hidden bibliography. They appear to take for granted a common participation in an established appreciation of society which requires no enunciation. It is as if the writings were chiefly intended to be connotative rather than denotative, conjuring up responses in an imagination which is assumed to be informed and sympathetic. Thus much interactionism rests on the strategic analytic tool of the 'sensitising concept', a device which I shall discuss in Chapter 3. That kind of concept is not organised to provide a definitive and clear description of an area:

> Hundreds of our concepts – like culture, institutions, social structure, mores and personality – are not definitive concepts but are sensitizing in nature. They lack precise reference and have no bench marks which allow a clean-cut identification of a specific instance, and of its content. Instead, they rest on a general sense of what is relevant.[15]

It is that general sense of relevance which is imputed to the reader. Some of the major themes within the perspective do become transmitted in this fashion, but their reception is mediated by intellectual contexts which lie outside the interactionists' control. Others are simply misconstrued.

There has been a tendency for portions of the sociology to be grafted on to other explanatory systems in ways that might seem bizarre if the larger interactionist vision were more fully comprehended. Such piecemeal excisions and syntheses are performed on all modes of sociology, but the checks on improper use are vastly weaker in the instance of interactionism. I shall take up this issue of misconstruction at later stages in the book when my argument has been more elaborately developed. Yet, parenthetically, it is possible to state that examples of the sociology have been radically bowdlerised. Thus some work on deviancy has been transformed into 'vulgar' labelling theory, a mechanical and deterministic account of a few simplied phases in the processes of formal social control.[16] The original authors have now disowned the title of labelling theorists,[17] but the work goes on. Similarly, political events have been given an interactionist gloss, but the supposed macrostructural deficiencies of the sociology have been remedied by yoking it to a glass of concepts which contradict its entire ontology. It seems to be implied that inattention to macrosociology flows only from neglect and not from reasoned argument.[18] I shall discuss these criticisms in Chapter 7.

Muddle and confusion are thereby compounded. The superficially intelligible and useable features of interactionism can be employed in ways that subvert themes within its more opaque core, exacerbating the formlessness of common versions of the approach. Without censors, interactionism is prey to abundant misconstructions. Without censors, its few critics can attack the misconstructions and purport to expose the contradictoriness of the whole enterprise.[19] Those sympathetic to the original misreadings may then attempt to do repair work which generates further distortion. A minor branch of sociology has developed around such play between mutant intellectual forms.[20]

When thought borders on the inexpressible or the unexpressed, its communication must be based on extraordinary procedures. The oral tradition thus provides and answers the particular demands of interactionism. Because the ideas of the sociology cannot be adequately conveyed in rational discourse, they have become tied to a mode of transmission which does not involve written language alone. To some extent, symbolic interactionism has evolved into a posture which cannot be presented as a series of propositions and conclusions. It has become, in part, a special kind of awareness or sensitivity whose constituent practices cannot be defined with clarity or precision. Such sensitivity proceeds most commonly from membership in an intellectual community and from an allied exposure to particular experiences and situations. The business of acquiring awareness cannot be so scripted that the student can foresee and comprehend all the structures of his initiation. Indeed interactionist essays on education themselves stress the dialectical and open properties of learning. Training becomes a matter of coaching by those who are already learned in the mysteries; a sponsored career into full membership of the community. Any deliberate effort to participate in the art must therefore tend to take the form of a personal tutelage under a trusted master. The interactionist tradition has taken much of its character from its similarities to the craft acquired through apprenticeship. Very largely it has been passed personally from adept to adept. Emulation, the simulation of experience, and the organisation of an intellectual career occupy strategic roles in the making of a sociologist. Of course, that process is neither mystical nor inarticulate. It does not represent a complete departure from orthodox styles of teaching, but it *is* a departure. Becker himself illustrates the manner in which conventional teaching was anchored in the oral tradition:

[The oral tradition was important] but while some of it was passed on that way, a lot of what I learned was handed on quite differently. It's right out of Kuhn – the way I learned was by studying *models* . . . of good research. I learned in the oral tradition which things to take seriously as models, to be sure . . . I can't overemphasize the degree to which I, and most of my colleagues, did just what Kuhn says novice normal scientists do: imitated those models and settled questions by seeing how the models dealt with them. It takes a good deal of work to grasp the implications of a model, and no doubt that was helped on by the oral tradition.[21]

A significant interdependence has developed between the incompletely formulated interactionism and the settings in which it is relayed and practiced. Sociological training in the Chicago manner encourages and is encouraged by the formation of small social worlds which centre on the maintenance of partially ineffable thought. It is necessarily a collective undertaking because ideas which cannot be neatly fixed, recorded and transferred by written words require complex underpinning for their survival. The symbolic interactionists consequently resemble what Karl Mannheim identified as a group based on conjunctive thought. They represent a community which sustains a common appreciation and understanding of the world.[22] The plausibility of an argument ceases to hinge merely on abstract and publicly available reflection. It can be resolved also by an appeal to a silently presupposed and shared sense of reality. Symbolic interactionism has thus become a candidate for more than intellectual interpretation. It has simultaneously become an aesthetics, an existential stance and a form of ethics. It is a way of being in the world. A member of its community will affirm and celebrate the interactionist vision in his writings and his conversation, and he will receive support from the affirmation of his fellows. For certain purposes, at least, the interactionists have jointly constructed a universe of meanings which serves as the implicit context of all their analyses. That context is the vital and accepted frame in which discourse is set.

It is of course the case that the very indeterminacy of symbolic interactionism leaves the frontiers of the community vague, Sociologists may remain fairly marginal members of the conjunctive group, or they may make use of its ideas in an instrumental fashion. Yet the main work of interactionism has been structured by the oral tradition, a tradition which has been cited by many who have attempted to discover the sources of the otherwise inexplicable coherence of the perspective. One such commentator, Huber, lodged her observation within a more general criticism of interactionism.[23] Her attack was itself assailed, but the defence of the perspective was constrained to assert that an adequate comprehension of interactionism must entail a prolonged exposure to its thought. In a sense, the defence maintained that a proper understanding of the position can be gained only by participating in the life of the conjunctive community:

> [There] is an already too prevalent tendency among many to reject SI [symbolic interactionism] in its entirety without adequate basis for judgement. The significance, implications, and complexities of SI are only realized through frequent, intimate and continued exposure to it. This is the major reason why many regard SI as simplistic.[24]

The roles played by the oral tradition and its supporting community are quite critical as practical expressions of interactionism and as influences which have guided its evolution. As practical expressions, they symbolise the particular incoherence which interactionism attains at the level of abstract exposition. As influences, they have contributed to the intellectual isolation of the interactionist. In its early phases symbolic interactionism and American sociology were virtually one. Until the 1930s and the rise of sociological functionalism, the influence of the University of Chicago and its satellites was paramount. But there were few resources within interactionism to ward off its displacement by more explicit systems of thought. The later history of interactionism may profitably be read as one which paralleled rather than interplayed with the development of the main body of sociology. Few sociologists pursuing other conceptions of man and society have had much commerce with interactionism since it was eclipsed by structural-functionalism. They

Interactionism as an Understated Sociology

have typically ignored its writings and its arguments. Rather, ideas have been elaborated in relatively closed intellectual circles which have impinged little upon one another.

America is vast and its population is geographically dispersed. It has an extraordinary proliferation of universities, and there is a tendency for their departments to lean towards a consistency of academic approach. In such a setting, intellectual worlds need never be in collision. They may pretend to a seeming completeness and self-sufficiency; reproducing themselves from amongst the ranks of their own students; devising, teaching and examining courses without any outside interference or scrutiny; being served by their own books and journals; and taking little stock of the positions held by others. Intellectual segregation suppresses reflexiveness[25] in copious ways. When the segregated cluster together in conjunctive communities, they possess a fully operational analytic apparatus that provides them with criteria for recognising reality, intellectual priorities and the successful demonstration of an argument. Unchallenged, that apparatus and those criteria may never be fully articulated. They remain largely unexamined, an invisible feature of the common-sense world of the intellectual. Many academic works are thus framed by an unstated context of meaning. The more isolated and integrated the social world which provides that context, the less specification will there be of background assumptions. The capacity to grasp an argument will be imputed to a reader instead of being coaxed into existence. When a community revolves around a common reality whose core is as inchoate as that of interactionism, shapelessness and elusiveness become further extended.

It is apparent that all scientific communities engage in some measure of conjunctive interpretation. Disciplined knowledge is a collective pursuit, and its manufacture does not rest on explicable or explicit procedures alone.[26] Even when coherent intellectual worlds do collide, there may be insufficient common territory for them to resolve all issues that are in dispute.[27]

Yet the matching and contrasting of perspectives can raise to awareness some of the implicit theoretical work that tends to be unrecognised in sociology. Indeed synthesis and confrontation form a substantial part of intellectual activity. Attempts have been made to reconcile Marxism with Weberianism, psycho-analysis with Marxism, and functionalism with conflict theory. The dialectic[28] of Lukács has been pitched against the rational and fragmenting processes of bourgeois thought. Idealism[29] has been set against materialism.[30] Marxism and phenomenology have been united.[31] Much of this work reflects the ease with which members of one conjunctive community can so organise the ideas of another that victory is assured. Much, too, conveys the impression of directionless fission and fusion. Nevertheless the process can lend definition to what had hitherto been ill-defined.

Although it may reasonably be considered one of the principal sociological stances,[32] interactionism is comparatively lamed as a system of ideas in competition with Marxism, functionalism, structuralism, phenomenology and the other ordered and formalised approaches. Unlike them, it does not represent a compact and organised body of thought whose implications for methodoloy, epistemology and ontology are clear. It reticence has prevented it becoming an alternative which might be awarded attention. Except in its own relatively isolated enclaves, it does not receive a prominent place. Indeed it sometimes appears to be chiefly written for the already appreciative members of the conjunctive community of interactionists. Outside that community, and particularly outside the United States, it constitutes at most a source of minor amendments to arguments, an irritant and wayward tradition which does not manage analysis in a routine or familiar fashion.[33]

Since important tracts of its thought appear to remain at a pre-theoretical level, it cannot be easily subjected to detailed comparison with other sociologies. There are few ways in which it can be grasped and transformed into a system whose epistemology might be contrasted with a Marxist epistemology,[34] its methodology with survey analysis, its ontology with that of structural-functionalism, and the like. This lack of ready juxtaposition has turned away those who might have attempted to translate the seemingly pre-theoretical into the theoretical, the unrefined into the refined. It has led to interactionism being rather neglected by the academic industry of explication. No one within the interactionist world eagerly courts or furthers such work, and outsiders do not seek it out. Contrived contrasts and confrontations which might have led to examination and reform are therefore missing.

As a further consequence, symbolic interactionism has been dwarfed into an inconspicuous and largely tangential tradition that plays little part in the polemical debates of sociology. After the waning of ur-interactionism in the 1930s, there has been little effort to offer it as a contender for intellectual dominance. Herbert Blumer and others may have occasionally deplored particular developments

Interactionism as an Understated Sociology 15

in sociology, but there is little reason to suppose that their episodic and unsustained attacks have been of much moment. After all, as I shall argue, the interactionists are less concerned with theoretical and metatheoretical issues than with the problematics of concrete research. It is not their bent to engage in the conventional debates of the philosophy of sociology.

Not only has interactionism been devoid of an imperialistic strain, but there have been few attempts to subdue the sociology itself. It has not undergone those revisions which typically follow upon a critical onslaught. Indeed there have been no appreciable attacks except those which were waged against the segments of interactionism that were transplanted to more systematic and obtrusive analyses. On the whole, interactionist productions have simply been treated as peripheral to the main sociological enterprise. Without substantial contact and criticism, interactionists have not been compelled to engage in prolonged and articulate reflection about their work. They have not been forced to address strange questions put by outsiders. They have been relatively unaffected by controversies and developments taking place elsewhere. They have not participated in the dialectic of assault and defence which distinguishes the evolution of most other forms of sociological thought.

Although interactionism may not be vigorously proselytising or imperialistic, it has nevertheless discovered itself occupying a colonialist role in some substantive areas. Thus, the sociologies of deviance, education and medicine have been radically transformed by interactionist conceptions of man, social process and the negotiated character of social order. Indeed, there are some grounds for arguing that there has been a break in the oral tradition.[35] Ideas have been transplanted to fields and areas largely uninhabited by members of the interactionist community. There was an efflorescence of published writing in the late 1950s and 1960s which made it seem as if the sociology could be prised out of printed materials alone. In part there was a curious substitution of a romantic context for the unstated environment which had been so carefully nurtured by the apprenticeship system.[36] That romantic context contained a number of qualities which were foreign to interactionism proper. In particular it stressed a politics and philosophy of experience whose origins and themes were very different from those of the Chicago School. Yet, for a while, an abundance of writings combined with a receptive mood. Interactionism became quite rapidly diffused so that it transformed the sociology of deviance. It acquired converts who had never personally known the authors of the works which influenced them. There were for instance pronounced affinities between those who espoused drug-taking and those who advanced an interactionist conception of rule-breaking.[37] However, it may well be that such an apparent expansion will not have long-term consequences. It has been accompanied by some vulgarisation of style and thought. It lacks the stability of the oral tradition. More importantly, it is deficient in those defences which the oral tradition provided. The distant novice is incapable of appreciating all the nuances and possibilities of his adopted sociology. The tenuously reconciled contradictions of interactionism have tended to destroy the exported versions.

Interactionism may have brought about minor intellectual revolutions in a number of fields, but they have provided no basis for more comprehensive revisions of the sociology. They remain localised, tethered to the region in which they first appeared. It is this interpenetration of the substantive and the speculative which has prevented the diffusion of interactionism as a general interpretative scheme. The perspective is not amenable to abstract manipulation or substantial deductive and inferential reasoning. It offers few specific recipes for mapping out new terrain. John Lofland has referred to this containment of interactionism as a source of 'analytic interruptus'.[38] He claims that those who would employ interactionist ideas often find themselves unable to proceed. Indeed one major treatise on interactionist methodology advocated the adoption of a virtually presuppositionless stance towards the social world, a shedding of all structured schemes which might order events in advance of enquiry.[39] This, and other principles lodged within interactionist epistemology, flow from a retrievable and describable mode of comprehending social life. It is with that description that the bulk of this book will be concerned. But it is apparent that symbolic interactionism is outwardly garbed with protestations which drastically curtail its capacity to be elaborated or applied.

There is another major formal constraint on the provision of a lucid and integrated account of interactionism. Vagueness has again fed on vagueness, perpetuating the distinctive incoherence of the position. Because its tenets have not been clearly laid down, because its contours and boundaries are imprecisely drawn, there cannot be any exact demarcation of the place of interactionism within the larger territory of sociology. There is sufficient uncertainty about what constitutes a peculiarly interactionist problem or argument for there to be substantial confusion at the margins of the perspective.

Interactionism merges and overlaps with numerous other sociologies. It is fused at its edges with ethology (in Goffman's *Relations in Public*, for instance); with conflict theory; with phenomenology; with ethnomethodology;[40] with functionalism (in Erikson's *Wayward Puritans*); with organisation analysis; with cybernetic and information theory (in Scheff's *Being Mentally Ill* and Cohen's *Folk Devils and Moral Panics*); with psycho-analysis (in Shibutani's *Society and Personality*); with Marxism; and with exchange theory.[41] Interactionism has thus swamped over into other areas, assuming something of their character and complicating the nature of its own. It is difficult to establish whether such ventures represent maverick forms of the sociology; whether the sociology is made up of a mosaic of minor syntheses; or whether it is polycentric, there being no one interactionism. If those syntheses are dismissed as impure, the unadulterated residue would be revealed as only a slight part of the writings that are conventionally identified as interactionist. It becomes apparent that any delineation of an unsullied interactionism must be highly contrived. What is or is not properly to be associated with the perspective remains problematic. As Kirson Weinberg observes, 'although considered a "school" in Sociology, consistent in frame of reference, Symbolic Interaction theory is fraught with divergent points of departure, interpretations of basic concepts and methodological emphases.'[42]

The resolution of that issue of the boundaries is not advanced by the interactionists themselves. In the main, writers do not overtly declare their allegiance to the perspective. They rarely proclaim themselves members of the conjunctive community or signify what issues keep them apart from it. They are involved in little explicit system-building. Their works are products of an ostensibly common-sense world-view which remains unvoiced. Intellectual purity and contamination are not presented as matters of any interest. The absence of such declaration is only partially remedied by an occasional acknowledgment of a master's aid. A statement of indebtedness to Becker, Hughes or Blumer might be the sole sign that the author considers himself a bearer of the oral tradition and a participating member of the informal community.

Curiously, when the contradictions and ambiguities of interactionism do foster reflexivity, the outcome is often desertion or recantation. Those who might have lent interactionism the appearance of a greater clarity or consistency have tended to abandon it altogether. During the 1960s, for example, an increasing analytic involvement with the politics of rule-breaking brought about the emergence of an intellectual movement which was to culminate in sizeable defection. The interactionist treatment of deviancy had stressed the role of power in the business of imposing meaning and process on experience. That emphasis on power was to become the focus of a radical, 'new' or critical criminology which jettisoned much of interactionism. Instead of repairing the sociology, defectors typically dwelt on the irremediable nature of its flaws.[43]

Interactionism may thus be likened to an orthodoxy whose adherents are sometimes given to sectarian division. Cleavage is encouraged by the permeable and indistinct nature of the orthodoxy's frontiers. To those who are unconcerned about the strict maintenance of purity, interactionism appears open to the manufacture of abundant syntheses. During the course of its evolution attempts have been made to meld the sociology with other, often conflicting, perspectives. An initial allegiance to the new synthesis typically gives way to a recognition of its untenability. Thus tracts of interactionism have been appropriated by Marxism, phenomenology or functionalism, but those reformulations have been eventually defined as inadequate and contradictory by sociologists who seek uniformity. There is a recalcitrant core within symbolic interactionism which defies complete assimilation by other sociologies. An intellectual outsider who tries to adapt interactionism is likely to encounter a set of fundamental ontological principles which negate his own stance. The history of interactionism may then be understood, in part, as a sequence of explorations conducted by sociologists who have sought to mine and exploit the perspective for a variety of purposes. Many of the major explorations have ultimately revealed that interactionism is built around an understated theoretical centre which cannot be modified. The sociology may thus be discarded because it is held to be ambiguous, inflexible, insufficiently schematic or unenlightening on critical issues.

As I shall argue below, the cultivation of a deliberately constructed vagueness is an integral quality of symbolic interactionism. It is intended to instill a certain aesthetic sensibility, a sympathetic responsiveness to special properties of the social world. It is a prime constituent of that sensibility that social phenomena should not be endowed with an excess of structure or definition. So defined, they can become molested and disfigured, analytically destroyed. Rather than risk such conceptual violence, the interactionists refuse to accede to demands that they should force coherence and system upon what

Interactionism as an Understated Sociology

they write. The cost of mobilising an effective defence against critics, renegades and apparent allies is believed to be the abandonment of a vital epistemological practice.

Almost liturgically, the editors of 'readers' and collections of essays declare themselves puzzled by the absence of a detailed exposition of symbolic interactionism. With some predictability, those collections fail to provide a graphic exposition. There *are* a few articles which attempt such a review,[44] but a comprehensive description of the school's history and major theses has still not been produced.[45] Undertaking that project would run counter to latent but quite discernible themes within the perspective. Chief amongst those themes is a methodical resistance to systematisation itself. It is almost impossible to offer a faithful account of interactionism without betraying it.

One argument of this book will be that the principles of interactionism celebrate an extremely unusual conception of sociology. There is an intellectual reticence which contrasts markedly with conventional styles of sociological reasoning. Most sociologies scrutinise and parade their intellectual technology. In some the preoccupation with strategy is so pronounced that it overshadows interest in the substantive world. Lukács, for instance, claimed that had Marx been faulted on every empirical question, he would still have remained in possession of the truth because he wielded the dialectic, the master logic of social life. Merton, too, has observed that the American sociology of knowledge subordinates all problems to its overriding concern with methodology.[46] Interactionism, however, systematically masks the procedures by which it generates description. The successful accomplishment of the school's projects depends upon their analytic organisation remaining covert. Effectiveness does rest on a form of methodological rigour and on logical cogency, but it depends above all on a recognisably faithful replication of the structures of social life. The prime issue is taken to be the problems of epistemology and ontology, not that of technology:

> Ordinarily, issues of the nature of reality and the modes of knowing are the main targets of methodological inquiry in any discipline, but the term 'methodology' unfortunately has come to mean in sociology the study of quantitative techniques of analysis and how to apply them to processing data gathered with such quantitative techniques in mind. The reliance on such techniques is, of course, naïve, and perhaps the reliance on techniques used by

symbolic interactionists, as we know them, is also naïve. Indeed, in a fundamental sense, the reliance on any technique is naïve.[47]

There is some variation in the attention which interactionists devote to methodological matters. Some, like Blumer,[48] are fastidious about the deployment of technique. Others, like Hughes,[49] display some methodological agnosticism. They appear to argue that a credible intellectual performance will be credible irrespective of the technical operations which brought it into being: if it is credible, the operations may be disregarded; if it is not, they have simply failed. Yet almost all the interactionists are directed by one guideline. They support a pragmatic conception of truthfulness, holding that interactionism can be properly defined as a natural part of social process, a way of being in the world like any other. Sociology will prove to be authentic experience if it is consonant with other features of everyday social life. The ideal of consonance is repeatedly invoked despite recognised difficulties which attend its attainment. It is asserted that the sociological experience which gave birth to work and the interpretative experience of the work's recipient must appear unfeigned, unforced and existentially at one with other modes of artless consciousness. The persuasiveness of an account will be gauged largely by its correspondence with the sentiments and responses evoked by active participation in the social world. The flow of interactionist logic must convey something of the flow and order of living experience itself. Thus Glaser and Strauss argue that one criterion of credibility is satisfied 'if a reader becomes sufficiently caught up in the description so that he feels vicariously that he was also in the field'.[50]

My imputation of an interactionist understanding of adequate explanation may be misconceived. But it does marry well with some basic arguments of the pragmatist epistemology which I shall discuss in chapters 3 and 4. It also explains what would be an otherwise puzzling discrepancy between two separate facets or phases of interactionist work. That work may be described as the harnessing together of imagery with an image-producing machinery. The artifice of presentation must not be exposed because the experience of appropriating knowledge would then be open to challenge as an instance of bad faith and the management of false appearances. The integrity of the perspective is thus retained as long as it is not shown to be significantly more calculated or engineered than other ways of grasping the world through activity and reflection. It is quite

Interactionism as an Understated Sociology

apparent that such integrity is manufactured and induced by processes which do not generally pervade ordinary experience. Yet the illusion of an organic connection with everyday life would completely vanish if analytic reflection appeared overly contemplative, scholastic, static or based on an alienating system of logic. The impression of authenticity must be attained by a thorough resort to the understatement of intellectuality. Just as drama employs numerous props and strategies to convey an illusion of the unrehearsed and 'natural', so interactionism resorts to intellectual schemes and devices whose presence is denied.

Collectively, the writings of the interactionists must be read on two distinct planes of interpretation. The one concerns the express intentions and achievements of the sociology. Occupied chiefly with a portrayal of the symbolic life of social worlds, it represents the semantic appreciation of the vision constructed by analysis. It is largely organised around an enlisting of the reader's imagination by means of a fastidious use of language and style. Works cannot be examined on this plane unless certain questions are suspended. They cannot be translated into a crude or definitive explanation without incurring the risk of defiling the impressions that they were designed to create. As Bruyn observes:

> If he works with the inner perspective [the sociologist] finds that his data are different from those of the traditional empiricist. That is, [he] does not initially explain his data in impersonal categories or definitive concepts; rather, he usually finds it more cogent to express his data in personal terms in the form of a portrait or an illustrative story . . . He finds he can explain his findings more adequately through rhetorical devices and cultural symbols . . . The meaning is conveyed to outsiders through such rhetorical means as metaphors, analogies, allegories, parables, and paradoxes.[51]

Similarly, Strauss introduced his analysis of identity by stating:

> As I began to write, I found myself drawn into using the essay form. . . . In a peculiar way, [that form] frees both the author and the reader by its very tone and style of attack upon problems. This does not make it any less a vehicle of thought, although the ideas do not necessarily march across its pages in clearly marshalled, or in propositional, order. If I have taken the long way around

stylistically speaking – drawing upon the connotative impact of language as well as upon its more denotative resources – my strategy has been purposive.[52]

The other level of interpretation may be likened to an understanding which reveals the syntactic organisation of the impressions. It illuminates the analytic machinery that furnishes ideas and structures for the reader's inspection. It is a concealed machinery whose operations can never be made explicit without some loss of effect. Drama is robbed of its forcefulness when it is watched from the wings. It becomes even less of a plausible semblance of reality when the preparatory and supportive work of the theatre is seen in its entirety. Interactionism, too, contrives to be an artistic simulation of the world. Attempting to convey the symbolic integrity of life, it can be betrayed and fragmented by obvious schematisation. For instance, Dalton reflected that his work for *Men Who Manage*[53] might well have taken a quantitative form, but 'I would have ignored widespread problems if I had quantified parts of the data in a way convincing to me. Where the problem was inextricably intertwined with others, I felt that too much injustice would be done to the whole to wrench it out for the sake of sampling and scaling theory.'[54] Totality would have been ruptured by the methodology of the physical sciences; phenomena would have been deformed; and faithfulness would have been lost. The insertion of methods and methodological descriptions can destroy illusion. Interestingly, interactionism can be understood fully only when it is not fully explicated.

Nonetheless this book will discuss the workings of that machinery. Such a prolonged examination cannot possibly recreate the perspective at the first level of interpretation. Instead it must necessarily illuminate the tension which is caused by an alignment of the conceptual universe of interactionism with the processes that create it. That alignment produces paradox. Interactionism rests on categorical assumptions which deny the possibility of categorical assumptions. It systematically repudiates systematisation. It maintains a comprehensive ontology and epistemology which assert that concise understanding about man and social knowledge is impossible. Matza argued that no extended argument rejecting philosophy can succeed in escaping a philosophical form for very long. It seems to be a major contradiction of interactionism that it has attempted to philosophically silence its own opposition to an exhaustive philosophy of social life. At a number of points, the perspective comes perilously close to proclaiming its own absurdity. By delaying such an announcement, by methodically neglecting the arguments which might lead up to it, it has managed to retain a reasonably viable grasp on the phenomena which it describes. The outcome is a particularly complicated form of ruse, best played by denying its very existence. The ruse can be successful because the two levels of interpretation may be treated as *sui generis*, offering quite distinct realms of understanding which need not clash. Interactionist imagery constructs a world which is available to conjunctive appreciation. That appreciation is not analytic but sympathetic – a matter of *verstehen* rather than *erklären*. It pivots on an application of the intuitive faculty, a kind of communion with truth. It is hostile to precise, neat definition and a firmly structured thesis. The semantic presentations of interactionism are thus, in part, an outcrop of an Americanised *Geisteswissenschaft*. The mechanical apparatus which furnishes such imagery is to be judged instrumentally and technically. It is a feature of a somewhat different order of phenomena.

Any attempt to impose order on interactionism must inevitably smack of arbitrariness. Indeed, the understated quality of the sociology reflects a tendency to treat the accumulated works of the school as an evolving whole which defies reduction to a single statement. In a sense, symbolic interactionism is defined by its adherents as the sum total of its component works. Its definition emerges as those works mount up.[55] When Blumer himself confronted the task of summarising interactionism, he asserted 'a view of human society as symbolic interaction has been followed more than it has been formulated . . . [There has been no] systematic statement of the nature of group life from the standpoint of symbolic interaction.[56] His own account was described as a 'personal version'. Mine too must be a construction rather than a report. Unstated intentions, conceptions and programmes must be inferred or invented in an effort to assemble an argument. The whole represents an imaginative reconstruction, a fabrication[57] which replaces the assertions and connections that are often mute in interactionist writing itself. The book may then be read as a kind of creation myth that describes the intellectual processes that would have to precede the logical accomplishment of the peculiar qualities of my understanding of interactionism. As a creative fiction, it cannot be anything more than idiosyncratic, and one that many interactionists may disown.[58]

2 The Roots of Symbolic Interactionism

Although it seems to be philosophically disinherited, symbolic interactionism is a full heir to the intellectual traditions and positions which were developed in nineteenth-century Europe. Like every other sociology, it offers one strategy for confronting the epistemological problems posed by the unresolved nature of social reality. Kant gave those problems a special clarity and poignancy, and it was Kantian philosophy which served as a basis for the evolution of sociology. Kant distinguished between discrete modes of apprehending the world. One such mode, the synthetic *a priori*, was adopted by Simmel as the pivot of a novel sociology which emphasised the organising part played by social forms. Formalism transmuted sociology into a viable enterprise, but it also challenged accepted definitions of the legitimate scope and task of social thought. It underscored the tentative and precarious character of knowledge; it emphasised the fluidity of social life; it dismissed analytic *a priori* reasoning; it reduced the scale of effective analysis; but it also provided some arguments for assuming that there was an identity between sociology and its objects. Those themes were incorporated through a direct process of transmission. They were absorbed to become some of the principal contentions of symbolic interactionism itself. Their origins have been forgotten, but they are an essential element in the reconstruction of the sociology.

Symbolic interactionism has undergone transformations since it first achieved a distinct identity, but the changes have not always been cumulative.[1] Discontinuities and erratic shifts of style and content have punctuated the history of the perspective, making it resemble a chain of loosely connected sociologies which have straggled together over time. The evolution of the position has not been controlled and

The Roots of Symbolic Interactionism

superintended in the manner common to other sociologies. Its ideas have not been codified and they lack an adequate historical record. Weak supervision has allowed arguments to become forgotten and developments of thought to become separated from the parent body. Thus critical intellectual possibilities have been emphasised or neglected at different phases, and substantive problems have been ignored sometimes to remain permanently suppressed.

Even the present state of interactionism lacks order. Indeed, in one sense, it is impermissible to describe such an unorganised sociology as a whole at all. Because there is no publicly accessible synopsis of the accumulated thought of the interactionists, the perspective can become problematic and opaque even to its own adherents. Lacking any articulate exposition, its evolution and structure have become somewhat mysterious and a subject for academic folklore. Huber argues 'much time was devoted to casuistical debating over questions of orthodoxy'.[2] Similarly, Kuhn observes:

> The oral tradition . . . has some generic peculiarities which are evidenced equally by primitive myth and by unpublished intellectual orientation: there tends to be much (almost ritual) repetition; there is a strain to 'get it right', that is, to be correct; there is much debate about orthodoxy, and whatever intellectual powers there may be, are more devoted to casuistry and criticism than to inquiry and creativity. . . . [Much work] has stemmed from the essential ambiguities and contradictions in the Meadian statement – ambiguities and contradictions which were generally interpreted to be dark, inscrutable complexities too difficult to understand as long as the orientation remained largely in the oral tradition.[3]

The refraction of the perspective through the talk of the interactionists has had multiple consequences. The talk has necessarily become a practical substitute for a written chronicle of the school. Being talk, however, it tends to be volatile, situational and selective. It lacks the structure of a meticulous bibliography and an accurate system of record-keeping. It is typically an emergent product of the particular concerns of central thinkers and their reading of the changing significance of past accomplishments. The very shape of interactionism is an eminently negotiable item, reflecting fashion and the careers of specific writers. At any one stage, the school's projects and horizons are defined by a peculiar constellation of problems and an intellectual past with which they entertain a dialectical relation. Changes in that constellation will lead to a reconstruction of the past, and the past will encourage different readings of current problems.

This unmonitored and unreported development appears in marked contrast to that of the other sociologies. Marxism, for instance, is produced by competing factions and distinct disputes; each typically bearing a name or an authorship, each locked clearly into the political and academic history of the theory. Bernstein, Kautsky, Stalin, Trotsky, Plekhanov and Lenin can be linked and plotted together, contributing to a more or less coherent movement of ideas. Interactionism has no such coherent or public past. Its creators have undertaken little of the work which might have lent a systematic or orderly appearance to their enterprise. Instead they have promoted a kind of intellectual invisibility for themselves and their thought.

In some cases, for instance, the interactionists have not always published strenuously. Thus George Mead was reluctant to publicly disseminate many of the ideas which were to give form to the sociology.[4] He chose instead to lecture, cultivating an informal intellectual community rather than an anonymous audience of readers. Many of his writings were published only after his death and at the instigation of his students.[5] It would seem, too, that the interactionists were not even anxious to distinguish their sociology by a special name. A title was awarded belatedly and apologetically by Herbert Blumer, and he called it 'a somewhat barbarous neologism'.[6] A group that is organised around conjunctive interpretation does not need to advertise itself or its ideas to strangers beyond its boundaries. When a position is celebrated in conversation, too graphic a description of its themes may simply signify that the writer is an intellectual outsider who feels compelled to discuss 'what everyone knows'. Such activity tends to be regarded as otiose by most members. As Faris remarks: 'Students at Chicago in the 1920's never heard the term *symbolic interactionism* applied to their social psychology tradition and no member of the department either attempted to name it or encouraged such naming. Every consideration was given to open exploration, none to naming or defending doctrine.'[7]

When understanding flows principally from current talk, much may be lost or deformed. Without the organisation of a comparatively firm intellectual base, without the materials that might serve a collective memory, thought is free to become mercurial. It can liberally redefine the past and obliterate its concerns. The reading of intellectual history is correspondingly recast. Historical periods become typically defined by the work and actions of men who are centrally responsible for maintaining the oral tradition. Prominent mediators of that tradition are forced to act as significant benchmarks so that many interactionists refer back to a few writers who bestow authority on ideas and methods. What was written or thought before those writers can be effectively bracketed. If it is not bracketed, a salient thinker may come to represent a convenient distillation or condensation of his predecessors' ideas. He will attain symbolic value as an organisation of perspectives, enabling a shedding of the past and a radical rewriting of the school's character. Just as Itzcoatl decreed that the memory of the Aztecs should be re-made by the destruction of all early records, so the interactionists periodically lose their past. Howard Becker may become recognised as the author of ideas which he himself later attributed to Edwin Lemert.[8] Erving Goffman may become the unacknowledged reincarnation of Georg Simmel. The Hegelianism and neo-Kantianism residing in the works of Fred Davis or Anselm Strauss can be masked.

An intense poring over the history of ideas is not necessarily a profitable activity. In the case of symbolic interactionism, however, some benefit may be gained. Many of the original problems and principles of interactionism have become the substance of a kind of silent language. They have become transmuted so that that which was once lucid and acknowledged has become part of an inexpressible vision. Having lost the clarity they initially possessed, the focal concerns of interactionism may hold a mystery for those who work with them. It is thus possible that the nurturing of the sociology as an aesthetic and conjunctive mode of interpretation may be understood as a partial response to an inability to articulate what were once salient themes. The muting of the past has rendered some thought ineffable and almost incommunicable. Much of that vanished history explains the preoccupations and problems of the present. It is an unappreciated repository of dilemmas and solutions which have shaped interactionism in ways that are now little understood. The tendency to seek for the roots of ideas in the work of a recent master has severely increased the difficulty. The interests of an Everett Hughes or a Herbert Blumer are not precisely the same as those of Hegel, Kant or the first pragmatists. They provide no more than a distorting lens through which to scan the past. Their location within an oral tradition has provided them with a context of taken-for-granted assumptions that were once clear and explicit. Some disinterring of early work is therefore vital.

Mine is not the first resurrectionist account of interactionism. John Petras, for instance, has published a series of essays which describe the evolution of interactionism from its very earliest American forms.[9] Yet, in the main, conventional histories ignore epistemological and ontological arguments that have had a critical impact on the developing sociology. They typically anchor interactionism in a debate about the authority of instinct theory and folk psychology. Kant is rarely cited, and Hegel is invoked only as a theorist of the collective mind.[10] Such a narrow construction tends to throw much out of focus. In particular, it deflects attention away from the two somewhat contradictory perspectives that infuse the style and substance of interactionism. Interactionism may be usefully construed as an amalgam of Simmel's formal sociology and a pragmatist epistemology. It combines much else as well, but an emphasis upon that synthesis should reveal some of the underpinnings of the central paradigm. I shall not offer a comprehensive discussion of all the ideas that flowed into interactionism. Rather, I shall dwell on a few principal themes.

Symbolic Interactionism and the Dark and Void Space

Running through sociology, and German sociology in particular, there is a great schism which affects the management of all intellectual problems. That schism bears on the fundamental nature of the material which confronts analysis. The problematic character of social reality brings in its train basic questions about the observer's powers to apprehend and understand what he describes. There are those who would maintain that the world can transform itself into a structure of pellucid truth, that it can be made to yield an unconditional and absolute logic. A sociologist's statements can so capture reality that subject and object become united in an undisputed communion. The essential character of the world may not be accessible to every man, but those who do not grasp it are blinded by mystification, by a disadvantaged structural position, by an unfortunate location in the flow of historical process, or by a lack of the proper intellectual weaponry. Analysis may then be construed as unequivocally correct or incorrect, true or false. It does not lend itself to diverse interpretation.

An accurate appreciation of social reality is mastered by wielding those techniques (dialectical, structural, psycho-analytic or scientific) which sift the relevant from the irrelevant and strip the world down to its inner core. Exploration may revolve around practical engagement as a device to bridge the gulf between the knower and the knowable; it may centre on methodologically scrupulous tactics; it may rest on the rigorous exercise of intuition; or it may be supported by the contention that the structure of rational argument is entirely symmetrical with the structure of social and natural events. Although individual thinkers or ideas may be cast as fallible, little doubt is entertained about the existence of an incontrovertible reality which lies open to discovery by an enquiring mind. A proper use of reason will make it apparent that a paramount and invariant truth organises all the visible and invisible features of life. The character of that organisation cannot be negotiated. Men are able to gain precise knowledge of it, and all constructions which impugn it must be derived from false consciousness. Such a stance is espoused by most Marxists, some structuralists, and some of the scientific sociologists. For many writers of the late nineteenth and early twentieth centuries, that version of truth was the only goal that would make a science worth pursuing. They sought to achieve a final reconciliation between the seeming dualities and contradictions of speculation: between subject and object, man and society, the moral and the empirical. Lukács, Marx, Goldmann, Mannheim, Adorno and Durkheim unearthed a solid order beneath a superficial chaos of impressions. Sociology came to be seen as a massive instrument of synthesis and unification which would dispel all the fragmenting appearances in which reality was lodged. Alienated and mischievous thought would surrender to a vision of life as a transcendental totality.

In conflict with such a strain, there is a tradition of thinking which disavows any pretensions to truth. It hinges on the assertion that there can be no single reality to which all science must defer. If an absolute truth exists, it must defy man's ability to comprehend it and is therefore void for all practical purposes. Every analysis is conceived to be irretrievably partial and perspectival, locked into the peculiar situation and problems of the sociologist. It contributes towards intellectual organisation, but much is also organised out of focus and cannot be handled by a solitary mind or a solitary theory. The search for the certain and the absolute may even be dismissed as a modern equivalent of the hunt for the questing beast. The real may be conceived to have no independence of the individual or collective thoughts which dwell on it.

Max Weber offers a major instance of an onslaught upon the pursuit of essential truth. He disowned the claims that were conventionally made for sociology. The fusions that sociology might accomplish were dismissed as chimerical: the good could not be derived from what was; practical activity was separate from speculative enquiry; the real and the theoretical are irreparably distinct; science and politics are autonomous of one another. In short, he denied the possibility of any overarching truth which subordinated all particular concerns and made them one.

His principal thesis was that reality is inexhaustible. It is too complex and dense to be fully comprehended, and no statement can ever reflect its infinite possibilities. A theory cannot be more than one of an indefinite number of legitimate vantage points on social process. No matter how detailed or substantial it may be, it cannot condense all that could be known about a problem. It may possess analytic strengths but, as a single perspective, it represents an abstraction which distorts, simplifies and curtails understanding. The deficiencies of limited knowledge cannot be amended by compressing an ever greater array of ideas into an argument. There may be little profit in synthesis or aggregation because reality can never be saturated by a description; because discrepant stances may not lend themselves to amalgamation; and because a parsimonious answer may be as practically serviceable as one that is extended. So vast and intricate is social life that it dwarfs any attempt to encompass it. Even a mammoth synthesis of theories or observations gains little in appreciable intellectual power. It would be absurd to assume that such syntheses offer greater approximations to truth. Indeed, it would be absurd to assume that even the smallest portions of reality can be intellectually subdued.

The sociologist must recognise that his inability to accommodate all perspectives renders him purblind. All that he knows is incomplete, provisional and open. The very formation of a perspective opens up further possibilities of knowledge which, in turn, furnish new ideas. Thought must generate more thought, just as action multiplies itself. At best, a synthesis can lead to a temporary freezing of knowledge so that it becomes available to inspection, but it cannot do more. No sociological understanding can attain a state of finality and closure.

Because the real can never be wholly known, there is a most profound difference between a description and what is described. All that may be accomplished is a cautious reconstruction by means of intellectual categories that enhance understanding. Those categories are constrained to remain parts of an imaginative contrivance only: they are not the same as the entities they purport to examine; neither do they enjoy an existence outside the mind of their employer. The assembling of a system of concepts may reinforce a sociologist's grasp, but it neither reflects nor encapsulates the real world. It is illegitimate to deduce properties of the real from those concepts. They illuminate only a limited segment of social process; they do not reproduce it; and all inferences drawn from them are liable to be in error. The lack of fit between model and the modelled cannot be repaired by tinkering: no amount of attention, embellishment or elaboration can transform the description into its object. No remedial work can bridge that gap. The workings of mind alone cannot engender truth. Instead, the sociologist must proceed most gingerly. He cannot claim some intellectual affinity with the march of man which empowers him to synthesise in advance of disciplined research.

Very few of the early sociologists maintained that the essence of social life was effortlessly available to the intellect. Even those who claimed that such an essence could be prised out of the welter of epiphenomenal appearances asserted that the task was onerous and problematic. The business of defining and grasping core realities was littered with obstructions which stemmed from ideology, parochialism, ambiguity and alienation. The divide between the essentialists and the nominalists was never complete. Both emphasised the metaphysical pathos of man alienated frm the Absolute. Both were heirs to the lingering preoccupation with estrangement that was celebrated in Plato's portrayal of the cave-dweller's divorce from the real and the true; in the tragedy of the Fall which was central to *Genesis*; in the Calvinist's apprehension that God is unknowable and untouchable. At the time when sociology was first taking form, the problem of alienation was the pivot and catalyst of virtually all speculation. Man was conceived to be blind and excluded, and sociology was nursed as a potential tool of his redemption.

It was in Germany that knowledge was initially organised into an industry, and it was there that the context of much sociological theory was structured. Within that context, the problem of intellectual estrangement was given poignancy and urgency by Kant's epistemology. Although Kant's assault on the status of pure reason had been anticipated before,[11] it was his argument that came to be seen as the most formidable and obstructive barrier to any scheme for the total comprehension of life. The entire development of sociology may be presented as a prolonged response to the questions set by Kant's depiction of the connections between matter and mind.

Symbolic interactionism can become intelligible only within the environment of uncertainties that was created by Kant. It houses one solution to the problems of philosophical dualism, and its hidden agenda is dominated by precisely the same concerns as those which precipitated the emergence of other sociologies. Instead of representing the fruits of an American version of the immaculate conception, it shares an intellectual parentage with Marxism, Durkheimian functionalism, phenomenology, positivism and the sociology of Max Weber. It appears disinherited because its particular resolution of dualism perversely encouraged its exponents to shed not only their intellectual past but also their arguments for adopting the resolution itself.

Kant and the Limits of Knowledge

David Hume brought about a massive fracturing of the claims of rationalism. It had been maintained that the systematic exercise of reason could lay bare the physiology of natural and social process. By contrast, Hume asserted that the realms of knowledge and reality were irrevocably distinct. Their relations were most problematic. There was no warrant for men to assume that they could describe the hidden workings of nature, because mind and nature did not mirror one another. Understanding was destined to be circumscribed, provisional and infirm. It was entirely illegitimate to imagine that the ordering principles of the world could ever be discovered by deduction or induction. For instance, the observation that the sun had risen every morning until now permitted one to have no more than an intelligent expectation that it would rise again tomorrow. The movement of the sun is not governed by any inexorable law which has to be obeyed. Law and causality are not parts of the domain of nature. They are merely features of an intellectual reconstruction of nature, categories which the mind foists on what it contemplates.

Kant attempted to rebuild epistemology by injecting some certainty into the knowledge which could be entertained about nonideal events. He offered a radical thesis which was to prepare the whole course of German intellectual history, philosophy and sociology. His argument was based on a criticism of Hume's account of the character of knowledge. He claimed that Hume had made an inadequate analysis of experience itself.[12] An experientially satisfactory epistemology would be organised on a foundation of distinctions between styles of grasping the world. Chief amongst these styles were the types of knowledge available to men. Knowledge could be analytic or synthetic, *a priori* or *a posteriori*. Analytic knowledge centres on deductive and logical operations of mind which proceed from axioms that have been established in some fashion. They refine and amplify what is already known, but do not add anything substantive to the stock of knowledge. They are complemented by synthetic understanding which consists of some concrete addition to the store of what people know. The synthetic must be empirical; that is, it must be rooted in an experience or observation of the world that generates new data.

There are thus three major modes of knowledge. The analytic *a priori* produces ideas independently of the observable, it anticipates the observable, and it depends for its cogency on logical rigour. It is a quality of pure understanding whose suppositions are insubstantial unless they are the material of a possible empirical experience. There is the synthetic *a posteriori* whose ideas stem from an active acquaintance with the world and are therefore existentially and retrospectively grounded. These two vehicles of knowledge provide different possibilities of negotiating an environment of objects.

Phenomena are the facets of materials which are available to experience. They are manufactured by us in the course of our dealings with them. Their apprehension is mediated by our senses, and it must always be contingent on the way in which they are presented to sight, touch, taste, smell and hearing. The encounters we have with objects yield the phenomena that we may grasp. How they reveal the inner essence of those objects must always remain problematic. There is no fashion in which the character of things-in-themselves may be established, because things are known only through their phenomenal manifestations. Understanding which is independent of such manifestations is rootless and unconnected with anything but the workings of mind itself. By definition, the phenomenal constitute the only sure knowledge we can attain, and that knowledge is necessarily limited to the immediate confines of experience. The quintessence of an entity, its noumenon, is for ever sealed from our certain understanding. The real, the fundamental and the true are decisively beyond the scope of objective knowledge. All that one knows about them is that they are literally unknowable. They are the boundaries around possible comprehension.

The noumenal constitutes the 'thing-in-itself': the unascertainable quality of an entity which can never be scrutinised or appraised. It can perform only a negative or limiting role, signifying the constraints that are imposed upon thought. Limited generalisation about appearances may be permissible if the arguments can be translated into the material of an experience. Conjectures about noumena must be relegated to the area of the permanently speculative. 'Objects of pure understanding will always remain unknown to us.' The absolute which sociologists and philosophers sought could be seized only in its problematic manifestations or through uncertain reasoning.

Kant introduced a third style of approaching the world, the synthetic *a priori*, which hinged on the contrast between form and content. People do not confront the world naïvely and without intellectual organisation. There can be no direct commerce with the contents of reality. All knowledge is mediated by forms of experience which shape what we can apprhend. The forms impart order, stability and meaning to an otherwise inchoate and unmanageable universe. Without such ordering structures of mind, nothing could become available to reflection or understanding. They are the means by which a thing is transformed into a possible object of knowledge. They enable the construction of the experience of a phenomenon. The synthetic *a priori* serves as a further block to the understanding of the absolute properties of things-in-themselves. Objects can never be seen as they *are*, independently of the shaping activity that is conducted by the intellect. The organisation created by mind denies all possibility of an unalloyed appreciation of the real.

Man as agent can proceed only by means of categories of thought which are largely pre-structured. His understanding grasps what surrounds him through pre-existing forms of interpretation. All that is moderately sure is the world of experienced data. Those data may be worked on to furnish modest inferences about the nature of events, objects and processes. Other modes of speculation must be recognised as relatively unsure. In particular, the analytic *a posteriori* is epistemologically inconceivable. The essence or general properties of items cannot be abstracted from experience. Pure reason must remain within its own sphere, and it is fanciful to pretend that the real and the true can be documented authoritatively. 'They have no objective validity and . . . are a mere play of imagination and understanding.' An *a priori* or *a posteriori* knowledge of things in general has no discernible bearing on its supposed objects. Rather it represents the procedures of an autonomous realm of intellect which is able freely to conjure up all manner of sports.

Such a formulation promised to lame all but the most humble empirical thinking. If man could not know the essential core of the social or natural world, if he were doomed to view the moral and the intellectual as an independent universe, then the philosophical search for truth, coherence and objectivity would be ever foundering in the unbridgeable abyss between subject and object, between reality and appearance. Fichte phrased the issue as one of 'the absolute projection of an object of the origin of which no account could be given with the result that the space between projection and thing projected is dark and void'. Sociological thought has continued to hover around this theme of alienated knowledge in an endeavour to neuter its more disabling implications.

Almost every sociological development may then be read as a reply to Kant. Weber, for instance, worked with a largely Kantian epistemology to produce a sociology which claimed no capacity to generalise, essentialise or establish truth. By contrast, the Marburg school of new-Kantian philosophy modified speculative dualism to argue that enquiry was not only responsible for the generation of an object's form but also its content. Kant had defined contents as creatures of the unapproachable 'thing-in-itself'. Like the latter-day Calvinist, members of the Marburg school contended that philosophy was the theory of the principles of science and, by its refinement, knowledge of the world could be progressively accumulated. Disavowing all such certainty, Positivism represents, in effect, an abandonment of the search for the true nature of reality and its displacement by a stress upon limited and scrupulously conducted empirical enquiry. All implicit and explicit questions of epistemology are dismissed as insoluble, metaphysical and practically meaningless.

In some variants, the programme of the phenomenologists abandoned all problems of the real and addressed itself entirely to the task of exploring how the universe of phenomenal appearances is constructed. The transcendental idealists may have retained a lingering interest in the world that lurks beneath surface appearance, but other schools have not. Schutz, for instance, adhered strictly to an examination of the symbolic constitution of society. Pursuing that search, many phenomenologists have rendered the character of the noumenon irrelevant.

The tradition carried by Vico, Marx, Hegel, Dilthey and Lukács denied the Kantian dualism of subject and object. It insisted instead on the fundamental unity of mind and social matter, knower and known, creator and created. It claimed that society is an alienated manifestation of mind which can be recovered by mind. The absolute could be reached either by replicating its animating logic or by some more immediate intuition of its nature. Resort was made to the dialectic or to an appreciative communion with works of art and literature which would afford privileged insight into the essence of a culture or an epoch.

Symbolic interactionism itself was compounded out of two of these routes to sociological certainty, Simmel's distinctive phenomenology and the pragmatist transcription of Hegel. In this chapter I shall discuss Simmel's formalism. In the next I shall focus on the manner in which Hegelianism was transmuted in American sociology.

Simmel and the Forms

Georg Simmel entered philosophy, borrowed Kant's intellectual edifice and put it to work in sociology. His affiliation with Kantian epistemology is immediate. His doctoral dissertation was occupied with problems which Kant had made salient; his language was neo-Kantian; and he conspicuously advertised the transposition which he had achieved. Thus, Kant had written an essay entitled 'How is Nature Possible?' and Simmel wrote a piece called 'How is Society Possible?' Almost all Simmel's work must be construed within the framework defined by Kant. His sociology is one effort to accommodate the crippling effects of intellectual uncertainty.

Simmel maintained that all objects, events and processes enjoy an existence which is intimately fused with the life of the observer who contemplates or produces them. Society and social action do not enjoy an ontological independence and they are not subject to their own immanent laws. The attempt to adjudicate what is the irreducibly real unit of social existence is an absurd exercise because all phenomena are the synthetic creations of those who deal with them. All that men confront is an environment of constructions which they have organised out of experience. Each of those constructions is as real as any other, and each may be the object of disparate and competing perspectives. Any comparison of phenomena in terms of their authenticity or conflicting qualities is profitless unless it is conducted with criteria that are set by a clearly defined problem. Similarly, social reality offers an inexhaustible reservoir of prospects which cannot be ranked. All judgments between them must be arbitrary and capricious. It follows that the attempt to discover the ultimately true must necessarily collapse because it is liable to become ensnared in an endless regress of ontological claims. If it is alleged that society alone forms the final reality, it may be asserted that society is a reified abstraction which lacks the tangible and visible qualities of the individuals who comprise it. Individuals themselves, however, may be described as little more than imaginatively assembled collections of traits, settings and qualities. A person is as much a reification as society. The components of personality, in turn, may be reduced down to drives, stimuli, responses and psychic process. Any elementary reality can be exploded into more basic realities in an infinite chain. The quest for the fundamentally authentic particle 'actually eliminates all knowable reality'.

An organisation, a style, an epoch or an experience represents a unified set of relations which is given form by the observer who uses understanding to carve it out, award it a structure, and impart characteristics to it. The field of potential experience which yields phenomena is bewilderingly massive. It is ordered selectively, collaboratively and creatively. All phenomena are artificial and, in the sense that they could be otherwise, they are also arbitrary. They are neither invented nor discovered, but *produced*. Society and its components are ongoing accomplishments, they are in a state of continual production as their members actively impose order on the world. They have no reality outside that accomplishment.

Society is made possible by a process of consciousness which bestows structure on otherwise incoherent happenings and things. That consciousness exists in the individuals who make up a society, it is the prerequisite of social life. But it represents more than the mere aggregation of the separate psyches of people because it possesses a distinctive character which is the properly social element of life. Men produce society in their interactions with each other. Such production flows out of conflict, intimacy, co-operation, struggle and competition. It is an endlessly fluid process which cannot be portrayed as a structure or a simple system. It consists of the myriad exchanges between men, not of the fixed, autonomous suprapersonal entities which some sociologists have claimed are ontologically superior to men.

Society thus assumed a particular significance in Simmel's sociology. He defined it not as a substance or an organisation but as an *event*. Indeed, he generally chose not to write of society (*Gesellschaft*) at all, but referred to the properties of collective interaction as sociation (*Vergesellschaftung*). Social reality is accomplished by innumerable people coming and going, meeting and parting, loving and hating, creating social order through their encounters. Any other identification would entail an unwarranted reification. Outside the constituent events of society there is nothing which may be witnessed or permissibly discussed.

Sociation arises when individuals encounter one another, are aware of the uniting situation in which they are lodged, and engage in some orderly and mutually responsive conduct. The awareness of any one individual cannot be the same as that of any other, but sociation requires a joint subordination to a common order even if the styles of subordination are complementary rather than identical. It is in those connections, the collaborative production of those connections, and the impact wrought by those connections, that society exists. Sustained interaction can engender seemingly autonomous social products such as classes, organisations and cultures that constrain and fold back upon people. Yet those products would not exist without the work of routine social encounters, and the encounters could survive without them. Analytically and ontologically, the petty materials of sociation are prior to the grand structures of conventional sociological theory.

One of the projects which Simmel set himself was the exploration of the constituents of sociation. He conceived society to be a continually unfolding process which was given structure by the routine and ostensibly petty. His analyses are littered with examples which most sociologists consider too trivial to report. But Simmel does convey an imagery of society as a pulsating web of relations whose interplay produces order and change.

Sociology was taken by Simmel to be neither a grand nor a minor enterprise. It was not, in Comtian fashion, to be regarded as the queen of the sciences, some vast overarching discipline which transcended all other approaches to reality. Neither was it to be understood as an approach which aggregated and synthesised all existing studies of man. It could not and should not purport to do the work currently performed by economics, politics, geography, psychology, jurisprudence, philosophy, philology and the like. Yet it was not to be managed as a latecomer to the scientific world which must scrabble around in the interstices of existing disciplines, piecing together what others had ignored. What distinguished sociology was not its subject-matter but its method. Simmel stated 'not its object but its manner of contemplation, the peculiar abstraction which it performs, differentiates it from the other historic social sciences.'

Sociology is thus presented as one of a number of possible ways of obtaining a grasp on reality. It is only a grasp, not a total embrace. Simmel does not claim for sociology any comprehension of totalities or essences or truths. Rather, sociology is simply another standpoint which a person might care to adopt. As a perspective it lends unity and coherence to its object, but it also methodically eliminates great areas of knowledge and it ignores innumerable features of phenomena. Simmel took the peculiar province of sociology to be the forms of sociation. In a sense, politics, economics and psychology provide the contents of social life. Life could not persist without political or economic activity. In themselves, however, politics and economics are featureless, shapeless and incapable of social realisation. Their expression must be mediated through social relationships before they become phenomena. They are moulded, channelled and directed by the limits and varieties of modes of sociation. A political event can become actual only if it is presented through one or more of the restricted styles of social display.

What is common to all contents, then, is their manifestation in the ritualistic, etiquette-governed forms of sociation. Sociology's business is the investigation and documentation of such forms. In so doing it becomes a companion to all the other social sciences; but unlike them it is concerned with the general properties of the socially possible. Sociology is thus an abstracting science which undertakes the discovery and chronicling of the ways in which social life is patterned. At bottom the contents of sociation are thrust into a relatively insignificant role in analysis. It is the general features of sociation that furnish an opportunity to compose a grammer or geometry of social relations. The unique and the substantive dwindle into a secondary importance.

The definition of sociology as an abstracting process offered Simmel a solution to the dilemma which was conventionally thought to bedevil sociology. Orthodox thinking on social analysis dichotomised science into two distinct realms of thought. Chiefly influenced by Windelband, analysis was divided up into the ideographic which comprehended the special features of the unique events of history and society, and the nomothetic (or rule-governed) which applied to the routine and general properties of the natural world. It was held that the social could not be mastered by methods which were evolved to inspect the natural. It was ontologically improper to act as if there were law-like regularities in social life. Instead the sociologist is restricted to the production of limited, focused descriptions of unique events. He cannot proceed to generalisation or the invocation of laws. By discarding the necessity to confront contents, Simmel furnished a strategy which could handle the social as if it were nomothetically analysable.

Forms became for Simmel's treatment of the social world what they were for Kant's discussion of natural phenomena. They were synthetic *a priori* modes of knowledge which lent unity and organisation to the potentially anarchic universe of experience. It was through forms that the sociologist and actor alike conferred order on what they did and saw. It was through the production, recognition and resolution of forms that sociation became structured, intelligible and concerted action. In forms, individuals transcend themselves. They cease to be isolated atoms and become parts of systems of sociation whose properties cannot be inferred from their separate characters alone. Whenever people speak, meet, make love, fight or play they realise the contents of their behaviour in social forms. Without those forms, the contents would be destined to remain permanently inarticulate and unknown. With those forms, they are transmuted and harnessed.

The distinction between form and content is practically impossible to define. Simmel himself confessed that he could not convey any body of communicable skills which would enable a novice to perform the operation of divorcing the two. Indeed he asserted that they are so interwoven that they can never be discovered independently of each other. He maintained that he was pursuing analysis by means of analogy only. Form and content should not be taken to constitute ontologically or analytically autonomous features of entities. Rather they represent convenient designations for facets of phenomena which must be disentangled before the work of sociology can be carried out.

Simmel's most common similes for forms are those which liken them to the relation between grammar and utterance, geometry and the actual substance of things which are geometrically ordered, logic and the assertions that logic permits. As grammar, geometry and logic, they are abstract properties of events which enjoy a life that can be assessed independently of the special circumstances of their occurrence. Simmel cited numerous instances of form: they include hierarchy, competition, secrecy, strangeness, domination, conflict, sociability, play, coquetry and subordination. In any specific event, the excision of form from content is problematic. Simmel maintained that the two are so indissolubly fused that they cannot be dismembered. No form would appear without content, and content could not become manifest without form. It is neither possible to examine a pure form which lacks all content, nor pure content which lacks all form. Any severing operation is thus artificial and contrived. Its justification lies in the observation that it is not only the sociologist who performs it. People in everyday life are inextricably wedded to the use and manipulation of forms. Unlike the components of Kant's nature, the forms of sociation lend coherence both to scientific speculation and to the materials which are analysed. Forms are simultaneously explanation and problem.

Simmel's form and content are virtually identical to the central structures of Kantian epistemology. Kant had argued that all synthetic knowledge is experiential, and the experiential cannot but be an understanding of the appearances of an object. It is impossible to gain an unfettered and unadulterated access to an entity. Phenomenon and noumenon have an entirely problematic relationship with one another. Since the noumenon cannot be directly known, it is not open to comparison with the experiences which people have of its manifestations. Those experiences, in turn, are lent structure by the categories or forms of thought which are the *a priori* and indispensable mediators between known and knower. Nothing can be grasped without them. Nothing can be known in its own innocent state by means of them. Simmel's forms play much the same role. Content is relegated, in the main, to matters of psychology. It is the substance of emotions, drives, interests and desires. None of these states can receive any guise in the world without the structures provided by the forms of sociation and social interpretation. They can thus have only the most spectral existence in analysis. Nothing can be said of them, and none of them can be given visible flesh, without the agency of forms which render them impure. Contents therefore are akin to the noumena of social life, and forms constitute the phenomena. Simmel denied the exact parallel with Kant's formulation. For instance, instead of being fixed and unalterable aspects of mind, Simmel's forms are fluid and negotiable. Yet the similarity is there. It enables the sociologist to defeat the problems posed by the uniqueness of happenings in social life; by an apparently unknowable social reality; and by the alienation of the commentator from the events which he describes.

Forms are not only ways of being, they are also ways of knowing. As soon as one broods, reflects or makes indications, one has transformed the pure content of experience into the form by which it is grasped. There are innumerable forms of knowing, each of which is as legitimate as any other, each of which lays the basis for a potentially comprehensive view of the world. Religious, artistic, political, musical, philosophical, sociological and practical forms of knowing and being translate the contents of existence into their own particular idiom. Groupings of forms can compose systematic wholes which then become worlds, self-contained styles of being which justify and interpret the social universe. Certain forms display an affinity for one another. Others are contradictory and not readily synthesised. Thus monetary calculation, bureaucratic organisation, democracy, mobility and rationality constitute a coherent whole because they place thematic emphasis on the mediation of unique events by general, logical and measurable criteria. They enable the reduction of all special qualities to one universal medium. They encourage the divorce of man from place and object. They subordinate quality to quantity, status to contract, aristocracy to democracy, and rootedness to deracination.

Forms therefore represent the currency of social intercourse. They make contents available, but they are regulated by properties which enjoy their own logic. As contents pass into form, so they are forced to submit to a grammar which has its own possibilities of evolution, synthesis and transformation. In particular, that grammar can confer autonomy on the forms of sociation and understanding. What may once have been instrumental and subordinate in the structuring of content can achieve the status of an independent end. The acquisition of autonomy by a form attains the greatest importance in Simmel's analysis. Central to it is the idea that life is also 'more-than-life', that existence produces an alienating organisation which simultaneously strengthens and negates it. In parallel with Bergson and the pragmatists,[13] Simmel conceived much life to be *durée*, lived experience in which a person is so immediately involved that he does not distance himself from what he is undergoing. Reflection imposes no shape on existence: person and experience are one, and content is directly apprehended. However, content cannot be grasped or pointed to. It must be lived immediately. *Durée* is interrupted when crisis, stress, frustration or contemplation alienates the person from what he has done and from the procedures which he employed to accomplish it. No sense can be made of that experience without forms of understanding which transmute content and render it foreign and problematic. As soon as forms become objects, they can become translated into phenomena that are autonomous of their producer.

Characteristic forms may be pursued for long periods because they offer a practical usefulness. People attend to sounds because they must be alert to danger, or to possibilities of food, or because they seek communication. The experience of being attentive may however become detached from its object. Involvement in the world of sound can foster the development of music, poetry, drama, literature, linguistics and phonology. Such forms are emancipated: they are separate facets of life which confront men as independent entities. Their cultivation may be utterly serious when everday concerns become the bases of abstract scientific work (the nursing of knowledge 'for its own sake'); they may attain triviality in pure sociability which is devoted solely to the artistic and playful experimentation with form; they may become sinister when the forms of domination confer legitimacy on tyranny and translate personal subjection into impersonal bondage. In all their manifestations, however, the forms can become so liberated that they are experienced as externally coercive objects which limit choice, restrict perspectives and infuse motivation.

Simmel located the autonomisation of forms in a dialectical process. He portrayed life as fluid, open and changeful; a fleeting meeting of past and future in which the past is endlessly reconstituted and the future is subject to shifting anticipations. Life cannot but generate more of itself, but its reproduction depends on forms whose stability and independence can thwart it: its realisation is achieved by the forms which imprison it. All transcending of those forms manufactures new forms which serve as new constraints. There is thus a constant war between man and the language of forms which he must employ. His life is forever being externalised into a fixed organisation which impairs his capacity to develop. Moreover, as those forms take on an autonomy, so they achieve an objective logic of their own. Practical activity gave birth to science which then established its own seemingly inexorable and impersonal mode of being. Life and its artifacts have fallen under the sway of two distinct logics: a subjective logic of the producer's unfolding existence, and an objective logic of his products. As time passes, so the world created by science and culture becomes enlarged. Man finds himself inhabiting an environment of objectified forms which he cannot control. Worse, he can barely understand the inner workings of that environment. So abundant and complex are they, that they appear as opaque and alien entities which threaten to submerge him. 'The cultural objects become more and more linked to each other in a self-contained world which has increasingly fewer contacts with the subjective psyche and its desires and sensibilities.'

Forms impose themselves on men's experience in complex ways. All life is seen as a generation of forms, a confrontation with forms, and a superseding of forms. Forms interplay with each other to weave most intricate patterns of evolution. In reality all forms are impure and distorted, they merge and intersect, and none can be discovered in a whole state. The stasis immanent within forms receives a dual challenge: from the life which is expressed in forms and from other forms themselves. Simmel's conception of sociation is not one of structure and system. Rather it stresses dialectic, change, confusion and process. It offers an imagery which is founded on the idea of life as tense, vibrant, emergent and melting.

The interweaving of forms is also complicated and animated by the gaps, the ignorance, and the fragmentary nature of social life and knowledge. No man can know all the facets of an individual, a process or a society. When he focuses on one aspect he must necessarily neglect others. He can tackle only minute sectors of life and then only momentarily. He is on the interface of countless world views and perspectives and cannot incorporate them all. As Simmel argued, 'we are constantly circulating over a number of different planes, each of which presents the world totality according to a different formula; but from each our life takes only a fragment along at any given time.' Life is thus made up of lacunae, uncertainties, pieces of partial knowledge, unsynthesisable elements which split men, forms and sociation up into disconnected parts. It cannot be other than open and incomplete. Few projects can ever be brought to a proper conclusion. The Simmelian cosmos is fractured and chaotic; it presents none of the coherence and simplicity which the other sociologies, particularly those wedded to the idea of system, espouse as themes. Von Wiese remarked that Simmel represented 'a very important advance over the older sociologists who founded on their mania for systems'.

Simmel and Symbolic Interactionism

The affinities between Simmel's formal sociology and symbolic interactionism are superficially clear, but it is always difficult to subject intellectual themes to an authoritative genealogical analysis. Ideas merge, are lost or are rediscovered in such a complicated fashion that their precise authorship and influence defy systematic detection.

Any dissection of the intellectual history of interactionism is made especially fraught by the methodical manner in which pedigrees are ignored, origins obliterated and syntheses are performed covertly. When it is discussed at all, the history of interactionist ideas is typically portrayed as a process built on two stages. It is as if no thought of consequence preceded the work of the Chicago School, and the Chicago School alone spawned the few seminal thinkers who lent decisive shape to the contemporary version of the sociology. Kant, Hegel and Simmel are forced to assume a largely invisible presence which has led to a frequent misreading of the origins and nature of their impact on interactionism.[14] False genealogies can be drawn up, themes thrown out of focus and problems deformed.

A sociology which forgets its past may be committed to the continuous rediscovery of old ideas. When the provenance of thought is unknown, authorship can be claimed by those who lack any proper title to it. Old issues are proclaimed innovations, only to recede again into the limbo from which they were retrieved. The unstated component of the oral tradition is a fertile culture for the emergence of a cyclical pattern of recovery and loss. It forms the dimly recognised and rarely scrutinised context of the perspective. As such it is an accessible source of anonymous ideas which bear immediately on the central concerns of interactionism. When areas of that intellectual penumbra are rescued and analysed, it is their familiarity which gives them plausibility. After all, they were initially responsible for the structure and cogency of the arguments that are used to examine them. Work undertaken in the early phases of the sociology's history is thus liable to be repeatedly disinterred and suppressed. Simmel's ideas could be exhumed a number of times under different authorities.

Within so clouded a perspective as symbolic interactionism, therefore, it is often moot whether an innovation is genuinely novel or simply a return to murky origins. It may well be that much of the interactionist resort to formalism is no more than a re-invention or rediscovery of Simmel's solution to the problems of dualism. Certainly, explicit references to Simmel's writings have appeared less and less frequently in interactionist analysis. The lack of express recognition may ape Simmel's own disdain for the rituals of acknowledgement and bibliographical propriety. But it may also signify the diminishing intellectual importance of Simmel as a source of interactionist themes. The exact scope and nature of Simmel's influence is highly problematic.

Another issue adds to the obscurity of interactionist genealogy. The reservoir of current sociological theories is neither vast nor varied. The core paradigms of many major sociologies are alike: they reflect their common roots in a few problems and a few theses; their evolution has been marked by diffusion and interplay rather than by dispersal and isolated growth; and it is conceivable that the absolute range of viable positions is circumscribed, that there are limits to the diversity of theories which can attract sustained attention. It is evident that many of the contentions of Marxism or phenomenology differ only slightly from those of pragmatism and formalism. They are phrased in a common language, celebrate common problems and share a common lineage. Only matters of context, programme and emphasis may serve to distinguish them. In the instance of interactionism, it is absurd to attempt any decisive attribution of principal conceptions. The various sociologies that have flowed into the perspective are not so unlike that their distinctive traces may be discerned. Formalism is akin to pragmatism in its stress on process, dialectic, the social construction of meaning, the illegitimacy of reification and systematisation, and the priority of the local over the abstract and the structural. It is impossible to prise the two apart and ascertain the particular refractions of Simmel in symbolic interactionism. It is as difficult to determine what other sociologies are at work in the theory.

Yet Simmel is demonstrably significant. At one level his works provide that set of supporting and connecting arguments that are required to transform interactionism into a substantial sociology. Without those props interactionism might simply fall apart. It would centre on strategies and interpretations which were incomprehensible and disjointed. Formalism must be injected into any intellectual reconstruction of the sociology. It represents a segment whose influence would have to be invented if it could not be documented. Simmel cannot but assume a salient place in a scientifically intelligible re-enactment of the birth of symbolic interactionism.

Such invention is not at all necessary. There are clear references to formalism and the social forms throughout interactionist writing, and the borrowing from Simmel is quite explicit.[15] Formal sociology was deliberately built into the early work of the interactionists. The *American Journal of Sociology*, published by the University of Chicago, contained numerous translations of Simmel's essays in its first volumes. Its editor, Albion Small, was active in sponsoring a massive importation of formalism. More importantly, one of the chief members of the original department of sociology at Chicago, Robert Park, studied under Simmel in Berlin. Indeed, Park observed 'with the exception of Simmel's lectures I never had any systematic instruction in sociology'.[16] Park fostered the establishment of the group which was to generate the oral tradition, and it was his work which fed the ideas of Simmel and the German university into American sociology.[17] As Hughes has argued, Park's absorption of formalism was critical for the entire course of American sociology.[18]

In conjunction with Ernest Burgess, Park produced what was probably the first sociology textbook of distinction in the United States. Their *Introduction to the Science of Sociology* harnessed an intellectual manifesto to a catholic collection of excerpts from sociological works.[19] Simmel's prominence is emphasised in that selection. He received the greatest individual number of citations in the index of names at the end of the volume. Further, of the 176 extracts, 10 were written by Simmel, 2 by Durkheim, 2 by Herbert Spencer, and one by Tönnies. There were no articles by Max Weber or Karl Marx.

The *Introduction* was intended to provide an authoritative review of existing styles and areas of intellectual organisation. It was written that many problems of epistemology and ontology had been settled, the major remaining task being the thorough exploration of the substantive social world. Sociology had evolved through three stages: the era of speculative philosophy; the 'period of the "schools"' in which factionalism had reigned; and the dawning period of investigation and research. The discipline was now established as an embryo science whose character was substantially based on the thought of Simmel. Indeed, all other European writers were dwarfed by Simmel. His ideas were reproduced in the *Introduction* and they gave order to its agenda. There are sections entitled 'The Natural Forms of Communication', 'The Forms of Accommodation' and 'The Elementary Forms of Social Control'. That language could have been borrowed from Durkheim or some other sociologist, but it does seem to have been part of a quite deliberate effort to lend a technical Simmelian vocabulary to American sociology.

The intellectual scheme of the *Introduction* largely replicates the focal concerns of formalism. It dwells on the forms of symbiosis, isolation, segregation, interaction, competition, conflict, accommodation and conflict. Of course, the book also aggregates many ideas that are foreign to formalism. But its programme does bear Simmel's mark. It laid the basis of the entire development of symbolic interactionism.[20] Many salient conceptions of early interactionism were prised directly out of formalism,[21] and they have continued to frame the writings of the school. More significantly, the epistemological and methodological style of Simmel permeated the sociology and left a permanent impression.

The Interactionist Translation of Formalism

I have claimed that it is fruitless to assess the minute ways in which interactionism is draped around a formalist skeleton. Because many apparently formalist perspectives were not taken from Simmel himself, it is impossible to distinguish the genuine from the spurious derivations. Yet I shall proceed as if it were possible to unearth pure formalist ideas in the sociology. By so doing I shall prepare the foundations of an incremental definition of interactionism. Rather than embark on an analysis of the theory in its present guise, I shall attempt to build it up from its real and fabricated components.

A formalist influence explains much of the typical looseness and tentativeness of interactionist thought. It tends to encourage a particular conception of the proper subject-matter of sociology, a conception which is not amenable to abstract or speculative reasoning. If social life is taken to be an event which is produced in innumerable exchanges, it becomes absurd to portray it as a totality. Indeed, as a totality, it need be no more than a shifting congregation of processes without necessary design or stability. Its very fluidity renders all but the most spartan and cautious descriptions improbable.

When the *a priori* imputation of structure to an unobservable 'entity' is denied credibility, there are no plausible means by which it may be restored *a posteriori*. The formalists and the interactionists retain something of Kant's distrust of the analytic *a priori* and the analytic *a posteriori*.[22] They dismiss the idea of scientific knowledge of the thing-in-itself of society as epistemoloical nonsense. From James and Dewey, through Znaniecki and Blumer to Cicourel, there is a fairly consistent posture towards the status of social structure.[23] Social structures may be held to reside either in the minds of sociologists or in the minds of those people whom sociologists discuss. In the latter form it has some phenomenological reality because it moves people to act. In the former, it is productive of mystification and reification. It makes quite impermissible leaps from observation to that which cannot be observed. In turn, the interactionists have tended to focus on the specific workings of phenomena, not on society as a whole, a system, or an entity whose character may be inferred from particular historical themes.

No sociology which entertains a vision of society as flux can resort to a language which is appropriate to social statics. Neither can it divide the social world into discrete parts which are united by invariant relations. The symbolic interactionists discount as myth-making any attempt to generate theory which rests on catalogues of nice distinctions between social phenomena. Sociological explanation would be impossible unless affairs were momentarily frozen for inspection, but flux defies precise description. The very idea of social structure is reduced to insignificance in a perspective that treats change and openness as chiefly characteristic of society. Indeed any definition is likely to impose excessive order on shifting phenomena. The sociologist can manage conceptual frames that deal with the forms of change, but he cannot amalgamate them into one all-encompassing scheme. Thus Janowitz's complaint that Park and Burgess neglect social structure tends to ignore their fundamental ontology. He states:

> . . . it was abundantly evident that society, the social organism, was in a never-ending process of flux. As a result [the *Introduction*] . . . focuses on categories of social process. At the heart of their analysis is a set of process categories which have become classical in describing social change . . . But their very concern with social process limited their identification of the essential stratification features of an industrial society and weakened their analysis of social structure. Instead of examining the macrostructures of society, at points they used such vague formulations as 'social forces'.[24]

Janowitz demands of symbolic interactionism that which it explicitly denies. Instead of the macrosociologist's clarity and interpretative scope, the interactionist is committed to a measure of imprecision, fragmentation and humility. He cannot erect coherent systems of thought which permit neat inferential work. Indeed, almost all interactionists have maintained that the social world is so confused and uncertain that the theory which reflects it must also be tainted by confusion and uncertainty. They hold that a lucid, programmatic statement which pretended to lay out all the connections between phenomena would be no more than a meretricious and deceitful portrait of the world. Its impression of integrity and comprehensiveness would subvert understanding. Thus Louis Wirth discarded deductive sociology as a series of 'mere exercises' in theory construction.[25] The rationality of academic thought finds no counterpart in the formative processes of society. W. I. Thomas, too, believed that the complexity and volatility of social life must translate sociology into a special discipline which could not parrot the procedures of natural science. It must recognise the instability and diversity of social processes.[26]

In the main, symbolic interactionism eschews the theorising which would make great tracts of social terrain intelligible. Whilst it does not wholly shun the idea of social structure, its stress upon activity and process relegates structural metaphors to a most minor place. It works instead upon the limited sections of visible social life whose evolution can be rendered comprehensible. Like Simmel's own analysis, it applies the forms of change to apparently trivial areas of sociation. The career of the high school teacher,[27] the organisation of a ward for tuberculosis patients,[28] the moral history of the taxi-dancer,[29] the career of a mental patient,[30] and transactions between police and juvenile delinquents[31] present materials for the dissection of elementary social forms. They are explored to illuminate a simple grammar of sociation, a grammar whose rules give order to the allocation of territorial rights, the programming of timetables, and the meeting of diverse groups. More important, it is a grammar which is intended to provide working recipes for an understanding of the abstract properties of social life. Except perhaps in the writings of Erving Goffman, there is a reticence about systematically expounding such a logic. The principles of its operation would appear to be provided by example and implication rather than explicit statement. The characteristic antipathy to overtly rationalised schemes has led to a radical understatement of the sociology's central work.

Forms encountered in the interactionists' ethnographic analysis are amputated from the contents which gave them life. Much of Erving Goffman's work, for example, may be read as an effort to reveal the basic logic of sociation, a logic which can be discovered in a variety of superficially diverse settings.[32] In this sense, interactionism has been consistently involved in Simmel's quest for the underlying organisation of forms. It provides a lexicon or a set of intellectual categories rather than a systematic theory. Unlike Simmel's own mathematical and geometrical imagery, the metaphors engendering the interactionist forms have been ethological,[33] ecological,[34] theatrical,[35] cybernetic,[36] and dialectical. The forms of symbiosis,[37] the career,[38]

The Roots of Symbolic Interactionism

commitment[39] and role[40] litter analysis. They are collated and related to manufacture descriptions of a rudimentary social order which shapes some of the seeming flux of society. It is in the display of those forms that social life is realised. They impose an organisation which is never more than incomplete, partial and precarious. They do not provide a firm disciplining structure, but a loose series of changing possibilities. Forms do not therefore constitute a social system. They are the ingredients of local and temporary processes. For the interactionist such forms nevertheless represent the elementary particles of sociation. Goffman's discussion of the etiquette that enables men to meet, discourse and part; Becker's analysis of the commitments which bind men to the routine and the orderly; and the work of Hughes and of Glaser and Strauss on the career, are all parts of a depiction of society as a combination of fluctuating contents and relatively stable forms. A listing of formal properties can contribute to an understanding of what makes social life possible.

Formalism also offers an opportunity to investigate the character of the synthetic *a priori*. Forms organise both the explanatory schemes which are invoked to make sense of behaviour and the behaviour itself. There is thus a symmetry between the sociology and its problematic objects which encourages the interactionist to imagine that description and described are not unlike. Some of the problems of philosophical dualism are thereby quieted. The analyst may feel that he has done little to misrepresent the material which he explores. He examines phenomena with the very techniques that first constituted them. As Simmel remarked, 'the unity of society . . . is directly realized by its own elements because these elements are themselves conscious and synthesizing units.' The sociologist may investigate those principles of synthesis and consciousness, achieving an internal and an external understanding of process.

Interactionism is permeated by a search for 'authenticity', 'faithfulness' and 'integrity'. In the work of Herbert Blumer,[41] David Matza[42] and Glaser and Strauss[43] may be discovered the same concern for a sociology that describes social life in a manner that could be recognised by the people whose actions are portrayed. There is a perennial interest in creating an intellectual style which reasonably mirrors the organisation of unselfconscious experience itself. It is argued that adherence to that style can alone guarantee that analysis has not become too independent of the world which it addresses.

Interactionism is restricted by its trepidation that theoretical reasoning may become autonomous. It defines theorising as a form of knowing that may delude those who employ it. Critical to that argument is the contention that any extended account of behaviour is given vitality by a set of mannerisms which rest on persuasive metaphor. The thematic core of all sociological models is structured around imagery which conjures up tangible and familiar processes. Explanation must apparently depict social life as if it were a mathematical system, a cybernetic process, a conflict between warring individuals, an organism, a human being, an ecological system or a dispute between schoolmen. It is this last model, the analogy of a debate between scholars, that furnishes interactionism with its own dialectical imagery.

Each dominant model is governed by a logic which is peculiar to itself. Mathematical transformations are simply not identical to the equilibriating processes of an organism. A logic may not be appropriate when it is applied to settings for which it was never designed. The internal consistency and plausibility of a model are no indication of its legitimate generalisability. When a phenomenon is observed through the perspectives provided by any model, incongruous features are typically thrown out of focus or given some explanation which reduces anomaly. As Kenneth Burke remarked, a way of seeing is always a way of not seeing. Thus, when society is likened to the body of a man or to a set of equations, there is always a risk that what it taken to be true of the model will automatically be taken as true of society itself.

The greater the level of analytic abstraction, the more central must an animating imagery become. All imagery is capable of providing some illumination, but it must be checked by a set of operations which can assess how well it fits what it describes. Since society is probably not regulated by a mathematical, cybernetic or organic logic, the models upon which those logics are based must be employed most gingerly. They require constant scrutiny by an outside monitor which is not ordered by the same intellectual procedures as themselves.

Sociology is not yet buttressed by a set of viable tests of correspondence. It is bedevilled by the tendency to confuse logical coherence with rigorous demonstration. In turn, the interactionists maintain that the abstract workings of metaphorical models have so problematic a relationship with those of the social world that they should be suspected as a guide. Unless it can be shown that there is a very close connection, highly abstract expositions should be jettisoned.[44] Clearly, symbolic interactionism is also constrained to employ metaphor, but it does so circumspectly and reflexively. There is a strain to prevent imagery from becoming analytically tyrannical.

The diffidence with which interactionists handle abstract analysis has given rise to a measure of anti-intellectualism. They do not usually discuss high academic matters in their works, use an abstruse vocabulary, fully observe the etiquette of a scholarly publishing style or claim a radical superiority for science. Most of that posture derives from the epistemology of pragmatism which I shall discuss in the next chapter. But it is apparent that formalism, too, has a substantial affinity with such reasoning. Like Simmel, the interactionists generally shun deductive system-building. For instance, Park and Burgess argue:

> It has been the dream of philosophers that theoretical and abstract science could and some day perhaps would succeed in putting into formulae and into general terms all that was significant in the concrete facts of life. It has been the tragic mistake of the so-called intellectuals, who have gained their knowledge from text-books rather than from observation and research, to assume that science had already realized its dream.[45]

A distrust of the reliability of logical extrapolation has propelled symbolic interactionism in two parallel directions. It has been maintained that sociology cannot proceed usefully if it merely explores its own axioms.[46] Knowledge can be advanced only by undertaking anthropological enquiry into the substantive world. That disdain for rationalism infused the work of the classical Chicago School: Park, in particular, organised a massive programme of ethnographic research which focused on such settings as dance halls, street gangs, Skid Rows, restaurants and lodging houses. Anthropology enabled the sociologist to evade the perils of excessive abstraction by becoming close to his objects. In turn, the mass of disparate and unique events unearthed in research was lent order and unity by a systematic resort to formalism. Content was transcended and compared by subordinating it to sets of social forms. The first works of symbolic interactionism thus married the local, the particular and the evanescent with the logic of Simmelian sociology. As Hughes observed of Park, 'he was interested in current goings on, but never content until he could put a news story into some universal theme of human interaction. Thus came the apparent anomaly, that the man who wanted to make sociology deal with the news was also the one who based his scheme on the work of the most abstract of all sociologists, Georg Simmel.'[47]

The interplay between the special abstracting methodology of formalism and a close attention to situated detail has continued to characterise the work of symbolic interactionism. Analyses would merely be trivial, fragmented and momentary were it not for their incorporation within a larger scheme which emphasises the form as a relatively permanent and generic principle of order. Interactionism is an accretion of studies which take their organisation from a common concern with the analytic development of forms. In Denzin's presentation of the business of theory construction, for instance, formalism serves as one of the principal theses of symbolic interactionism: 'with Simmel I argue that human conduct presents itself in behavioral forms that differ only in content. The job of sociology is to discover the forms that universally display themselves in slightly different contexts.'[48]

If society is compounded out of synthetic *a priori* forms of knowing, the processes by which it is produced must be understood phenomenologically. The inner logic of social action rather than the inferential logic of science must govern enquiry. Hence there has been a companion thrust towards the reproduction of the subjective life of the worlds that were chronicled. That life cannot be revealed simply by intelligent surmise. The construction of symbolic worlds has accordingly become a prime centre of all interactionist analysis. Thus Thomas and Znaniecki argued, 'social science . . . must reach the actual human experiences and attitudes which constitute the full, live and actual reality beneath the formal organization of social institutions . . .'[49] Not only is that social reality the true subject-matter of sociology, but its documentation offers some reassurance that explanation has not gone adrift. Two strands in interactionism— pragmatism and formalism—work together to proclaim the necessity of studying the subject's own perspective. Simmel's charting of sociological possibilities suggested that analysis must dwell on the observable. It also suggested that the affinity between the forms of explanation and the forms of the phenomenon is so great that the inner structures of social life can be appraised. The fundamental identity of science and common-sense knowledge is a theme which receives considerable recognition in interactionism. Louis Wirth, for example, asserted 'in my work in theory, especially through my years of teaching it to graduate students, I have tried to emphasize that theory is an aspect of everything they do, and not a body of knowledge separate from research and practice.'[50]

Formalism therefore supported the phenomenological strain that runs through interactionism.[51] Simmel's emphasis on the procedures by which social reality is constructed has been retained by his successors. In particular there are elements of the dialectic in Simmel's work which bolster up those flowing from pragmatism. As I have argued, Simmel organised much of his analysis around the conception of experience as both more-life and more-than-life. He maintained that existence continually reproduces itself, realising itself in phenomena which then act as its own boundaries and obstacles. It is inextricably caught up in a process of contradiction and conflict, a process in which alienating forms are created and superseded. Social existence cannot then be conceived statically; it is no mere occupancy of a series of roles or functional positions. Neither is to be explained by the simple following of rules or norms. Rather it represents a flurry of negating and transcending movements. Built into such a conception is the pivotal idea of sociation as process. That idea is also critical to interactionism. Thomas and Znaniecki cultivated the word 'becoming' to affirm the emergent properties of social life. The forms of becoming are strategically important to interactionist analysis.

Social behaviour is explained in an imagery of intertwined dialectical processes. Change occurs not in simple chains of actions and reactions or of disorders and adjustments. It is taken to be a complex series of fluid transformations. Mediating between people and the contents of their experience are the forms of interpretation which define situations. Through those forms, old elements are continually being worked into new shapes and combinations. Man's capacity to interpret the world allows him to transcend and synthesise contrasting facets into qualitatively new configurations. Those configurations feed back into the world and present new possibilities of action, response and understanding. It is in this sense that interactionism holds the world to be in a state of constant evolution. It denies the possibility of explanation by reference to a limited set of initial conditions because those conditions do not exercise an unchanging influence over social process.[52] They undergo progressive translation over time, sometimes reversing or ceasing their connection with the emerging phenomenon.

Indeed the interactionists generally choose to shun the vocabulary of causality altogether. They have created complex ways of attempting to manage analysis without citing causes. Part of their rejection of causality may be attributed to the transforming work performed by sociation itself: the effects of conditions are so unstable that the invocation of causality does not usefully capture them. Prediction cannot be based on a foundation of original causes because the causes themselves are transmuted in often unforeseeable ways. The influence of the past is endlessly reconstituted as the social world changes.

An example of the recognised or unrecognised application of Simmel's dialectic is afforded by Howard Becker's treatment of the emergence of marihuana use. He argues that conventional models of deviance typically rely on static analyses of supposed originating causes:

> But, in fact, all causes do not operate at the same time, and we need a model which takes into account the fact that patterns of behavior *develop* in orderly sequence. In accounting for an individual's use of marihuana . . . we must deal with a sequence of steps, of changes in the individual's behavior and perspectives, in order to understand the phenomenon.[53]

Becker's advocacy of 'sequential causation' focuses on the manner in which a process is built up out of stages, each stage being ordered by a fairly distinctive form. It is an extension of the 'process categories' of Park and Burgess, the form of the moral career fostered by Goffman,[54] and the idea of becoming espoused by Thomas and Znaniecki. More especially, it displays a pronounced similarity to the Simmelian dialectic. In 'Marihuana Use and Social Control', Becker undertakes a staggered analysis of the structures of drug-using experience. He argues that the old forms which organise the meanings of use must be transcended if one is to move on to consuming marihuana. The typifications of social control must be rendered alien and neutral if they are not to be permanently binding. Definitions of drug experiences as 'distasteful, inexpedient or immoral' have to be replaced by those which translate them into 'a conceivable possibility to the person'.[55] The 'more-life' of the user may then overwhelm the 'more-than-life' forms of convention. Interestingly, John Auld has subsequently observed that the once liberating forms which opened up the world of drugs have now themselves become alien and alienating. He argues that the movement into a religious revivalism may be understood as one response to the existential constraints imposed by what have become the routine rituals of drugs.[56]

The Simmelian preoccupation with the dialectics of form may also be discovered in much of the work on the organisation of existential careers. Interactionism is replete with descriptions of the systematic way in which identities are negotiated, assumed and discarded.[57] It focuses extensively on the alienative quality of definitions,[58] on the management of status contradictions,[59] and on the social control work performed by labels. Indeed, this last area has emerged as a virtually independent subdiscipline of interactionism. The sociology of deviancy has centred most of its thought on the transformations that are wrought by the application of villainous typifications.[60] It has sought to explain the origins, consequences and negations of labelling processes, formulating a perspective which examines the imposition of deviant identity as an archetypal form of self-estrangement. Thus Matza's *Becoming Deviant* and Lofland's *Deviance and Identity*[61] are extended essays which concentrate on the dialectical development of deviant forms.

There are similarities too between Simmel's phenomenalism and the particular intellectual incisions made by the interactionists. In distinguishing form from content, Simmel had rejected the substance of social life as irrelevant and inaccessible to the abstracting activity of sociology. Contents were vaguely and generally delegated to the province of psychology. Some interactionists have also disowned interest in the contents of sociation. Edwin Lemert, for example, pursued his analysis of deviance by distinguishing between its primary and secondary manifestations.[62] The primary form of deviation may be defined as an act of mere rule-breaking which need not be accompanied by any symbolic implications for the self of the deviant. Secondary deviation constitutes the organised reply to the reactions extended the primary deviation. The rule-breaker may be impelled or may choose to adopt a penitent, sick or devious role-style to accommodate the effects of others' responses. In like fashion Thomas Scheff explored the process of being mentally ill.[63] His principal analytic object was the development of the mad role, a role which was selectively ordered in the transactions between the deviant and his significant others. In both works may be discovered a disinclination to explore the contents of behaviour before it receives organisation from the stock of deviant forms. Lemert starkly asserts that primary deviation 'abounds' and Scheff maintains that mental illness may stem from any one of a crowd of causes. What is critical to both is the manufacture of social phenomena through the mediation of synthetic *a priori* knowledge. Both have been lambasted for having neglected the 'causes' of deviance,[64] for ignoring 'secret' deviance,[65] and for paying excessive attention to definitional work.[66] Such criticism has the phrasing of a sociology which is radically incompatible with symbolic interactionism. It raises the possibility of lay and scientific minds being able to appraise the noumena of social life. In such a phrasing, the focal interpretative forms and processes studied by the interactionists may be contrasted with some independent version of essential truth. Failure to recognise those contrasts, and an accompanying failure to act on them, can then be attributed to wilful obstinacy,[67] blindness[68] or false consciousness. The conflict about the metaphysical status of knowledge thus lingers on in disputes about the sociology of deviance. Interactionists themselves might respond by stressing their vision of social life as an ongoing event which is produced by men. Society has no real or deep structure outside the forms that emerge during the course of sociation. Secret deviance may exist, but it is phenomenally distinct from public and alienated rule-breaking. It is distinct for the deviant because it is not necessarily experienced as a wholly estranged facet of his existence. Primary and secondary deviation are not identical. Neither is interpretative work unimportant.

Conclusion

I am aware that many of the areas which I have discussed are affected by other sociological perspectives. Indeed some of them derive very little from formalism. But it is apparent that there is an unusual elective affinity between interactionism and Simmel's expression of sociology. It is not at all certain whether many of the authors of interactionism themselves appreciate that affinity or whether they make deliberate use of it. However, formalism does serve to cement some portions of the sociology together. It is indispensable to an imaginative reconstruction of the sociology even if its influence must largely be imputed. It is one vital part of the interactionist compound. Pragmatism is another. Their synthesis leaves only a small portion of the sociology unexplained.

3 Pragmatism and Symbolic Interactionism

Formalism was one vital constituent of interactionism. Pragmatism was the other. Superficially at variance with formalism, it offered yet another solution to the problems posed by the gulf between observer and observed. It may be read as a transcription of the Hegelian rejection of Kant's dualities between mind and matter, subject and object, knowledge and known. Hegel denied the reality of those dualities, asserting instead the fundamental unity of seeming opposites. His thought was exported to America where it laid the base for a variety of schools of philosophical idealism. The pragmatists were exposed to those schools, and they modified their thought into a philosophy of personal action. Blending Hegel, Darwin and the philosophy of science into a distinctive compound, they stressed the practical and emergent character of valid knowledge. Contradictions could be resolved, and provisional truths established, by treating man as an unalienated participant in the natural order. Practical knowledge was no less unnatural than any other facet of that order. Procedures which nursed it were held to be the vital prerequisites of a tenable epistemology. Contemplation and speculation were thereby discredited, legitimate understanding becoming a part of praxis alone. In turn, a measure of anti-intellectualism was introduced into American thinking and, eventually, into interactionism itself. Formalism and pragmatism were joined to stress common themes in symbolic interactionism: the evolutionary and embedded character of enquiry; the unreliability of axiomatic thinking; and the central importance of the thinking and observing self.

Introduction

Max Weber, Georg Simmel and the phenomenologists performed a kind of alchemy on Kant's epistemology. What had originally appeared as a massive bar to the emergence of sociological thought was transformed into its chief catalyst. The structure of Kant's thought suffered little violence, but it was made to undergo a major change of significance. A curb on knowledge became a formula for generating knowledge. Symbolic interactionism itself celebrates some of the dualistic themes which the phenomenalists had preserved and exploited. Yet it has also been fed by other sources which seem to deny philosophical dualism altogether. When they are fully extended, the component theses of interactionism provide some scope for contradiction and disarray.

In particular, interactionism is constructed out of materials provided by the pragmatists. The influence of John Dewey, William James and George Herbert Mead is paramount. They brought to the sociology a modified Hegelianism which retains traces of a fundamental opposition to the perspectives accepted by Simmel. All three collaborated to produce a peculiar metamorphosis of the Hegelian philosophy which dominated much speculation in England and America of the late nineteenth century. Emphases lodged in that philosophy were not entirely lost in the process, and they were passed on to be synthesised in interactionism.

Kant's delimiting of the possibilities of knowledge had hinged on the irrevocable divide between subject and object, knowledge and things known. Mind must eternally scan a phenomenal field which cannot reveal its real and essential character. Dualistic definitions of mind, the social world and their connections are thus of strategic importance. They had first to be emasculated if any competing possibilities for knowledge could be advanced. Those who preferred an alternative stance were obliged to maintain that a Kantian construction of society was radically misconceived. They asserted that the business of understanding social process was qualitatively different from all other pursuits. When people engage in that business, they are not surveying a natural universe which is alien, external and forever sealed from enquiry. On the contrary, they are actually trying to interpret themselves and their own productions. An exploration of society and history is a process of self-exploration. In Hegelian metaphysics, the Kantian opposition between a philosophy and its objects simply disappears. They are not different entities. Rather, subject and object are fundamentally one. Thus Hegel argued: 'the terminus [fixed for knowledge] is at that point where knowledge is no longer compelled to go beyond itself, where it finds its own self, and the notion corresponds to the object and the object to the notion.'[1]

Men and their social environment are alienated constructions of mind, but they are not irretrievably distinct from mind. Philosophy is capable of reuniting them and, in Hegel's thought, that restoration has been accomplished. Men's thought about the social world is really a disguised self-knowledge. Subject and object can become a single identity, and the dichotomies of Kant's critique of reason are revealed as false and misleading, evidence of an unreal consciousness which does not recognise itself in its own externalised form.

The fused subject-object of history was never conceived to be a static entity; rather, being was defined as becoming. It was a moving synthesis of evolving parts which systematically transcended itself and its past. Man's history was the progressive revelation and documentation of an unfolding consciousness which was constrained to take on an alienated guise. For many of the Idealists, and for Hegel especially, history was a chronicle of alienation. As consciousness emerged in the process of creating social and natural phenomena, so it lost something of itself in the world which it had constructed. By developing, it engendered a reality which seemed to stand independently against it, a circumscribing reality which restricted its possibilities. Since that reality was a realm constituted by mind, it was an alienation of mind from itself, an alienation which could be overcome only by mind attaining a higher level of consciousness which transcended contradiction and made subject and object whole again. Hegel conceived his own thought to represent that ultimate unity, a final overwhelming of alienation in which all was comprehended and ordered.

In pursuing this thesis the Idealists offered a vision of the world which attacked the very base of philosophical dualism. They claimed that philosophy was capable of unravelling the workings of *Logos*; that the operations of philosophy were essentially the same as those of the emerging reality of the world; and that any anomaly or confusion between the observed and the asserted must be resolved by resorting to the superior principles of reason and logical speculation. In philosophy, content and method are one. The structures of the noumenon and metaphysical thought are identical. Reality is not what it appears to the vulgar impressions of the senses. Lichtheim states 'while philosophy provides the general categories for the understanding of history, it also turns out to be the secret of history, inasmuch as the latter is revealed as embodied reason, now brought to self-consciousness.' At this level all practical concerns are irrelevant, bizarre and false. The manner in which men appropriate the world in thought becomes all. When mind has alienated itself in the empirical, any investigation of the empirical merely celebrates and perpetuates alienation. A toying with phenomena affirms false consciousness. The noumenon becomes available only when phenomena are seen as the cloaks which shroud truth, and it can be grasped by reason alone. Thus Hegel observed that the emerging Absolute and the emerging science of history are merely different facets of one another:

> The goal, which is Absolute Knowledge or Spirit knowing itself as Spirit, finds its pathway in the recollection of spiritual forms as they are in themselves and as they accomplish the organization of their spiritual kingdom. Their conservation, looked at from the side of their free existence appearing in the form of contingency, is History; looked at from the side of their intellectually comprehended organization, it is the Science of the ways in which knowledge appears.[2]

It is a central feature of the Hegelian or counter-Kantian thesis that the world of appearances should be recognised as a collection of snares and decoys. The synthetic *a posteriori* does no more than prepare an observer for a shallow acquaintance with the disunited epiphenomena of life. Empiricism may seem sure, but it is illusory because it fragments and disconnects processes which are fundamentally whole. The enquiring mind must probe beneath the surface manifestations of an entity for the deeper, indivisible reality which is its essence. 'We have to put the *whole* of sense-certainty as its essential reality, and no longer merely one of its moments . . .'[3] It was axiomatic that noumena are wholes which lend coherence and integrity to their objects. Fundamental essences cannot themselves be partial or fractured. They are the irreducible truth of experience and life, awarding significance to everything that surrounds them.

The Idealists insisted that all things and processes make up a totality. Seeming discrepancies and discontinuities either reflect the deceits of the phenomenal world or else they are the contradictions whose transcendance brings about transformation. At bottom, the world is a moving whole. Any partial science, such as economics, sociology or economics, which attempts to carve that whole up into analytic segments is then conceived to be a violation of the principle of totality. As an affront to the real nature of the world, it is to be dismissed. Anything that departs from the effort to comprehend totalities must be flawed and, at its worst, it must be a basic deformation of reality. Totality in an Idealist dialectic is a most complicated conception. In part, it refers to the complete systemicity of processes. Social life and history are not composed of 'things' or autonomous entities that interact; rather they form a *Gestalt*, a whole, whose parts are transformed and transform as they move. In the context of totality, no part can ever be properly understood in itself because it does not exist in itself. It takes its significance only from the entire universe from which it has been severed. In part, too, totality alludes to the complex interplay of occurrences within the whole. The *Gestalt* is not internally undifferentiated. Rather it is animated by inner movements which propel it through a sequence of transformations. Those movements exemplify the workings of partial totalities which must be analysed both as components and as wholes.

If the character of totality is denied, alienated sciences develop which fail to comprehend the real structures of life. Such sciences dwell on local features of the here-and-now; neglect their connections with totality; neglect the mediating processes which transmute them; and identify them as sources of adequate knowledge. When that adequate knowledge is translated into a statement about properties of the natural or social world, it becomes disabling, mystifying and an exercise in self-estrangement. Empirical science is held to sustain the subject-object gulf. Instead of recognising the fundamental unity of subject and object, it reifies the object, makes it a thing of nature, and then aligns the observer with it. Any discussion of objectivity, therefore, smacks of alienation. Typically, with the division of intellectual labour, science dismembers and explodes totalities, replacing them with partial treatments of epiphenomena. Empirical thought is riddled with reification. Its science proceeds from that reification, its rationality enhances it. It makes and is created by a consciousness that transforms the human into the inhuman, the created into the alienated.

Truth can then proceed from a methodology which shuns empiricism and the rationality of bourgeois thought. The Idealists constructed various formulae for the manufacture of such a methodology. Lukács, for example, claimed to have discovered the identical subject-object in the proletariat. Proletarian knowledge constituted an historically underwritten truth because it was potentially the furthest removed from the reifying structures of capitalism. Karl Mannheim lodged truth in the deracinated community of intellectuals which replicated in microcosm the fragmented and conflict-ridden larger society. The intellectuals were capable of breeding a synthesis which transcended all the partial truths of classes and factions. That synthesis would enhance the rebuilding of totality from its severed parts. Others fostered an intuitive understanding of the spirit of an age or a culture. Works of art and literature were held to offer an undistorted access to the noumena of the past and the present. A creative disinterring of the inner life of totality would accomplish what no fracturing empiricism could achieve. The pragmatists evolved yet another solution. Their methodology represents an implosion of the Hegelian dialectic, a massive concentration of a transcendental epistemology in the body and mind of the observer.

Hegelianism and Pragmatism

My review of pragmatism will be brief and focused. I shall be principally concerned with the fashion in which pragmatism mediated the infusion of Hegelianism into interactionism. There must be some recourse to condensation, simplification and stereotyping. Pragmatism is a most complex system of thought, and I can merely distil a few of those ideas which are salient to interactionism. I shall also gloss over the features which divide the principal exponents of the philosophy,[4] discussing them as if they contributed to a happy unanimity of thought.[5]

Pragmatism is deeply embedded in Hegelianism. The American university of the late nineteenth and early twentieth centuries was most responsive to the philosophical movements of Europe,[6] although its teachings were to domesticate them. In a sense pragmatism itself may be read as an Americanisation of Hegel. The environment of speculation in which it took shape was imbued with the Idealist systems of Harris, George Morris, T. H. Green, Bradley and Royce. Even William James, who constantly assailed the metaphysicians of the Absolute, was forced to address the issues which Hegel had raised.[7] Other pragmatists had flirted with Idealism. John Dewey was a member of the circle which once celebrated the work of Hegel and introduced it to American philosophy.[8] His own doctoral thesis confronted the problems of a Kantian psychology, and he found in Hegel a weapon to transcend the dualisms which that psychology and philosophy had emphasised.[9] Hegel was to provide the materials for an analysis of life and experience as continuous and whole rather than as a collection of 'facile disjunctions, hard and fast alternatives, sharp separations.'[10] Hegel, and Darwin his supposed successor, were conceived by Dewey to be the only thinkers who proferred viable alternatives to the 'spectator theory of knowledge', a theory which pitched a passive observer against 'a blind rhapsody of particulars, without meaning or connection.'[11]

Similarly, George Herbert Mead studied under Josiah Royce and borrowed much of his intellectual approach.[12] He recalled, 'Professor Royce opened up the realm of romantic Idealism. What had been barriers of thought became but hazards in the game. Contradictions, instead of marking the no thoroughfares of reflection, became the guide posts toward higher levels of reality. To have achieved the dialectic was to have won a liberty . . . '[13] When Dewey and Mead eventually abandoned an Idealist metaphysics, they nevertheless retained much of the formal analytic apparatus and many of the problems that Hegel had first crystallised.[14] Both produced arguments which may be described as examples of Hegel writ small. Their reasoning is consistently dialectical and it reinforces the sociology which flowed from Simmel's rewriting of Kant. Its commerce is with wholes, unities, negations, contradictions and transcendental developments; not with the discrete oppositions and syllogisms of Aristotelian logic. Indeed, in the embryonic interactionism of Charles Cooley, little of Idealism has been rejected. To Cooley, society constituted an organism which derived its life from the collective existence of its members. Participation in a common consciousness furnished a unity which is redolent of the Idealist totality:

> A separate individual is an abstraction unknown to experience, and so likewise is society when regarded as something apart from individuals. The real thing is Human Life, which may be considered either in an individual aspect or in a social; that is to say a general, aspect; but is always, as a matter of fact, both individual and general.[15]

The cosmic interpretative scheme of Hegel was transcribed by the pragmatists into a matter of practical epistemology; the unfolding of Absolute Spirit became personal biography;[16] a grand historicism became an emphasis on the pervasive moulding of meaning by context; the machineries of historical change were transformed into the processes by which man's dealings with the world display emergent properties; and the identical subject-object became the individual thinker. In all this, Hegel framed the work of the pragmatists. But their thought was also to take up other themes which largely displaced the Idealist strains of Hegel. Those themes rooted epistemology in a new comprehension of man's being, and they were made chiefly possible by Charles Darwin's account of evolution. Intelligence became explained by a novel amalgam of phenomenology,[17] evolutionism and biological science.[18]

Mead himself explained pragmatism as the convergence of scientific method and Darwin's evolutionary theory.[19] The approaches complemented each other well: both demonstrated the incremental and progressive character of life, and both underlined the emergent rather than the absolute quality of things in change. Mead's own work has been described as a philosophical generalisation of Darwin's stance: it is an exploration of the orderly change which distinguishes all facets of the natural and social world.[20] Cooley, too, adopted evolutionism as an axiomatic principle of his sociology.[21] Similarly, Dewey conceived Darwin to be a fitting companion for Hegel: each writer stressed the developmental nature of the world; each emphasised the systematic interconnectedness of evolving phenomena; each grounded the structures of process in history; each attacked the empiricist theory of mind; and each suggested 'the impossibility of considering psychical life as an individual, isolated thing developing in a vacuum'.[22] Yet Darwin's particular significance was his encouragement of a radical ontology. Mediated principally by the writings of William James, Darwin's impact upon pragmatism was to become his erosion of the conventional dichotomies of organism and thought, mind and matter. James united emotion, biology and instinct into a compound,[23] a 'biological matrix', which permitted the shedding of the dilemmas posed by philosophical dualism. Simultaneously, James's adaptation of Darwin permitted a rejection of the Hegelian identification of mind as an antecedent reality which manufactured matter in a curious game of riddles. The *Origin of Species* enabled man to be defined as a part of nature like any other. Man was an integral aspect of evolution, and all his works were in and of nature. 'For Dewey the distinction between the organism and its environment is only a distinction in phases of the process, whether this process is called psychological or biological.'[24] If the doings and adaptations of men were natural forces, there was no plausible reason to suppose that thought itself was a stranger to the universe of natural events. It did not represent some mysterious outsider which was permanently exiled from what it beheld. As James argued:

> ... constituting the inner life of individual persons who are born and die, our conscious states are temporal *events* arising in the ordinary course of nature, – events, moreover, the conditions of whose happening or non-happening from one moment to another, lie certainly in large part in the physical world.[25]

If thought was not unnatural, the vision of man as an alienated spectator could be superseded. Knowledge could no longer be regarded as uniquely privileged or disprivileged because it was not completely distinct from what it comprehended: it was a grounded part of nature and a grounded part of the active experience of nature. 'Experience is *of* as well as *in* nature. It is not experience which is experienced, but nature ... Things interacting in certain ways *are* experience.'[26] That unity prepared the basis for a thoroughgoing epistemology that Hook has described as the naturalisation of 'Hegel's historical approach by a biological theory of mind.'[27]

Kant had portrayed mind as the witness of an external and opaque world. The uncertainties and limitations of speculative reasoning stemmed mainly from the abyss that separated thought from its objects. The pragmatists, by contrast, denied the existence of any such abyss. They mounted an attack on an imagery of mind as passive spectator. They claimed that mind and matter were but phases of a single process, phases that shaped one another in an ongoing development which could not be pared down into isolated units: 'what had long been viewed as disparate ultimate entities, mind and world, became two factors in a process, necessarily related through the process, neither having any existence independent of the other'.[28] Mind defined nature just as nature defined mind. Thus Dewey reflected, 'life denotes a function, a comprehensive activity, in which organism and environment are included.'[29] In an early article he had challenged another form of dualism, the developing behaviourism which asserted the analytic independence of stimulus and response in the unfolding of an act. He maintained that mind constructs its own environment so that what comes to be represented as a stimulus has already been predefined by the organism which responds to it.[30] The critical feature of all valid knowledge is its anchorage in activity. That anchorage dispels all the bedevilling problems of philosophy, psychology[31] and sociology: 'complications attaching to the questions of the relation of mind and body, or the self and its stream of mental states, are disentangled, and the elements in question fall into ordered perspective when viewed from the standpoint of the growth of an intelligently effective action, and so with the other questions of philosophy'.[32]

This interdependence of thought and object subverts any epistemology which proceeds as if man were not a true part of the natural world. Pragmatism translated the observer and his field into an organic unity which is akin to the structured totality of the Idealists. Organism, mind, self and society are the conceptually contrived movements of an evolving whole. Morris comments:

> Mead's view denies the reality of mind as such in separation from action or from social co-operative process. Role-taking, which is an ideational process, has its seat in an acting biological form, which in turn involves the inorganic world. Reflective thinking, role-taking, is in itself an emergent of the highest order and involves the three major systems of reality: the inorganic, the organic and the human social system. By this social interpretation of the emergent, Mead escapes a metaphysical dualism.[33]

The identical subject-object of the pragmatists is the individual thinker who is experientially grounded in an environment that he has created and which creates him in turn. The existential world does not inhere solely in the mind which experiences it. As Peirce observed, 'some things are *forced* upon cognition . . . there is the element of brute force existing whether you opine it or not.'[34] Neither does the existential world inhere only in sensed objects. It is a fused and complicated amalgam of both aspects of process. It is not possible to trace out the logical or temporal priorities of either aspect. Mind does not antedate matter in an Idealist universe. Matter does not precede mind in a simplistic empiricist universe. Rather, both are the emergents of transactions in which thought and its objects constitute one another. Thought works on nature, just as thought wells out of its physical and physiological context. Minds and selves arise in a conversation of gestures between organisms which are at home in the world. For Dewey, it followed that the content of experience is an inherent feature of nature itself, not an attribute which contemplation foists upon it: 'the habit of disposing of the doubtful as if it belonged only to *us* rather than to the existential situation in which we are caught and implicated is an inheritance from subjectivistic psychology'.³⁵ Problems are qualities of the total situation in which an individual is lodged, not parts of conciousness alone.

The pragmatist conception of the organic unity of the self and its environment denied the dilemmas posed by the solitary surveying intellect or by the uncertain character of an unsurveyed material world. That conception was held to detonate all the props of conventional epistemology and philosophy. They receded into an intellectual prehistory to be replaced by a new understanding that was free of alienating and false problems.³⁶ Because selves and knowledge are aspects of acting biological forms, epistemology becomes translated into the psychology of the act. It is in the act that empiricism, phenomenology and philosophy meet and become one. Acts themselves are problem-solving processes: they are always addressed to unsettled features of a world or self that require alteration. They are organised to relieve inhibition or express impulses. In that guise, all valid knowledge becomes practical. It is attentive to the mundane world, not to the sphere of metaphysics. The acting organism proceeds by reducing the problematic facets of its environment and in so doing generates knowledge about that environment and itself: 'the problem of knowledge then is not to find out how we can get from a state of mind to an object outside of mind, but how an intelligence that lies within nature can so reorganize its experience that the activities of the inhibited individual can proceed. Knowing is then as natural a process as running or eating or bearing children, as living or dying.'³⁷ Thus conceived, knowledge is an activity which moves from incertitude to determination by manipulating its context and, correspondingly, itself. The redefinition of knowledge as a grounded and emergent stage of action further rendered invalid the claim that thought could comprehend its objects in advance of exploring them. Authentic thought becomes praxis and contemplative reasoning becomes absurd: 'we are carried to a conclusion where reference to useful action ceases to mark an invidious contrast with reality, and, accordingly, indicates a standpoint from which the need of any rival mode of knowledge, called philosophical, becomes doubtful'.³⁸

There can be no immediate understanding of an event or experience: 'our own experience in so far as it is not reflective does not involve knowledge. . . . Experiences simply are, like other occurrences in nature.'³⁹ The significance of phenomena unfolds as the enquiring individual engages in an active investigation which progressively transmutes them. By discarding the idea of an antecedent reality which may be somehow known, Dewey and Mead gave birth to a theory of knowledge which anchored the truth in praxis alone. Dewey stated, for instance, 'the problems of perception and science are straightened out when looked at from the standpoint of action, while they remain obscure and obscuring when we regard them from the standpoint of a knowledge defined in antithesis to action.'[40] Practical experience and action become a multifaceted entity, synonomous with existence, the objects of knowledge and nature itself.[41] Knowledge as an experiential process had radically different implications from knowledge imagined to be a mirroring of some independent reality or an incision into an unchanging universe. It suggests that men cannot grasp essences or absolutes because there are no such fixed noumena. Reality shifts as men build it up in their transactions with nature and with each other. It shifts as their problems and vantage points change. Indeed, there is no one reality but a pluralistic universe[42] in which perspectives jar or become amassed. The result is indeterminacy, an abandonment of the quest for the phantom of certainty and its usurpation by an acknowledgement of openness.[43] Knowledge can never be complete or confident. It may possess a limited authenticity when it is embedded in experience. When it pretends to convey truths about Absolutes, when it becomes foreign to everyday existence, it may lose every sure hold on the world:

> It is the personal experience of those best qualified in our circle of knowledge to *have* experience, to tell us *what is*. Now what does *thinking about* the experience of these persons come to, compared to directly and personally feeling it as they feel it? The philosophers are dealing in shades, while those who live and feel know truth.[44]

Authentic knowledge then becomes tiered. It carries less and less of the truthfulness invested in the identical subject-object as it retreats from lived experience.[45] The most authentic appreciation of the world is lodged in an immediate confrontation with it. Yet, typically, that appreciation is akin to the formless content of Simmel's naïve actor. It is ineffable and incommunicable. It does not lend itself to abstraction or replication unless the audience is empowered to undergo that experience itself. 'Quality is not something that can be expressed in words for it is something that must be *had*.'[46] In turn, quality and experience provide their own emergent contexts for each other which render them further distinctive and resistant to description. They can attain states of coherence, patternings, which serve as fields for the grasping of new events.

Such coherent environments are *situations* and, in an epistemology which denies existential boundaries around the organism, situations are indefinitely extensible. The mind is lodged in a setting which is potentially infinite. Yet it is more than merely lodged, it *is* that setting. In its pre-reflexive state, experience is 'double-barrelled in that it recognizes in its primary integrity no division between act and material, subject and object, but contains them both in an unanalyzed totality'.[47] What lends structure to a situation and sets limits about it are the specific foci and interests of the acting individual. As those foci and interests change, so his system of relevance shifts. In turn, the situation itself is transformed by the evolving thought which lends it definition. The situation is thus another aspect of action and of the interdependence of organism and environment:

> In actual experience, there is never any . . . isolated singular object or event; *an* object or event is always a special part, phase, or aspect, of an environing experienced world – a situation. The singular object stands out conspicuously because of its especially focal and crucial position at a given time in determination of some problem of use or enjoyment which the *total* environment presents.[48]

Situations order and direct the process of knowing. Yet that process is encouraged only when situations are questionable, confusing or doubtful. An individual would address a situation only when it is problematic enough to provoke activity. Environments are not simply contemplated to no purpose. Indeed, Dewey defines inquiry as 'the controlled or directed transformation of an indeterminate situation into one that is . . . determinate in its constituent distinctions and relations . . .'[49] Not all situations are indeterminate, but it follows that what organises knowing is often brought into being because it requires organisation itself. The context is an emergent which unfolds as action progresses.

As knowledge becomes deracinated and available to reflective examination, so it incurs the risk of losing authenticity. Qualities cannot be conveyed in description; objects cannot be properly understood outside their situations; and the 'situation as a qualitative whole is sensed or *felt*'.[50] Indeed, in the reasoned anti-intellectualism of the pragmatists, talk and analysis correspond to the alienating forms which threaten to strangle the more-life of the experiences that are discussed. Experience as more-life, and as the warrant of communion with unalienated understanding, cannot be mastered by words:

> As long as one continues *talking*, intellectualism remains in undisturbed possession of the field. The return to life can't come about by talking. It is an *act*; to make you return to life, I must set an example for your imitation, I must deafen you to talk, by showing you, as Bergson does, that the concepts we talk with are made for purposes of *practice* and not for purposes of insight.[51]

If truths cannot be divined by speculation, if there is no unwavering essence that awaits discovery, if knowledge and its objects are indissolubly fused in what Dewey called the 'knowing-known transaction', then truth itself is suspect. Knowledge may be variably authentic, a facet of experiences which are more or less corrupted by abstract intellectuality. But certain truth lies outside human reach.[52] In its place there must be inserted a modest questioning of the practical consequences of the different outcomes of ideas. Some outcomes may be so inconsequential that, with the positivists,[53] the pragmatist can reject them as meaningless. They can be dismissed as 'non-utilitarian, haughty, refined, remote, august, exalted'.[54] Other outcomes may be assessed by their impact on the lives and problems of those who are likely to be affected by them. In a sense, pragmatism offers a utilitarian canon of personal truthfulness which is regulated by the socially organised nature of experience.

When the search for absolute truth is abandoned, the practices of knowing are themselves transformed. The rooted and contextual nature of enquiry, the incompleteness and incoherence of many projects, and the multiplicity of perspectives that can be trained on any problem, conspire to make systematic reasoning absurd. When no clear truths exist, and the only criteria are afforded by experience and a current problem, there cannot be a general propositional scheme that is capable of performing a useful service. That scheme would merely reanimate the dualistic conception that severs reality into an unchanging essence and a mantle of fleeting impressions. If impressions are more authentic than most Idealists supposed, and if they are the emergent properties of existence, then philosophy must concern itself solely with the forms of change that order experience:

> The laws in which the modern man of science is interested are laws

of motion, of generation, and consequence. He speaks of law where the ancients spoke of kind or essence, because what he wants is a correlation of changes, an ability to detect one change occuring in correspondence with another. He does not try to define and delimit something remaining constant *in* change. He tries to describe a constant order *of* change.⁵⁵

The pragmatist thus 'turns away from abstraction and insufficiency, from verbal solutions, from bad *a priori* reasons, from fixed principles, closed systems, and pretended absolutes and origins. He turns towards concreteness and adequacy, towards action and towards power.'⁵⁶ As a consequence of his emphasis upon the grounded and the emergent, he also recognises two distinct spheres of knowledge which correspond roughly to the styles of competence which flow from contemplation and from praxis. That dichotomy is critical to both pragmatism and interactionism. It elevates active reasoning to become the sole source of substantial knowledge. A knowledge *of* events flows from a specific focusing of attention which renders them problematic. They become actively studied with a diligence and a curiosity which cannot be extended to all affairs. By contrast, a knowledge *about* events merely enables men to accommodate them in their lives, but it is neither detailed nor based upon rigorous examination.⁵⁷ It is the stuff of the habits which pragmatists maintain are the major components and buttresses of social order. Habits are the unthinking, routine contexts of most action. By extension, it is also argued that broad speculative systems of thought can themselves generate little more than knowledge *about* the objects they purport to describe. They do not usually rest on an intimate acquaintance with all their phenomena, they do not entertain close experiential links with them, and their statements depend on abstract surmise alone. That surmise is no substitute for scientific enquiry and it does not produce sure truths.

A philosophy which entertains such a vision of knowledge cannot itself be laid out as an axiomatic scheme. Knowledge is held to arise out of a process of detailed enquiry, not from the application of a propositional logic. Dewey, for instance, rejected the claims of formal logic throughout most of his life.⁵⁸ He insisted that that logic was tainted by a 'formalism' which failed to accommodate the basic unity of humans, experiences and objects. A principled objection to systematic thought has rendered much of pragmatism unorganised. Although they wrote copiously, the pragmatists chose to define their works as incomplete, provisional and unschematic. Thus Mead's major works were largely published posthumously, assemblies of unfinished papers and lecture notes which were edited by his students. Dewey, too, refused to identify his philosophy as a system, stating at the age of seventy that it was 'still too much in a process of change to lend itself to [definitive] record'.[59]

Significantly, the very person of the thinker becomes redefined in pragmatism. The knowing person cannot be regarded as a detached and unchanging monitor of events. Neither can he be understood as an all-comprehending consciousness. Deeply implicated in those events, indeed taken to be fused with those events, he evolves as they evolve. An idea for the pragmatists is a plan of action, a symbol recapitulates activity in the imagination, and all knowledge is processual. Thought thus entails a real or a projected engagement in the world, and it necessarily transforms both its object and its thinker. A decision must always have existential ramifications because it works back on the self which initiates it. It refers not only to things but to the emergent self which it creates.

Selves are always in the making. They cannot be construed as static, fixed entities which manifest themselves in different settings. Any such attribution would only revive the dualisms which pragmatism was designed to suppress. It would pit the rational against the emotional, the thinker against the animal, the social against the non-social. Human nature must not be defined as an absolute or an essence which is imperfectly grasped in its phenomenal forms. On the contrary, it is a phase or aspect of the 'knowing-known transaction' like any other. Selves are built up and known in the pursuit of projects. They are objects amongst the other objects of a situation and, as objects, they may be either the ends or the means of action. If nothing can be the topic of a specially privileged knowledge, selves themselves are just as problematic as any other portion of the social and natural world. They are not entities which lie open to immediate understanding or to definitive characterisation. They arise in interaction, display different possibilities in different contexts, and must always be incomplete and ill-structured. 'At any given moment in the historic movement of events human nature cannot altogether say what it is, simply because it has no adequate idea of its possibilities, of what it can be.'[60] The only authentic knowledge of the self is that knowledge which flows from consciousness turning on itself, and it is fraught by all the uncertainties which distinguish the process of understanding.

The self is taken by the pragmatists to be a social construct that emerges in the general process of evolution. It is a product which arises when thought is provided with forms that can fold back on themselves and make an object out of their thinker. Sheer experience contains no self because it is unreflective: the process of generating a self must involve knowledge and consciousness. It is when one is able to react to oneself as others do that self-awareness and self-estrangement become possible. The medium for translating inarticulate experience into reflexivity is held to be language, and the pragmatists defined the self as a stage in an inner dialogue which was built around the forms of conversation. That conversation enables a person to confront himself, make indications to himself, discourse with himself, assess himself, and survey himself from without. Selves are then aspects of an inner forum in which social individuals encounter themselves and interpret their own experiences. They emerge from imploded transactions which mirror the symbolically mediated exchanges of social interaction. In this sense an individual is in continuous conversation with himself, and it is that conversation which Mead designated 'thought'.[61]

Problematic Features of Pragmatism

It is apparent that there is much opaqueness and contradiction within the scheme which was to become symbolic interactionism. They have continued to plague interactionism, infusing most of its central themes and rendering many of them virtually incommunicable. Chief amongst that legacy of dilemmas were the anti-intellectualism and the unresolved Idealism of pragmatism.

The special status awarded immediate experience threatened the authenticity of any analytic or academic commentary. Reflection produced a critique of reflection which neutered itself. The pragmatists had represented their epistemology as a charter for scientific method, but it is evident that any knowledge which is appreciably alienated from immediacy becomes suspect, unnatural and reifying. Mead, for instance, stated that pragmatism was distinguished by two arguments:

> one the reference of thought to conduct, and the other the inclusion of intelligence within the sweep of biologic evolution. That these should lead to anti-intellectualism implies that intelligence and thought are not so native to human conduct and behavior even in

their most elaborate social expressions, but that they deform experience. . . .[62]

In that formulation, pragmatism and symbolic interactionism themselves become false. They may direct the thinker into the world of experience, but they discredit any of the reports which he brings back. The very claims made for experience become untrustworthy: interactionism is patently self-destructive. Not only the explicit statements but the methodology of symbolic interactionism are thrust into a pathetic and absurd guise. Participant observation, for instance, urges an immersion in immediacy which is unattainable and ineffable. It is with that dilemma that I shall concern myself in Chapter 6. There is then a methodical invalidation of all the achievements of interactionism which interactionism is forced to neglect. In that fashion the sociology is required to escape its own epistemology in a complicated exercise of evasions and omissions.

The claims made for immediacy pitched one form of knowledge against another. Although the quest for direct understanding is ruled intellectually barren, it has continued to dominate interactionism. The undistorted and true mastery of meaning has become the grail of the sociology, although it is tacitly acknowledged to be beyond rational reach. The consequence has been a Quixotic cast for the discipline: an advocacy of unattainable ideals and impossible missions.

A further ambiguity undermines the certainty of the interactionist enterprise. There is a fundamental equivocation about the ontological status of nature and phenomena. Two conflicting assertions have been made about the character and relations of man. As parts of nature like any other, men are not represented as privileged participants in the empirical order. They do not know and cannot be known in any way that singles them out from other objects. The self and society represent problematic phenomena whose significance is contingent on practice: it appears as the knowing-known transaction proceeds although knowing and known are one. Yet it is also asserted that immediacy throws up understanding which is somehow distinguished, that it offers an unbarricaded entry into the truth of society. More problematically, it is maintained that society and nature are constituted by mind in a dialectic which is ordered by principles that cannot be reduced to a simple phenomenalism. Thus Morris argues:

> The predominantly biological emphasis will stress the fact that the world which appears for observation is a function of impulses

seeking expression — and this point of view, carried to its extreme, would result in some sort of metaphysics of action, a biological version of Leibniz or Hegel. On [one] emphasis the organism is one unprivileged object in a world of objects; on the second, other objects appear only as stages in organic activity.⁶³

Idealism in the form of an organic solipsism then confronts a particular version of empiricism. That unclarified opposition has also scarred interactionism. There is a tendency to move from an assertion of the inherent meaningfulness of phenomena to an attribution of bestowed meaning alone; phenomena are sometimes alleged to 'talk back' to man, sometimes to be entirely responsive to man's purposive imagination. It is unclear what ontological autonomy is supposed to be conferred on society and nature. Lacking systematisation, interactionism tends to make use of different epistemological poses at will, contributing to an incoherence which is often recognised. There is thus a basic obscurity in the pivotal theses of the sociology, and it is an obscurity which makes many problems insoluble at the abstract level. They may be answered on the plane of practice, but theoretical contradiction remains.

Pragmatism and Symbolic Interactionism

Pragmatism and formalism together compose a fugue-like theme. They both stem from what Gouldner identified as the Romanticist strain in Chicago sociology, a strain which emphasised the role of intuitive understanding, a distaste for rationalism, and a pluralistic realism.⁶⁴ Gouldner does indeed remark that the interactionists were the result of a profound exposure to the German critics of the classicist tradition. Despite their divergences, the pragmatist and formalist voices refract and play with one another, reiterating a number of primary themes. Their arguments denied important strands in much idealism and orthodox sociology, stressing those which were to maintain a concerted opposition to any reading of society as a welter of phenomena circling about an absolute core. Few interactionists have offered a definition of what 'society' *is* because they claim that there is no warrant to imagine that society actually does possess an essential nature. James, for instance, protested: 'Damn great Empires! including that of the Absolute . . . Give me individuals and their spheres of activity.'⁶⁵

Dewey, too, asserted

society is of course but the relations of individuals to one another in this form and that. And all relations are *interactions*, not fixed molds ... I often wonder what meaning is given to the term 'society' by those who oppose it to the *intimacies of personal intercourse*, such as those of friendship ... We should forget 'society' and think of law, industry, religion, medicine, politics, art, education, philosophy – and think of them in the plural. For points of contact are not the same for any two persons and hence the questions which the interests and occupations pose are never twice the same.[66]

By extension, 'society' could not be intellectually managed as a totality which displayed sets of structured characteristics. Social process, whether in microcosm or macrocosm, may be unravelled as an evolutionary and dialectical sequence of movements. But only the forms of the movements, not the things moving, can be subjected to examination. If there is a social structure, it must reside in a patterned organisation of changes and not in the static physiology of a social system. The eschewing of Idealism by the pragmatists and the formalists led to a companion suspicion of the abstract schemes devised by the rationalists. Reason and essence are not symmetrical, and a rational system maps nothing but the principles of its own manufacture. When formal logic, the analytic *a priori*, and rationalism are jettisoned, all inferential sociology becomes impossible. Indeed, interactionism embraces a profound distrust of the very language which must be deployed to describe social phenomena:

> we must admit our misgivings about the fact that our very conceptions of logic are totally ethnocentric. Conventional logic ... is merely a formalization of Greek grammar ... Greek grammar breaks down the world as a number of objects acting upon other objects to bring about certain observed results or consequences ... We miss the processes that may well alter the very identity of things we have observed.[67]

The production of authenticity and integrity must then be inseparably wedded to the small, local settings in which social life is built up. As Gouldner argued, 'the world of Romanticism was seen as a mosaic, each tile of which had some unique reality or value in itself. The whole itself was often seen, however, not as a harmonious and integrated entity, but as an incongruous assemblage and as a tensionful conjunction of parts.'[68] Simmel's intertwined forms of analysis and action, and the pragmatists' experiential truth, combine to lend authority to only a limited range of sociological styles. Social exploration must be grounded, focused and situated. It cannot proceed from or to analytic abstraction without forfeiting its legitimating connections with the reality in which social transactions unfold. The practical consequence has been the catalysis of abundant ethnography and the barring of logico-deductive work. Conjecture can never retreat to a phenomenological distance from the scenes that first furnished understanding. Thus, ironically, the emerging union of pragmatism and formalism was to produce a sociology which disinherited itself. The ban on abstraction and rationalism brought about an abstention from the philosophical reasoning which might justify the interactionist stand. Interactionism is embedded in a philosophical resolution of the problems of dualism which denies the authority of philosophical resolutions. It is plausible that the paradoxical nature of its mandate encouraged interactionism to mute its more perplexing themes by consigning them to the limbo of the community's silent language. Any other course would have further enfeebled the intellectual perspective by submitting it to a sustained assault from its own pronounced anti-intellectualism. Freedom from paradox was bought by renouncing parentage. The tacit myth of interactionism's virgin birth may have arisen as a result of such a sacrifice.

Both stances lean towards a concentration on the dialectics of the emerging self and its environment. As I shall argue in the next chapter, that self is not an atomised and discrete phenomenon. On the contrary, it is produced in the social act and the act is itself mediated by forms which are not reducible to individual psychology alone. But the self is the centre. The formalists and the pragmatists alike cast the individual as one who negotiates the world with socially fashioned thought. He is alone entrusted with knowledge that has been ratified by the social forms or the organic unity of experience. He is thrust into the role of an archetypal explorer of social settings, a puppet and scout who lays bare the social reality about him. The actor of interactionist anthropology is tantamount to the identical subject-object navigating the world. His experiences and encounters belong not only to him, they are also the sociologist's and, vicariously, the reader's. The epistemological status of his doings is relatively sure; he is a peripatetic guarantee of authenticity. Matza's deviant, Paul Cressey's taxi-dancer, Donald Cressey's embezzler, Sutherland's professional thief, Marvin Scott's jockey and Becker's marihuana user are assembled and then set free to bring back intelligence about the nature of social life. Interactionists are thus the authors of picaresque analyses which pit their heroes against an obscure world.

There would clearly be no need for sociology if the reports produced by the identical subject-object were comprehensive and adequate. All men would then become practical sociologists whose knowledge required no amendment or supplementation. However, the interactionists' actor is not quite so competent. He is locked into a sequence of situations which he cannot wholly grasp, which are dimly perceived, typically uncompared and often unscrutinised. They are ordered by limited perspectives, open and unfinished. Unlike the sociologist, the actor is unable to put questions to those about him without breaking the flow of action, appearing incomprehensibly impertinent and destroying the very situation which he is attempting to understand. His system of relevances cannot be quite the same as those of the sociologist. After all, he usually has some practical project at hand which requires more attention than any academic problem. Then, too, he emerges out of experiences and situated interpretations which are rarely touched by the formal concerns of sociology. Thus Becker advised that it was more sensible to ask people 'how' they put action together than 'why'.

Yet the actor remains the only sure source and site of knowledge. Documents about him and by him are the indispensable base upon which all speculation must rest. W. I. Thomas claimed that the undesigned personal record is the most significant material for sociology. The life history and the case study constitute the representations of reality which serve as criteria for all other constructions:

> The case study method and the 'natural history' method must not only precede the more scientifically acceptable method in order to produce realistic hypotheses and indicate what units should be defined and isolated; they must also be used as a general background of reference to the more limited statistical findings. . . .[69]

Such detailed natural histories abound in the works of symbolic interactionism.[70] *The Jackroller*,[71] *The Professional Thief*,[72] *The Polish Peasant* and *The Natural History of a Delinquent Career*[73] are annotated accounts of experience which explore hitherto unknown regions of social territory. They display the fashion in which people build up their lives and social worlds. They provide an insider's perspective which is unavailable to all but the intimate members of a particular group. In a sense, then, they play a role akin to that of the native informant in social anthropology, but more is made of them because of the central place of the self in interactionist ontology. There is an attractive ambiguity in the metaphor of *natural* history; it suggests that these chronicles enjoy an unfeigned veracity. Becker remarks that the life history provides the sociologist with an existentially authentic context for reasoning: it 'gives us details of that process whose character we would otherwise be only able to speculate about, the process to which our data must ultimately be referred if they are to have theoretical and not just an operational and predictive significance'.[74]

It is also the case that interactionist writings are unusually replete with long quotations from the people who have been interviewed or observed in the work of research. Those quotations not only substantiate arguments and develop the phenomenological texture of a report, they also convey the impression that the reader has direct access to the subjective life of the world that is under scrutiny. An ambience is created which suggests that the writing has some semblance of an intimate connection with that life. Interactionists typically describe the minute detail of the worlds they are observing, report the language and symbols which the world's inhabitants themselves employ, and give little space to abstract reflection of their own. There is thus a stylistic delicacy which conveys the sense that a faithful reconstruction has been accomplished. More important, however, the sociologist himself attempts to stand aside so that the immediacy of the knowing-known transaction may bestow authority on his ethnography.

The critical significance of the idea of the self may then be appreciated. It is the pivot on which interactionism turns, and some have identified it as the unifying theme which lends coherence to the entire sociology.[75] The journeyings of the self, its definition, and its negotiation have been the focus of much work.[76] The self constitutes more than a substantive area, it is a touchstone. It is for this reason that the anthropological strain within interactionism has been reinforced. Distrusting his puppets and his respondents more than he does himself, the interactionist engages in the participant observation of unfolding social processes. That strategy has been peculiarly identified with interactionism, and it is wholly consonant with the sociology's epistemological foundations. As Denzin remarks, 'such a strategy implies a commitment — either conscious or unconscious — by the observer to basic principles of symbolic interactionism.'[77] The sociologist treats himself as a research instrument, cutting into the variety and nuances of meaning which organise any activity. It is only by locating himself in the flow of social life that he believes himself entitled to issue authentic reports. As the identical subject-object, he can claim to *know* the objects of sociology in a fashion forever foreign to those who rely on questionnaires, surveys, secondary analyses or *a priori* reasoning. Participant observation is only one among many interactionist strategies, but it assumes a special potency within the sociology's scheme. However temporarily, the sociologist can claim to have been the scene he has described. Thus Bruyn observes 'we must find a unity between subject and object. The participant observer, as observer, must know by 'separation', but what has not been thoroughly examined in social research is his alternative role as participant, which means becoming identified with the lives of the subjects he studies.'[78] Only when it is treated as praxis can research be valid. It is an active encounter with the world, not contemplation, which furnishes interactionist material.

The Situation

Pragmatism impressed itself upon interactionism in another important fashion. The focus upon the organic unity of experience had led to a projection of the knowing self into an environment of objects which was both organised and organising. Men were in and of situations: each constituted the other in an endless interplay. Contexts, and their symbolic ordering, then became an integral part of the knowing process. For interactionism, too, the context came to assume a massive significance. A sociology that is wedded to an analysis of consciousness must explore the realm inhabited by mind. Only mediately are men held to respond to a universe of forces and reactions, stresses and equilibriating adjustments, demographic data or vast historical transformations. The mediations are accomplished by an organisation of symbolism, and that organisation must be mapped if action is to become intelligible. Cooley had maintained that the solid facts of life are the imaginations we construct of people.[79] We do not respond to people, but to our definitions of them. Society and its components are no more than ordered imaginations themselves: 'an institution is simply a definite and established phase of the public mind. The various institutions are not separable entities, but organized attitudes of the public mind, and it is only by abstraction that we can regard them as things by themselves.'[80] Social reality is thus the accomplishment of processes of knowledge. It has no ontological independence outside those processes. The manner in which knowledge bestows structure on the world, manages the world as problematic, and takes action to contend with such problems, is then treated as the principal topic of sociology.

The interpretations which are made of settings and possibilities create the objects of social life. Objects have no meaning outside the situations in which they are lodged, and the sociologist cannot approach them as if they enjoyed some invariant scientific or common-sense standing. Indeed, the early interactionists had denied the very existence of discrete phenomena which are not fused into a potentially infinite field of experience. The apprehension and genesis of situations thus became of consequence in establishing the self that was observed, the knowledge which it employed, and the objects which it confronted. Without that understanding, all became literally meaningless. In the first instance, at least, the primary reality is that of the knowing self which is scrutinised, not that of the sociologist. The analyst must defer to the sense which the subject has of his world because it is that sense which generates behaviour. As Thomas observed, 'if men define situations as real, they are real in their consequences.'[81] Men's definitions, and the environments which they reveal, are the chief focus of interactionist work. From Anderson's *The Hobo*[82] to Becker's *Making the Grade*,[83] there has been a preoccupation with the procedures that are used to build and maintain symbolic worlds. The programmatic description of those procedures can be the end of research; but it is also taken to be the essential base of any further enquiry.

The low level of analytic magnification that attends such work commends a reluctance to generalise features of social settings. When it is observed in detail, any social scene contains contours and materials which can never be wholly reproduced elsewhere. Even superficially similar events or phenomena become unique under prolonged examination. Over time, the progressive synthesis and elaboration of meanings that distinguish any enduring process will create an organisation of symbolism which is totally distinctive. Two delinquents or schoolteachers, for example, will never share identical biographies, situations, experiences or contingencies. They cannot be the same social objects. Although language conveys the impression that phenomena are alike because it offers the ability to describe them in generic terms, it may well simply mask the grounded nature of the items which it abstracts and groups. Terms such as *prostitute*, *fishmonger*, *exchange* and *competition* maintain an illusion of a world divided by discrete contrasts, general properties and independent objects. On inspection, however, the prostitute does not only play a different role from that of the fishmonger, she is the inhabitant of a different world. Some of their behaviour may be explained by alluding to a community of economic experience, common problems in dealing with customers, and difficulties in handling competition. But competition, customers and economic exchange are situationally defined and have no exact symbolic equivalence in the worlds of fishmongers and prostitutes. Sociological analysis must defer to this lack of equivalence, but it cannot defer too religiously. It is constrained to recognise some correspondence between the constitutions of different worlds, however problematic it might be. The only alternative is the virtual abandonment of attempts to understand social life; a slumping back into a torpor of utter subjectivism; and the building of a Tower of Babel in which each social world is awarded its own untranslatable language.

The Unique and the General

Interactionism manages this central dilemma of the sociology of knowledge by resorting to three discrete strategies. Firstly, the import and scale of contextualised meaning cannot be appraised from outside the situation. It is impossible to gauge on *a priori* grounds, or from knowledge *about* social process, exactly what the internal topography of a situation might be. If the topography is problematic, sensible and pertinent questions cannot be put until it is known. That critical informational void can be filled only by an immediate inspection of the setting and its symbolic composition. Participant-observation recommends itself because 'we must become involved in the everyday lives of the individuals we wish to study so that we can come to share enough of the commonsense meanings of those activities to the individuals doing them to be able to understand what those meanings are'.[84] The simple application of generic terms is no substitute for an embedded understanding of a situation.

A companion solution jars with this stress upon the grounded quality of experience. The pragmatists and the formalists had defined the contents of existence as ineffable. Indeed, Jack Douglas[85] himself observed that certain sentiments 'are almost completely outside of verbal language, which often disrupts them more than it builds in these realms.'[86] There are tight limits placed around any sociology which portrays its contents in such a manner. It can rarely make systematic advances without encountering formidable blocks. In fact it continually risks being overwhelmed by the fragile and incommunicable nature of its materials. Simmel had proposed an analytic strategy for bypassing those blocks, and interactionism turns to Simmel in need. Formalism constitutes a reservoir of solutions to the problems posed by the densely woven, unique and virtually indescribable content of action. Many interactionists have never actually moved very far from formalism. For instance, Becker, Hughes and Strauss have largely ignored content, occupying themselves with the institutional structures in which experiences are realised. Unburdened by questions of the substantive character of the social world, their sociology is relieved of abundant dilemmas. I shall discuss those dilemmas in Chapters 5 and 6.

Interactionists are variously exercised with the description of contents. A few have emphasised the phenomenological strands running through formalism and pragmatism by synthesising their work with the thought of Alfred Schutz and his successors. Yet, at some point in their analysis, all must suppress substantive work and take up a formalist stance. Every sociologist is intellectually committed to some version of formalism. Thus prostitutes and fishmongers must be described as if they shared moral careers, commitments, the constraints of role-playing, the problems of gathering information and the like. There can be no precise symmetry between the intellectual forms of the sociologist and the rooted and modified forms of social life, but it is by forms that the sociologist remains both faithful and competent. Formalism lends order and stability to an analytic style which might otherwise founder on the imponderables of authenticity. Pragmatism advocated a treatment of the world which might well have incapacitated any sociology that it influenced. Its portrayal of the qualities of true experience and true knowledge could not easily provide recipes for disciplined research. Its more disabling principles must therefore be simply abandoned at critical junctures.

The third strategy addresses the problems that arise when analytic knowledge is itself defined as a process which cannot promote certainty. The pragmatists had injected into interactionism a reasoned incapacity to work with systematic thought, *a priori* schemes or propositional logic. It was argued that understanding would be corrupted if it were framed by a precisely structured explanation. In turn, sociology must itself reflect the emergent and open properties of learning. It is committed to exemplifying the principles of its own epistemology. In this emphasis interactionism shares common features with other sociologies that claim to adopt a dialectical approach to knowledge. Karl Mannheim, for instance, argued that inconsistency and formlessness may be necessary features of any discipline which explores consciousness: 'in a simple empirical investigation or straightforward logical argument, contradictions are mistakes; but when the task is to show that our whole thought system in its various parts leads to inconsistencies, these inconsistencies are the thorn in the flesh from which we have to start.'[87] He contrasted an epistemology which adhered to a belief in unchanging realities with one that was itself evolutionary:

> we become aware of the fact that we are observing the world from a moving staircase, from a dynamic platform, and, therefore, the image of the world changes with the changing frames of reference which various cultures create. On the other hand, epistemology still only knows of a static platform where one doesn't become aware of the possibility of various perspectives and, from this angle, it tries to deny the existence and the right of such dynamic thinking.[88]

The position adopted by Mannheim and the interactionists thus stands in pronounced contrast to other sociological epistemologies. In a radical Idealism, for example, the Absolute is the one essential truth which is not divisible into dissonant elements. Perspectives will differ in time and space, but they must finally submit to ranking, comparison, sifting and synthesis. Reality cannot be ultimately revealed as an irresoluble disharmony. In a similar fashion a sociology which is under the sway of natural science methodologies cannot readily accept irreconcilable contradiction. There are standard analytic instruments which were designed to dispel confusion and produce a demonstrable order. The instruments reflect a logic which is outside space and time: they can be improved or replaced but the logic itself cannot be changed. In Mannheim's scheme, however, multiple truths can coexist. They lose or gain in authority as their situations are transformed. An evolving knowledge must include provision for its own displacement. It cannot be guided by absolute principles which irrevocably determine its future forms.

An epistemology which is committed neither to the Absolute nor to Aristotelian logic may then countenance a state of continuing intellectual disarray. It may further adopt an exploratory style which upholds different truths as it advances. Such an epistemological style can be more or less pronounced in any sociology. Strains of it are certainly to be discovered in pragmatism and they have been inherited by symbolic interactionism. The major consequence has been a marked caution which manifests itself in a reluctance to set down firm conclusions or well-defined structures of explanation. Instead of occupying a central place, interactionist analysis unobtrusively accompanies the unfolding processes which it describes. In turn, it reflects its opposition to *a priori* reasoning and the idea of fixed structure by subscribing to emergent sociological definitions of events.[89] Instead of laying out hypotheses and definitions at the beginning of a description, the interactionist will typically coax those statements out of the unwinding discussion itself. Thus Strauss committed himself to vagueness and openness when he chose to discuss 'identity': 'by deliberately choosing an ambiguous, diffuse term like identity I sensed I could better look around the corners of my problems, and be less likely to slide down the well-worn grooves of other men's thought'.[90] Intellectual system is then itself regarded as an emergent property of sociological enquiry. It must not be established *ab initio*.

A propositional sociology is then replaced by a stance which relies on the loosest of ideal-types which are progressively modified and refined as they become applied in substantive work. Rudimentary definitions are assembled to direct the sociologist at possibly important areas of the social world: 'whereas definitive concepts provide prescriptions of what to see, sensitizing concepts merely suggest directions along which to look'.[91] Instead of firmly prestructuring the world, they are designed to entice description out of the ongoing experience of the sociologist. Sensitising concepts reflect the pragmatist concern with the illusions of abstract intellectuality. Interactionism holds that knowledge must be an integral part of the analytic process, created in that process rather than setting or misinterpreting its forms. If understanding is grounded, it cannot be other than an evolving property of investigation. Any attempt to anticipate its organised state will stem from an analytic *a priori* judgment which irreparably violates and distorts its objects. There is thus a determined commitment to induction and a great hesitation about deductive reasoning:

> Many of our common errors come from assuming that what is known in some cases is also knowledge for the case in hand. This kind of subsumption is the essence of all dogmatism. Deductive reliance upon old knowledge ... is precisely the thing against which the inductive function has to safeguard us.[92]

Analytic induction and the employment of sensitising concepts are rooted in the pragmatist distinction between modes of knowledge. They derive especially from James's contrast between knowledge of intimacy and knowledge *about* the world. As I have argued, knowledge about social life serves most practical purposes well, but it cannot act as a sure foundation for a tenable sociology. What men take for granted or what some authority has approved cannot stand without independent scientific support. Hence Becker remarked that his work with Everett Hughes taught him to be 'skeptical of conventional wisdom; just because everyone thinks something is so does not make it so. At the same time, one must not dismiss conventional wisdom altogether, but rather see it as one of the elements people use in interpreting their experience and organizing their own actions.'[93]

The adoption of a dual definition of knowledge clearly opens the way for a limited paradox which plagues interactionism. Phenomenalism and a belief in the irreducibility of symbolic reality clash with the scientific posture. The claim to a special knowledge of intimacy threatens to divorce the sociologist from the world which he acknowledges to be alone authentic. In Becker's observation, for instance, it may be seen that common-sense suppositions are equivocally 'genuine' *and* 'false'. At one level, they *are* social reality. They constitute the situations in which men act and, phenomenologically, they cannot be dismissed as mere instances of false consciousness. The interactionist cannot countenance the idea of false consciousness because it would serve to resurrect the dualistic gulf between the real and the phenomenal. Nevertheless, those suppositions cannot be taken as a definitive account of the social world because the sociologist makes particular demands which they cannot satisfy.

Curiously, the interactionist is compelled to become intimately acquainted with lay interpretations but discount them; defining them simultaneously as adequate and inadequate explanations of social behaviour; and responding to them as both 'real' and 'less-than-real'. His analyses must not only transcend but defer to common-sense conceptions of the world. There is a tension in interactionism which may be observed in Lofland's statement that we must 'recognize that to know about – to know through stereotype and typification – is not enough. We want a more direct sense of what other people are about and what their lives are like than that provided by casual and unexamined typifications.'[94] The paradox is, of course, that 'other people' organise their lives through 'unexamined typifications'. Symbolic interactionism is then caught up in a refined interplay between forms of awareness which may become tortuous and indecisive. 'Knowledge about' process must be suspended so that scientific enquiry can reveal the internal and embedded 'knowledge about' process. Common sense then becomes a vehicle, a resource, a complement and a problematic object.

Interactionism recognises that the special status of knowledge about processes handicaps the development of sociology. Such knowledge serves as a reservoir of inferences about the nature and flow of social action, and it seems to direct decisions with competence. It transforms life into an orderly and predictable series of events. So effective are its workings that we are not often incapacitated by the totally unexpected or the inexplicable. In this sense, practical reasoning and practical knowledge are entirely serviceable. Yet their very unproblematic quality may make them deceptive. Our mastery of those forms should not make us suppose that we perfectly understand them. We are not able to precisely describe their origins, nature and functioning. Like language, they are exercised with an ignorance and skill which may mislead us into imagining that we have an intellectual grasp on phenomena which we dimly understand. In the instance of language, Kwant observes 'we . . . remain in the situation of not knowing fully what we say . . . No matter how much we search for light, the words arise in our mind from a certain darkness; we do not know why these words came forward and not others . . . These words combine, as it were, spontaneously into sentences, and we do not know how this combination takes place.'[95] The capable speaker is not then necessarily a capable linguist. Neither is the socially astute layman a proficient sociologist. The operations of mind may be competent, but consciousness cannot be easily turned on itself to provide a coherent account of what it is and does. The interactionists conceive mind to be a problematic object to itself, not an entity which is pellucidly intelligible. In their emphasis on the unemancipated nature of reflexivity, they refuse to share a common ground with the phenomenologists and subjective Idealists.

Knowledge about society is intellectually perilous because it might persuade us that we can readily interpret ourselves and the situations with which we are connected. The blandishments of such thinking are resisted by most interactionists. They would only deceive us into constructing common-sense interpretations which deform the common sense which is explained. Reasoning must be conducted by a disciplined knowledge of phenomena. Although it must inevitably arise out of common sense, it becomes phrased into sensitising concepts which are most uncommon-sensical in use. The analyst is therefore compelled to systematically mediate the contradictions between his everyday ideas and the social reality which he seeks to elucidate.

A distrust of any recourse to knowledge about society will severely limit the scope of possible generalisation and argument. Interactionism enjoins its adherents to adopt a posture of humility before a world which is defined as more opaque and mysterious than is commonly supposed. Irony, subtlety and change so abound that the simple logical extrapolation of arguments will lead thought astray. Old knowledge cannot always anticipate new objects. Indeed Everett Hughes asserted that knowledge *of* one institution merely produces knowledge *about* institutions as a sociological category.[96] Similarly Becker dismissed as spurious many of the problems that are raised about the failure of studies to yield the 'same' descriptions of the 'same' phenomena: 'we should never assume that two institutions are alike simply because they belong to the same conventionally defined sociological category . . . If two studies uncover . . . differences the result is anomalous only if we insist that things called by the same name therefore *are* the same.'[97] Thus detailed understanding cannot be extended without warrant. Grand schemes embracing many instances must give way to the gradual mapping-out of areas of relatively sure knowledge. However pressing social or intellectual problems may be, they cannot be settled unless they have been submitted to properly scientific investigation. The complaint that interactionism neglects macrocosmic process[98] would then be met with the reply that such process has a most suspect ontological and empirical status. It might be tempting to furnish great master systems, but it is more sensible to refrain from unfounded and grandiose speculation.

Pragmatism and Symbolic Interactionism

Unlike Marxism, structural-functionalism and other architectonic constructions, interactionism builds its conceptions of society up from modest analyses of a host of minor occurrences.[99] It ascends from earth to heaven, and refuses to descend from heaven to earth. This strategy of limited analytic induction is an integral part of the interactionist understanding of scientific procedure. By practising a systematic distrust of what passes for authoritative understanding, interactionism cannot take for granted the validity of accounts provided by others. Park used to observe that, like Goethe's Faust, he had wearied of books and turned to the world of men.[100] His successors have done likewise. They have become *faux naïf*, addressing social reality as if it had never had been described before. In particular, the conventions of sociology itself are methodically disregarded. Analytic attention is primarily engaged by the common-sense interpretations which structure the social world. Those ideas, rather than the theories of colleagues, are taken to be chiefly instructive. If they are neglected there is a danger that processes will become reified — translated into seemingly autonomous occurrences which have severed their linkages with the people who brought them into being. As Becker argues, 'we often turn collective activity — people doing things together — into abstract nouns whose connections to people doing things together is tenuous.'[101] By turning his back on the sociological common sense that 'can delude us', the interactionist confronts the fount of relatively authentic knowledge. He dissociates himself from the stock wisdom that 'includes social-science generalizations about the nature of social phenomena, correlations between social categories . . . and the etiology of problematic social conditions . . .'[102] The interactionist's pursuit of humilty thereby commits him to the arrogant severing of his work from virtually all the ongoing concerns of sociology. Ironically, it also detaches him from the work of his own intellectual ancestors. Those who prepared his rejection of others' knowledge brought about their own intellectual rejection. The ancestors of symbolic interactionism ensured their mortality.

An overthrowing of most *a priori* classifications and explanations forces the interactionist to become a stranger in even the most familiar scenes. He must regard as anthropologically bizarre and problematic what others take to be commonplace.[103] The interpretations of others become ethnographic data or distractions rather than competing or complementary sociologies. Such an intellectual position makes only the most tentative categorisations possible. Every social event must be viewed as if it were novel; its connections with other events as yet undemonstrated; and its characteristic developments as yet uncharted. Every study is then conducted as if there were little or no sociology to support it. As Bruyn remarked, 'the social scientist... looks at the world phenomenologically... as though things were happening to him for the first time.'[104] Interactionists tend to write each of their analyses in a style which suggests that they are building sociology anew on raw foundations, not adding to an established body of knowledge. Their constant return to new beginnings accounts for the haphazard appearance of the sociology. Rose described the growth of interactionism as 'an idea here, a magnificent but partial formulation there, a little study here, a program of specialized studies there'.[105] The cost of purposeful and incremental system-building would be the loss of anthropological naïvety. Interactionists would become engrossed in axioms and uninvolved in ethnography.

The Emergence of the Ethnographic Tradition

Symbolic interactionism is perhaps the major segment of sociology which has devoted itself to the detailed ethnography of small social worlds. The anthropological materials most readily at hand for the early interactionists were those scattered around the university itself. Robert Park exhorted his students to chronicle the myriad phenomena that were developing in the Chicago of the 1920s and 1930s. For a time at least, Chicago sociology was virtually identical with the sociology *of* Chicago.[106] It was nursed as a cartographic exercise, studying Little Sicily, the Jewish ghetto, Polonia, the Gold Coast, the slums, Hobohemia, rooming-house districts and the gangs of the city. Each of those areas was treated as a symbolic world which created and perpetuated a distinctive moral and social organisation. Each was subjected to an interpretative analysis which attempted to reproduce the processes by which that organisation was brought into being. They were collectively identified as *natural areas*: 'natural' because they were themselves part of the natural evolution and selection which shaped society; because they were different from the structures produced by planning and science, and because they represented a unit which allegedly framed American thinking on social and political life. According to Mead, 'those larger communities which political and economic activities have always implied and involved . . . have had little or no existence in the retrospect and historic structures of the American mind.'[107] American philosophical and sociological perspectives carved the small community into the natural context of thought and action: the American's 'most comprehensive institutions of social control and organization have found their reason for existence in the immediate problems of the community'.[108]

Ecology[109] and formalism[110] were combined to explain the emergence and interplay of natural areas. Dewey had observed that social life rested in communication, and the social ecologists translated communication into a spatial and moral process. The physical and economic map of the city was read as a patterning of opportunities and restraints which shaped the possible development of social worlds. The natural area was a locality carved out by people and endowed with a distinctive social character. Its boundaries and contours were structured by features such as roads, canals, railroads, lakes and parks. The content of its life was acquired, in part, by the role which the area played in the city's division of labour. It was also formed by the varying capacities of groups to appropriate social space and hold it against the competition of others. Organised configurations of territory and social process emerged, reflecting the evolutionist themes of increasing structural complexity, integration and conflict. Evolutionary theory, ecology and formalism together offered a master logic which hinged on the metaphors of symbiosis, competition, struggle, conflict, succession and adaptation. Specialisation of function, segregation and selection ordered the spatial components of sociation. Those components in turn established the possible limits and substance of the collective situations in which selves, careers and moral meanings could appear.

The social flux that accompanied rapid social growth engendered some interest in the investigation of social disorganisation. Pathology, in particular, was examined as an outcrop of the disintegration of conventional controls.[111] But flux also evoked another style of intellectual response. The sheer novelty of many urban phenomena led to a radical revision of sociological and philosophical assumptions. The pragmatists of Chicago, for instance, were encouraged to abandon the static Idealism of the European metaphysicians. They embarked instead on a programme which portrayed man as a problem-solver in an open and relatively unstructured world.[112] The interactionists, too, shed much of the theoretical edifice which had been prepared by European sociologists. Conceptions of estate, class and moral solidarity became seen as increasingly untenable when they were placed in the context of the expanding Chicago. The forms of society were being redrafted in America. Although Thorstein Veblen may still have explored the workings of class, many of his contemporaries simply bracketed them as inconsequential and anachronistic. European thinking was interpreted as appropriate only to the background which the immigrant had left.

The Chicago sociologists reacted to the city as their English counterparts had done some seventy years before. Henry Mayhew and John Binney had been part of a journalistic movement which surveyed London as a new Babylon, a mysterious and kaleidoscopic array of strange worlds and unknown groups. Their ventures into hitherto 'unexplored' metropolitan territories produced reports which had all the fascination of anthropological tracts. They framed their observations in a special interpretation of political economy, but their writing itself emphasised the tasks of ethnographic description and an appreciative understanding of the capital's subworlds. That work still stands as unexcelled reporting of the mundane and deviant facets of urban life. The early ecological tradition did not survive in England for very long. It was stifled by the rise of medical and Lombrosian readings of social and moral processes. But the expansion of Chicago excited a similar response in the beginnings of American sociology. In the instance of Chicago, however, an intellectual stance was preserved both by a permanent institution and an existing body of supportive ideas. Ethnography and journalism could be grafted together into a reproducible and continuing tradition.

The city of Chicago grew so rapidly that it was not thought to represent a fitting subject for the application of established theorems. It unfolded such a number of unfamiliar and shifting phenomena that imported perspectives were simply seen as incompetent. It became proper to describe the novel in a modest fashion, a fashion which often reflected no more than the desire to capture an entity before it changed or disappeared. People discovered in the problematic situations were themselves transformed into guides. They elucidated what existing sociologies were incapable of analysing. Their management of social life had to be sympathetically examined. Thus Matza remarks of *The Hobo*, 'the conception of a peculiar world, albeit deviant, with its own logic and integrity is introduced early in Anderson's volume and occupies a fundamental place in the study.'[113] The conjunction of pragmatist epistemology, the journalistic urgings of Robert Park, and the efflorescence of new and unknown social terrain led to the growth of an interpretative sociology which rejected almost all the major European paradigms. One *a priori* model, suggested by Warming's *Plant Communities*, had been transposed to the sociology, but it was initially mediated by the forms of Simmel. It was linked to the anthropological posture which feigned ignorance about the social world, could not derive useful hypotheses from conventional abstract schemes, and was committed to a stance of sophisticated naïvety.

It may also be the case that the larger character of American immigration contributed to the special style and foci of symbolic interactionism. Chicago's growth was largely made up from the influx of Poles, Scandinavians, Jews, Italians and Irish. Within the United States itself there was massive geographical movement. The deracinated character of American society, its construction out of diverse national and regional materials, and the accompanying dilution of communality may have thrown analytic attention on to the self as a salient object. When the larger structures of society are apparently dismantled and confused, the individual world of the self stands out and becomes prominent. As Shaskolsky argues, the absence of a firm sense of stratification and hierarchy made possible an imagery of action which was fluid and free. The individual's 'definition of the situation' became analytically pronounced when structural regulation was depressed.[114] He states, '[symbolic interactionism expressed itself] in the belief in the uniqueness of each member of society and his freedom to plan and perform his everyday actions in interrelationship with others unencumbered by . . . the impinging rules of a structural society. . . .'[115]

The early intellectual world of Chicago was embedded in the grosser phenomena of capitalism and urbanisation. In that context estranged men could become the primary units of morality and understanding. Capitalism engenders rootlessness and an erosion of communal conceptions of identity. Those organised ideas which are attached to estate society give way to others which emphasise the isolation of a person in a society of markets, contracts and flux. For example, *honour* refers to the participation of a person in a collective identity, a participation which partially submerges individuality.[116] *Dignity*, by contrast, is the attribute of the atomised man. An emerging class society encourages ideas of dignity and devalues honour. It is plausible that the greatly accelerated processes of capitalism in early twentieth-century America gave ontological primacy to the individual above all other categories. Theories which centred on estate society, or on the European forms of class, could be discounted as irrelevant. The self became chiefly problematic.

The Reversals of Formalism and Pragmatism

I have argued that interactionism is a diffuse and ill-defined enterprise which has formed around a reasoned rejection of systematisation. Part of that rejection entailed an act of self-amputation, a disregard for the school's prehistory and its legitimating theses.[117] Academic knowledge was itself discounted to be replaced by an emphasis on the integrity of everyday understanding. Thus Park recalled that James had taught him 'the real world was the experience of actual men and women and not abbreviated and shorthand descriptions of it that we call knowledge'.[118] Within that intellectual context, reversals of significance and intent can occur. There has been little industry devoted to superintending orthodoxy or maintaining coherence. Themes fed into interactionism are thereby subjected to the risk of being rudely severed from their originating contexts of meaning. The exact purposes of their authors can be forgotten.

Ironically, the influences implanted by the formalists and pragmatists culminated in a series of abandoned twists and reversals which transformed some of their pivotal arguments. That series did not play itself out through the entire interactionist edifice. An unsystematic sociology is not prey to systematic change. Yet formalism did lose some of its emphasis upon the creative and mediating role of the individual, and pragmatism was pulled apart to release Idealism to interactionism.

Formalism and pragmatism instilled a pervasive resistance to abstraction, reification and schematisation. They could do so only by developing complex, abstract schemes of thought which addressed central problems of epistemology and philosophy. In a sense, they had to be the first and the last philosophically literate creators of the sociology. Fidelity to their principles required a form of intellectual suicide: a ritual death of the originating abstractions and the birth of a cleansed and uncontaminated sociology. Interactionism represents the paradox of anti-intellectualism being sustained and justified by a wholly intellectual foundation. When the more impeccable interactionists turn back to those who first bore the oral tradition, they sometimes recognise an affinity but they may also disown Simmel and the pragmatists. Glaser and Strauss, for example, observe the correspondences between the thought of Simmel and Goffman;[119]

they take Simmel to be a fertile source of 'unintegrated' theorising;[120] but they nevertheless regard him (and Weber, Cooley, Mead and Park) as the source of a hagiolatry which stifled innovation.[121] The business of exegesis and explication suppressed new sociology.

Formalism was subjected to greater irony. The forms of ecology became candidates for a drastic autonomisation. In examining the unfolding dialectic of ethnic succession, competition and conflict, Park came to ascribe an ontological independence to macrostructural process.[122] In this work he was at one with Durkheim in his championing of the social as a sovereign order. The significance of men was radically reformed: they could achieve little as the creators of the forms of life. Instead, they were subordinated to the inexorable workings of social forces, becoming mere vehicles for expressing the interplay of forms.[123] That tyranny was not exercised by alienated products of mind. It was the property of a realm that was *sui generis*, propelled on by the logic of its own inner transformations. Indeed, the principal historian of the Chicago School was to detach ecology from interactionism, identifying the two as virtually separate intellectual traditions. He relegated interactionism to social psychology, and assigned the ecological model to its own independent sphere: 'the most important discovery was that a complex ecology does exist, and that it operates in important ways to select populations, to control the direction of their flow, and variously to influence behavior, especially in the variety of manifestations of social disorganization.'[124] Faris does not dwell on Simmel's place in interactionism, and it is clear that he holds the forms of ecology to be very different from synthetic *a priori* knowledge. In the vulgar versions of the labelling school of deviance, too, that drift has been sustained. It has become translated into a depiction of society in which men no longer display choice but are simply shepherded into simplex roles by an irresistible authority.[125] The idea of the more-life of men has been thrust aside, and the more-than-life forms have been subjected to a thoroughing reification. Simmel's careful stress upon the anchorage of all forms in the doings and thoughts of men has been obliterated. The forms are turned on people as if they were agents of the suprapersonal forces which Simmel sought to discredit.

Similarly, some work has destroyed the precarious fusion of organism and consciousness that the pragmatists had nurtured. That fusion was brought into being partly to transcend the dualism of mind and matter. Whilst the self was analytically independent of the body,[126] the contemplating consciousness did not create the social and natural world. To the contrary, it was an integral part of it. Consider James's reflections about psychology:

> The only conception at the same time renovating and fundamental with which biology has enriched psychology, the only *essential* point in which 'the new psychology' is an advance upon the old is, it seems to me, the very general, and by this time very familiar notion, that all our activity belongs at bottom to the type of reflex action, and that all our consciousness accompanies a chain of events of which the first was an incoming current in some sensory nerve, and of which the last will be a discharge into some muscle, blood-vessel or gland . . . Viewed in this light the thinking and feeling portions of our life seem little more than half-way houses towards behavior. . . .[127]

Thought was inextricably lodged in the realm of nature. Any other stance would raise the demons of crude empiricism or rampant Idealism. The integrity of the knowing-known transaction required preservation if the epistemological superstructure of pragmatism was not to collapse. But it is apparent that emergent consciousness could become interpreted as an independent agent which was liberated from all but itself. The delicate balancing of organism, mind, self and society could easily be upset by a determined emphasis on one facet of the totality. If the self arose to survey and control the rest, pragmatism could return to its pre-Darwinian source.

The intellectual world of the early interactionists was ill-equipped to preserve and transmit pragmatism in an undistorted form. Although there was a relatively viable working collaboration between its members, it was always so fractured that it refracted themes in diverse ways. The various founders of interactionism were largely untrained in sociology. Indeed, they were principally engaged in establishing its contours for an American audience. They came to the nascent discipline with perspectives that were different compounds of biology, history, philosophy, journalism, social reform and the study of languages. Some had had no formal exposure to philosophy, others were steeped in it. There was thus little of the unity that might have flowed from a common subjection to a single intellectual tradition.

Many of the early interactionists were attempting to fabricate their own distinctive syntheses and charters for the discipline of sociology. Almost all tried to impose a special stamp on the emergent and substantially undefined enterprise. In so doing they gathered around them small groups of sympathetic students and colleagues who became the centres of increasingly independent perspectives. The apprenticeship structures of symbolic interactionism may be traced back to that first phase of factionalism: students were absorbed into academic fiefs and received their training from one or more of the competing masters. In some cases the bulk of intellectual exchange took place within the fief. Thus W. I. Thomas stated in 1927: 'I have now lived to the point where my most stimulating contacts are with the younger sociologists, such as Bernard, Burgess, Thrasher, Zorbaugh, and Shaw, some of whom have been my pupils.'[128] Factionalism and disunity fragmented the original Chicago School. Some of those who had been associated with it became socially isolated. Cooley, for instance, sustained no great intimacy with his fellows.[129] He was able to retain an Idealism unreformed by pragmatism, arguing that 'mind is an organic whole made up of co-operating individualities'.[130] His particular methodology was 'sympathetic introspection', an Idealist simulation of the thought and life-word of others.[131]

Pragmatism and formalism were thus differently received and defined by the early interactionists. W. I. Thomas, for example, recognised that he had been influenced by Dewey but claimed 'Dewey has always seemed to me to be essentially a mystic and a metaphysician and I found – or thought I found – that I was repudiating almost everything he said, or ignoring it'.[132] By contrast, Everett Hughes stated that Park had referred to Simmel, Dewey, Royce and James as his 'special mentors'.[133] Park himself alluded to the profound impact worked by Simmel, James and Dewey.[134] Significantly, Mead became estranged from Cooley, arguing that he 'cannot or does not wish to identify the self with the physical organism'.[135] Mead deplored the segregation of the animal organism from social process. There was then no uniform mediation of pragmatism by interactionism.

In the welter of disparate versions of interactionism, Cooley was one of the principal champions of the retention of Idealism. There is a great affinity between his work and the more developed treatments of consciousness in the sociology. He exploded the organic unity of mind and sought to achieve a disjunction between the material and the reflexive. Cooley asserted that the material can become consequential only when it is mediated by imagination:

We are accustomed to talk and think, so far as we do think in this connection, as if a person were a material rather than a psychic fact. Instead of basing our sociology and ethics upon what a man really is as part of our mental and moral life, he is vaguely and yet grossly regarded as a shadowy material body, a lump of flesh, and not as an ideal thing at all. But surely it is only common sense to hold that the social and moral reality is that which lives in our imaginations and affects our motives.[136]

The deracinated imagination conjures up a social reality in concert with other imaginations. It is discontinuous with the physical and physiological substrata which carry it along. The organism can then become significant when mind renders it significant and in the fashion that mind forms. People are no longer embedded in the entangled existential situation of Mead and Dewey. Rather, they work and act on one principal plane of reality which summons and transmutes the objects of all other planes. Thus Cressey denied the authority of explanations which sought to trace the aetiology of 'motiveless crimes': motives are not 'inner biological mainsprings of action but linguistic constructs which organize acts in particular situations'.[137] In Cressey's ontology, motiveless crimes are themselves part of a vocabulary of motives which organise and elicit behaviour.[138] Many interactionists have attended primarily to the symbolic organisation of experience and have put to one side the 'biological matrix' of Dewey. Taylor, for instance, rejects the stance that 'accords purely epiphenomenal status to the deviant's verbalized reasons, believing that inner drives, instincts, conditioned reflexes, internalized goals constitute necessary and sufficient motives for action.'[139] Similarly, Scheff advocated a methodological agnosticism about the 'causes' of mental illness, 'for the social scientist . . . the symptoms of mental illness have human meaning and human consequences regardless of their origins'.[140] What for Dewey had been 'a withdrawal from reality' became a strategy for analysing withdrawals from reality.

It matters little whether deviation from orthodoxy has enhanced or undermined the intellectual power of the symbolic interactionists. What is important is the manner in which the original integrity of the pragmatist totality has been violated by thought which was once given coherence and cogency by that totality. There is a looseness and play within the interactionist appraisal of sociology. Such freedom has permitted the appearance of perverse ideas which fold back on the main body of interactionism. In a sense, contradiction and confusion have emerged to liberate and complicate the work of the sociology. Liberation is promoted when a lack of system and convention enables innovation and a pragmatic responsiveness to the business of enquiry. Confusion abounds when procedural and interpretational directives clash in a vortex of opposing ontologies. Practically, the issue is again resolved by a sustained dedication to ethnographic and applied research. The befuddling contradictions of the perspective are partially stilled by a comparative neglect of the abstract ramifications of interactionism. The sociology has become progressively decentralised, yoked to the different substantive regions in which work takes place. In this fashion it still adheres to the pragmatist conception of experience as a form of grounded knowledge which cannot be regulated by abstract ratiocination. Becker illustrates this position well. Replying to those who criticised the interactionist perspective on deviance, he observe 'labelling theory . . . is neither a theory, with all the achievements and obligations that go with the title, nor focused so exclusively on the act of labelling as some have thought. It is, rather, a way of looking at a general area of human activity; a perspective whose value will appear, if at all, in increased understanding of things formerly obscure'.[141] Manifesting the interactionist distaste for the intellectualisation of enquiry, extending no welcome to the citing of theory, he casts interactionism as an unfolding transaction with the world which cannot be assessed *a priori*. He thereby conserves the tendency to focus away from the mires of exegesis and explication. Becker attends to the ongoing experiential reality of the object of sociology, not to that of the sociological subject.[142]

4 The Self

Pragmatism and formalism had both raised the self of the observer to a position of special prominence. Not only was the self a source and synthesis of all viable knowledge, it constituted the elemental unit of sociological analysis. It was thus simultaneously an intellectual subject and an intellectual object. The self is taken to be a social construct, emerging from language, which lends order to all interaction. It is man made conscious of himself as a social process, and its basis is a reflexive turning-back of mind on itself. Reflexivity is made possible by the social forms and it advances the evolution of those forms. It is in the self that a fundamental grammar or logic of the forms is allowed to unfold. All social phenomena stem from that logic so that a socially formed mind and the processes of society display a unity.

Introduction

My discussion of formalism and pragmatism has already emphasised the extraordinary significance which the idea of the self was to receive in symbolic interactionism. The self is not merely a convenient analytic focus for an emerging microsociology. Neither is it to be regarded as a token device which was introduced simply to breathe a little life into descriptions of social structure. Rather it constitutes the very hub of the interactionists' intellectual scheme. All other sociological processes and events revolve around that hub, taking from it their analytic meaning and organisation. For certain purposes, at least, they are forced to become extensions and phases of the self's activities, possessing no autonomy or substantial interest of their own. The doings and evolution of the self are elevated to a central place.[1] They create and refract every important social phenomenon. They are alone 'real' sociological objects, although the nature of their reality is often obscure and their wider boundaries exclude little.

More importantly, interactionists regard the self as the only process which can produce and distil useful knowledge. It is in this last guise that the special quality of the process appears: the self is neither a simple physical entity nor an elementary unit of a social system which is *sui generis*, it is a particular expression of consciousness. So close is the symbolic interactionist identification of the self with knowing that the two have sometimes been collapsed together. For instance, William James stated 'the thoughts themselves are the thinker'.[2] Similarly, Perinbanayagam observes that 'selves are rhetorically constructed'.[3] Thus conceived, the self is synonomous with embedded reason; it furnishes all knowledge, and speculation about knowledge must turn to the self for the solution of its problems. Philosophy, logic, epistemology and metaphysics are translated into a detailed exploration of the reflexive act.[4]

The self then becomes both the vehicle and the object of knowledge. Its possibilities not only outline the claims of philosophy and sociology, they also form their distinctive territory. The ramifications of examining the self must reverberate in a discipline: they define the examiner, the examination and the examined. In that sense, there is a beguiling affinity between the symbolic interactionists' self and the identical subject-object of Hegel and certain Idealists. It is undoubtedly an affinity that would have been recommended by exponents of the intellectual tradition which first nurtured pragmatism. The Absolute Idealists expressly awarded utter potency to mind: they 'sought to sweep all activities of the spirit, scientific, aesthetic, religious, and political, within the logic of the development of the self'.[5] Indeed the interactionists did cast an ambiguous penumbra about the self, laying it open to incorporation by Idealist and behaviourist schemes alike.

Mind was represented as a complicated and diffuse unity made up of subordinate phases. Surveying itself, mind became both subject and object, 'I' and 'me'.[6] Its dual aspect rendered it a candidate for use by Idealists. Its remarkable scope further encouraged that candidacy. Generously defined, the self became tantamount to the totality of things touched by humanity. Ploughing through an environment of objects, mind shapes and rearranges the phenomena which it encounters. Unknowable outside praxis, and transformed by praxis, an object becomes the ambiguous creature of consciousness: 'the physical object is an abstraction which we make from the social response to nature'.[7] The world can then become an adjunct of the knowing mind, giving rise to what Charles Morris described as a biological transcription of Leibniz or Hegel. Consciousness does not only enjoy what is virtually a transcendental relationship with nature, it also uncertainly subtends society itself. Mind is held to generate the communal forms by which it is produced, bringing about a dialectical fusion between the individual and society.[8] Society may analytically precede mind, but the individual has a concreteness which community lacks. In a sense, society flows through him. More comprehensively, intelligence and society are integral parts of nature themselves. Mead, for instance, stated that mind may have singled man out but 'social or moral intelligence . . . is entirely the same as the intelligence evidenced in the whole upward struggle of life on the earth . . .'[9] So formulated, organism, mind, self and society are little more than the intellectually-severed manifestations of a totality in which consciousness is the dominant phase. There is a corresponding temptation to portray the self as a process which has only to know itself in order to yield absolute understanding about all things social.

In the main, interactionists have resisted that temptation. They have prevented the self from evolving into the identical subject-object which can attain certain knowledge by exercising introspection. Such a prohibition has not been universally enforced: there are quite prominent Idealist strands running throughout interactionism, and phenomenology has begun to redefine the methods and tasks of the sociology. But the movement towards subjective Idealism has not been uniform and the central strain of interactionism has remained faithful to phenomenalism. Phenomenalism awards no privileged place to mind or to the self which takes mind out into the world. Indeed the two movements of mind, the 'I' and the 'me', are taken to be problematic to one another. A man cannot know his socially-situated self with any clarity. Neither can that self understand the processes that are lodged within the inaccessible immediacy of lived experience. One must cautiously and uncertainly make sense of oneself, being awarded no exceptional interpretative powers.

Yet the very unprivileged status of the self is a source of particular strength. Symbolic interactionists assign men to an unalienated place in the cosmos. People are held to be neither estranged from the physical world nor the representatives of some grand synthesis of all lesser orders. They are, instead, integral parts of nature, ontologically indistinct from the rest. The universe is thought to be constituted by objects which existed before any contemplating mind could gaze upon them. Those objects develop in an orderly fashion, and humanity itself is totally caught up in their evolution. All its associated experiences and practices are entirely objective events, and there is no warrant to describe them as if they were part of some foreign domain. The forms of existence may be rooted in mind, but mind itself is a fundamental emergent of evolution. That peculiar rooting should not belittle or aggrandise the character of human experience. The attribution of 'subjectivity' can refer only to the special site of processes. The subjective is not discontinuous with nature, and it does not possess some less-than-real quality: 'pleased palates and irritated or suffering members are there in the same sense as other percepts or objects'.[10] Sensations, sentiments, thoughts and even the complex structures of social organisation must be ranked with other happenings as objective phenomena.

The processes of thought and investigation are thereby translated into exchanges between different sets of empirical events. As a man explores an entity by touching, smelling, hearing or scrutinising it, so he may change both its physical constitution and its significance for him. Its altered meaning is as much real as its altered form. Such transactions within nature cannot be reduced down to the unfoldings of a sovereign consciousness or to the inconsequential examination of an unchanging object by an unchanging mind. Practical activities do transform the world, but only as movements between its different parts. They are neither an imposition from without nor an irrelevant occurrence on another plane of reality.

Activity refers to the commerce between men and the things which surround them. It is both the product and the producer of perspectives which shape purposes and other actions. As activity proceeds, so there is a rearrangment of the environment and a trading of meanings between knower and known. Such meanings inhere neither in mind nor in the objects to which they are attached: they are natural properties of the two, being revealed as conduct unwinds. Indeed pragmatists took the prime difference between prereflexive action and its objects to be functional and not ontological. Action moves and objects are moved.[11] Any examination of knowing processes must therefore dwell on conduct, meaning and objects as an evolving whole. Further, that whole must be surveyed as if its parts were scientifically equivalent. Some of the parts might be locked into private experience, others may be publicly visible, but all enjoy the same status as real events:

> In evolution not only have new forms appeared, but new qualities or contents in experience. It is the sensitivities of forms that are the occasions for the appearance, in the world of these forms, of new

characters of things, answering to all the senses, and new meanings answering to their new capacities for conduct. And these new characters and new meanings exist in nature as do the forms of physical objects, although they are relative to the sensitivities and capacities of the individual forms.[12]

In its uncontaminated state, then, knowledge is an objective occurrence which is not a member of a unique or autonomous realm. Despite its intangibility and seeming insubstantiality, thought is as solidly a component of the factual world as any other. It is merely another facet of that world, not a Laputan sighting of it: 'perspectives of nature exist in nature, not in the consciousness of the organism as a stuff'.[13] So defined, unreflected knowledge is transformed into an unproblematic process. It is fraught by no uncertainties or metaphysical doubts.

Such innocent knowledge tends to represent an assured anchorage for philosophy but it does not yield the contents of a system of thought. It may not be adequate for many social or intellectual purposes because it is almost invariably partial and incomplete. More disturbingly, it appears to be wholly alienated from reason and consciousness. It cannot be tapped for its understanding of the world. Similarly, prepredicative experience is ordered by a private language of the self. It is not consensual. A common stock of knowledge and perspectives arises only with conscious co-operation and the use of an organising symbolism. But the variation and utter subjectivity of that experience cannot render it less sure. There may be an abundance of visions, each one being valid in its own situation. In this sense there are as many truths as there are people. Truth can no longer be investigated in spurious isolation from the specific circumstances of its appearance for an individual. In short, situated and unselfconscious knowledge is not only 'real' but the undisputed possession of actual individuals. Sociology and philosophy alike must turn to those individuals. The human being is the vehicle which incorporates and guarantees all the items that might be useful to a discipline.

The Emergence of the Self

The self is a peculiar construction of consciousness which translates a person into his own object. The interactionists maintain that there is no consciousness or selfhood in prereflexive knowledge. Rather, lived experience is structurally similar to the responses which an animal makes to its environment. There is an imagination of objects and of the animal's effects on those objects, but no turning back to the animal itself as an uncertain object.[14] The creature is all subject, existing in an undifferentiated wholeness and unable to survey itself from some fabricated external standpoint. It cannot know self or self-estrangement because it houses no inner division of awareness. By extension, there is no relativity in immediate experience. An organism merely *exists* in an environment that *is*:

> in our moving about in a world that is simply there and to which we are so adjusted that no thinking is involved, there is a certain amount of sensuous experience such as persons have when they are just waking up, a bare thereness of the world. Such characters about us may exist in experience without taking their place in relationship to the self.[15]

That unmediated awareness precedes the rise of mind and it persists after mind has been stimulated into existence. But it can never be grasped reflexively.[16] Any attempt to recapture or remember it will impose alien forms upon it.[17] Pathetically, it can be known only when there is no effort to examine it: it disappears as soon as an examination proceeds. It represents what is tantamount to the unstructured content of life, its organisation destined to remain nothing more than a matter of surmise. The reconstruction of immediate experience is as conjectural and absurd as a projected portrayal of the quintessence of an entity. Mind must impute its own consciousness to experiences devoid of consciousness. There is thus a vast tract of human existence which can never be framed analytically. Any person is built around a stream of events which resemble the noumenon of the dualists. He is composed of experiences which do not lend themselves to description:

> Since 'I' is known to our experience primarily as a feeling . . . it cannot be described or defined without suggesting that feeling. We are sometimes likely to fall into a formal and empty way of talking regarding questions of emotion, by attempting to define that which is in its nature primary and indefinable. A formal definition of self-feeling . . . must be as hollow as a formal definition of the taste of salt, or the color red; we can expect to know what it is only by experiencing it.[18]

Symbolic interactionism takes much of its style from the attempt to convey what is ultimately indescribable. Its arguments are often embedded in a framework that is woven out of connotation and evocation. Accordingly its central theses can be fully understood only when an audience colludes with the sociologist in constructing an interpretation of a problem. The audience is necessarily endowed with a sympathetic and sophisticated imagination that can reproduce the prereflexive experience which no sociologist can portray. It must arouse in itself those contexts and sentiments which defy explicit development in a formal analysis. Interactionism is thus forced to offer its ideas in a partial imagery which will remain incomplete until fleshed-out by its recipients. Great play is made with words and syntax in an effort to coax impressions that are never demanded in conventional sociology. It follows that the persuasiveness of interactionism depends on an observance of the implied contract between writer and reader. When that contract is not recognised or honoured, the sociology is revealed as elliptical, banal or stark. It is this tacit appeal for aid that makes the sociology most vulnerable to the attacks that could be mounted by a hostile critic.

Exchanges do take place at the level of unreflecting existence, and some attempt has been made to comprehend them. Interaction without symbolism or selves is at one with the rest of the world known to immediate experience. In that world, a being's gestures and responses are objective phenomena which can excite an antagonistic, complementary or similar reaction in others. What distinguishes such acts is that they are only accidentally private and relative to thier producers.[19] They appear as natural, external events which stand against creator and observer alike. They are not therefore experienced as subjectively problematic, seeming merely to be emitted without any appraisal of the complexities of their reception.

When gestures are made, then, there is no anticipation of their socially mediated consequences. Neither are those consequences themselves part of the unfolding gestures. At most there is a mechanical sequence of action following upon action without imaginative rehearsal or retrospectively imposed order. What is chiefly distinctive about unmediated activity is its segregation from the structures and effects of sociation. An act does not represent some symbolically collapsed section of larger social process. It is not so phrased that it encloses others' real or possible responses. It is not progressively tailored to incorporate or direct future responses. Instead it is entirely encased in the undifferentiated subjectivity of a being. In this sense, any sustained collaboration between beings must rest on simple habit, on a fortuitous integration of various responses, or upon something equivalent to a physiological division of labour. Ants, for instance, form complex societies because they are structurally dissimilar, not because they can consciously program each others' activities into a co-ordinated whole.[20]

Selves arise when unreflexive activity is superseded and an environment of processes and objects attains social significance. They become possible when the simple 'thereness' of phenomena gives way to negotiated meaning. Gestures are then shaped rather than exuded, complex rather than simple, intertwined rather than isolated. The significant gesture indicates an object's meaning to oneself and to others. It fosters a shared identification instead of a mere accidental convergence of perspectives. Such deliberate symbolisation is qualitatively different from the unreflecting act. Its realisation demands the introduction of an entirely new set of forms. In particular there must be a special structure of consciousness which permits a detailed anticipation of the consequences of behaviour. The possible impact of a gesture cannot remain unproblematic and tangential. If meaning is to be created or supported, the other's answering gesture must be assessed and built into the very fabric of the nascent act, serving as a stimulus to the person who initiates an exchange. Without that vicarious stimulation the projected behaviour would be deficiently social. It would be unresponsive to the different replies which it might receive. After all, ratified meaning may be defined by the likelihood of a common attitude towards an object. In turn, the promotion of a common attitude must hinge on the successful imputation and control of identities and identifications. Unless a person can adopt the other's perspective and treat it as his own, he will be unable to appreciate the effects of what he does. He must enlarge his imagination so that it offers workable facsimiles of others' minds and attitudes.

An expressive act is thus compounded out of the various stances that might affect its evolution. When a person gives birth to a significant gesture, he is simultaneously himself and the others for whom it could be an object:

> We must indicate to ourselves not only the object but also the readiness to respond in certain ways to the object, and this indication must be made in the attitude or role of the other individual to whom it is pointed out or to whom it may be pointed

out. If this is not the case it has not that common property which is involved in significance. It is through the ability to be the other at the same time that he is himself that the symbol becomes significant.[21]

A reflexive act is a most complex rehearsal of social activity. It encompasses what one might do, how other might reply, and what one's answering actions could be. Each of these phases is an uncertain prediction which must be modified as activity unfolds and as one's own and other intentions are revealed. Each of these phases will itself be a stimulus, the person imagined in the future and the past guiding himself in the present. One has to assume multiple identities that are related and staggered over time. He must not only be himself, but also comprehend the amalgam of himself and others evolving around the incomplete act. In selling an item, for instance, a vendor will indicate what his intentions are to himself and to the buyer, he will excite in himself the buyer's response, will attempt to grasp how his own role has been assimilated by the buyer, and then repeat the sequence through its more distant stages. He must further be sensitive to people who are physically absent but nonetheless implicated in the transaction. They too proffer perspectives which must be recognised. He must attend to the more anonymous etiquette that governs legal and economic exchange. In so preparing himself, he will appreciate that others are making similar but largely invisible preparations. They are also required to act on tentative plans and inferences which shift as he illustrates his intentions in action. Projected gestures are therefore lent form by what are thought to be the attitudes and anticipations of others, just as those anticipations revolve around his own assumed moves. In this fashion, he can only become himself by being someone else. Transactions are awesomely complicated: each man is his own panopticon, an external monitor of himself and others, and an interpreter of the hidden dialogues that prompt others to act. He surveys all that complex process through different perspectives and from scattered points in the constructed past, present and future of the action. Exchanges can take on the appearance of an infinite chain of reflected images, akin to the interplay between opposing mirrors but made elaborate by their shifting relations.

None of this intricate imaginative work can be performed solely on the prereflexive plane. A distinctive set of forms must arise to organise and simplify the conversation of significant gestures. Meaning and consciousness are held to be creatures of the special medium of language, emerging from the discourse between and within individuals. Indeed, Mead claimed that language is so vital to the growth of mind that its development must have been historically prior to the development of thought itself.[22] The prime function of the linguistic gesture is to serve as an alienated stimulus. Speech and writing can become estranged from their authors and confront them as objective symbols.

Consciousness, Language and the Self

Such is the place of speech in interactionist analysis that it is important to emphasise its contrasts with other types of gesture. A person can acquire diverse perspectives on the expressions which attend his activity, but most are affected by his authorship of what he examines. He cannot enforce a distance between himself and the symbolism which organises his appearance. Gestures and qualities remain stubbornly tied to his experience, resisting objectification. So dependent are they that he is very often deprived of expressive information about himself. He can generally see and know less of himself than others do. His own physical and facial gestures are typically concealed from him although they may be entirely visible to those who are about him. He can never be quite certain what he looks like or what meaning he might be conveying. Indeed others may be able to predict and understand his intentions more accurately than he can himself. Unless he constantly refers to a mirror, he must elicit his own symbolic character from their reactions. Borrowing from Emerson, Cooley described the accumulated effect of such reactions as 'the looking-glass self'.[23] Similarly Znaniecki wrote of the 'reflected self'.[24]

More critically, there is a profound difference between the experience of producing symbolic expressions and the experience of observing them. There is no necessary parity of meaning for the communicator and his audience. A person's understanding of what he does is uniquely and intimately shaped by his place in the flow of action: he provides contexts, purposes and a history which need not be commonly shared or known. Each assigns his own framework of meaning which cannot be properly imparted to others. Much expressive activity is also mediated by personal forms which cannot be transcribed into an articulate public description. They are locked into private experience, inextricably identified with the individual who employs them.

By contrast, language is a form which can liberate itself from its producer. The vocal or written gesture is relatively emancipated because it may be heard by its author as if it were the product of someone else. It can become detached from its source, exciting the speaker as it does others.[25] Unlike most other modes of expression, the utterance can attain an anonymous and external appearance. When speaking, a person can provide his own stimuli. In turn, a man can become his own other, a social object or self, which may be manipulated and monitored. Words promote a fissure in awareness, creating the divide between subject and object, 'I' and 'me', ego and self. They permit one to constitute oneself through an internal conversation, compressing the interaction between gesture and response into the site of the conscious mind: 'the self arises in conduct when the individual becomes a social object in experience to himself. This takes place when the individual assumes the attitude or uses the gesture which another individual would use and responds to it himself . . . he talks to himself as he talks to others.'[26] Language makes it possible for a man to scrutinise his phenomenal self, the self that is visibly present to others. But it also enables that self to work back on the secluded I which can never be exposed to the senses. The autonomy of speech allows one to simulate the other's role in a transaction. He can survey his actions as if he were a stranger to himself, building up meaning as he proceeds. The socially-situated phase of a person thus establishes itself as a process which can turn on its creator. The possibility that a vocal gesture can evoke common reactions in an audience does not entail an absolute identity of response. Every person will be excited in a different fashion. It is enough that the gesture should be so objective that people can make adequate inferences about each other's responses. Speech then furnishes the self: it accomplishes the symbolic transformation of a person into a publicly known phenomenon.

More obviously, language objectifies the self by providing names, classification and definition to an otherwise amorphous phenomenon. Phenomena could barely exist without language. Words prise objects out of the stream of immediate existence and award them structure and an enduring identity. By employing names to point to an entity, a man can put boundaries about it, impart coherence to it, and enforce a shedding of the irreproducible experiences which engulf it. Paradoxically, context is both lost and found in naming because language furnishes the environment from which it detaches its objects. Without a distinctive name, the entities would not only be ephemeral and unique, they would also merge imperceptibly with what 'surrounds' them. Indeed there would then be no instrument for outlining what is object and what is context: the two would be one, they would form an irreplaceable cluster, and they could be grasped only by experiencing them in some evanescent present. There would be no possibility of recalling or anticipating them.

Language bestows other qualities on the world. In particular, it permits the emergence of a seeming continuity between events over time. Such continuity is necessarily essentialising because it suggests the existence of an unalterable substance behind all the forms of process.

Yet even the spurious attribution of sameness to things in change enables a person to construct an identity for himself and for the objects that are around him. A person is palpably not the same being as he was ten or twenty years before. In a Heracleitian sense, he is not even the same person from second to second. However, names can repair such broken histories. They can lend a semblance of stability and permanence to what could be seen as a discontinuous series of chameleon selves. Language not only checks the potential disintegration of experience, it also fosters an apparent harmony between the selves of different settings. Unchanging names do provide tenuous links and uniformities that would otherwise be missing. The calling of oneself and one's significant objects by enduring terms enhances one's ability to impose sense on flux.

Words tend to transcend the confines of personal existence. They universalise that which is basically experienced as parochial by forcing affinities and identities on disparate phenomena.[27] They join objects in classes, summoning up connections and separations. In so doing they manufacture an appearance of communality and order. There are few compelling reasons to suppose that one's own private world resembles that of any other person. Names alone create the overarching forms which advance confidence in the presence of a shared world. They engender the contexts in which regularities and an assumption of invariance can emerge. Common names can then lead to common imputations. Thus, the experience of a student at the University of Calcutta may seem to reproduce that of a student at Yale University: they are both subjected to lectures, students, curricula, teachers, examinations and graduation rituals. A close inspection might reveal that those similarities are misleading, but they serve adequately for many purposes. A shared terminology disciplines knowledge about events. If permits one to compare oneself with others, participate in a commonwealth of experience, and distinguish oneself from those who are differently named. If he considers his Indian counterpart at all, the Yale student might believe that he shares more with him than he does with a New Haven shopkeeper. Similarly, many North American Blacks fail to appreciate how American they are until they visit Africa.

The interplay of words becomes crucial in the objectification of oneself. The act of assigning a common label to various phenomena leads to the presumption that there are, in truth, shared characteristics amongst them. Words and classifications thus represent the principal means by which characters and structures may be inferred. As Strauss argues, 'any particular object can be named, and thus located, in countless ways. The naming sets it within a context of quite differently related classes. The nature or essence of an object does not reside mysteriously within the object itself but is dependent on how it is defined by the namer.'[28] Definitions organise facets of the world. What is or is not aligned with a self reflects the operation of classificatory procedures rather than some determining principle in nature. A self may then be inflated or deflated, grandiose or modest, eccentric or ordinary. Its constitution and linkages centre on social recognition, convention and the limits of language. If, as Cooley maintained, 'the social self is simply any idea . . . drawn from the communicative life, that the mind cherishes as its own',[29] the major constraints on the building of a self will be drawn from the forms of thought. The fecundity of vocabulary and grammar shapes the complexity and variability of objectified personality. The richer are words, the greater will be the shades and textures of meaning that can be introduced into the presentation of a self. The casting of oneself as a social object therefore pivots around the use of language. Words make innumerable and diverse selves possible, they encourage reflective experimentation, and they allow a kind of existential toying with oneself. Indeed, Peirce claimed 'my language is the sum total of myself.'[30]

Moreover, it is not only 'my' language that establishes 'me'. The languages of others open up perspectives which would otherwise be unavailable. By resorting to alien words a man can more fully see himself as others do, extracting the widest significance out of the organised stances that are offered in a society. The movement into any sector of social life is likely to bring about the provision of new visions of oneself. Each sector tends to be ordered by a distinctive vocabulary and accompanying articulation of meanings.[31] Each affords a distinctive reading of what one is and what one does. Combined, the resources of those sectors can issue countless different imaginations of oneself: 'the extent of knowing is dependent upon the extent of the naming'.[32]

Finally, and most evidently, language is a vital mediator of the discourse that takes place within and between the minds of people.[33] The 'I' and the 'me' are phases of a process which has been likened to an inner conversation. The 'I' is that stage of the organism which is buried in immediate experience. It emerged as the dialectical partner of the 'me', representing the inaccessible and unknowable core of social man. It is fused with nature, ultimately anchoring all practice and social organisation in the physical world. No impulse of the 'I' can attain social expression without a mediating symbolism which renders it remote from organic experience. The impulses of the 'I' lack clear definition, structure or frontiers. They have sometimes been characterised as the direct emanations of animal and physiological life. So defined, they must remain inarticulate until they are expressed by the other phase of being, the self.[34] The 'I' may be mediated by the self, but it also works back on it. People attend to themselves as they would to others. They can control their appearance by administering praise, reproof or guidance. In turn, the self feeds the products of outer relationship to the 'I', censoring and informing what can be expressed.

Language is the vehicle of that conversation, and man's ability to create, shape and support himself revolves around its possibilities. The flexibility and innovativeness of conversation transform the dialogue between 'I' and 'me' into an open-ended and indeterminate dialectic. So potent is language that it can become phenomenologically autonomous, building up its own realm of meaning and establishing the self as part of that realm. A word can displace its object, becoming independently available for manipulation and combination with other words. It can furnish meanings and objects that may never be encountered in nature or society. Indeed, much conversation treats with physical objects in only the remotest fashion. It can be mercurial and sweeping, rarely involving a parallel train of immediate sensory experiences. Such talk can translate phenomena into their symbols alone. In many instances words acquire a totemic character. Their emancipated quality frees them to manufacture every kind of remarkable thought. Verbal exchanges are therefore confined merely to the limits set by intelligibility and reasonable syntax. By extension, the process of constructing appearances and identities is itself unchecked by constraints imposed by the empirical world. It can become the plaything of fantasy, being restrained only by the credulity of oneself and the audience which observes one.

The forms of language mediate the workings of consciousness, the self and social interchange. In turn, those forms provide symbolic interactionism with its own logic of explanation. Society is held to emerge from discourse and symbolisation. The metaphors which phrase that vision borrow heavily from an imagery of everday speech. Interactionism portrays social life as an ongoing series of conversational encounters.

The Self as an Object in Interaction

One salient focus of interactionist analysis is the dialogue between the twin aspects of the self. It is a focus that is necessarily clouded by the ambiguous nature of its objects. Ambiguity stems in part from the sheer intellectual intricacy of the dominant description of the self. The self is not defined as a state, a substance or an object. At bottom it is conceived to be rooted in neurological process, but mind has rendered it vastly complex. The rise of mind brought about the possibility of the organism becoming self-constituting. The self is a facet of consciousness appearing out of itself, reproducing itself, and transforming itself by transcending or accommodating its own contradictions. It is variously and sometimes confusingly depicted as totality and duality, as empirically known and metaphysical, as observable and unobservable. It is an analogy that has been drawn from such diffuse sources as behaviourism, the philosophy of science, phenomenology, biology, formalism, Darwinian evolutionism and Idealism. Adequate for many descriptive purposes, it tends to lose some of its coherence when it is examined closely. Its different parts do not lend themselves to complete reconciliation.

More generally, ambiguity has been generated by the difficulty of incorporating the 'I' into analysis. Pragmatism and formalism both espoused versions of phenomenalism. They were hostile to any sociology or philosophy which purported to expose the inner structures of a noumenon. Indeed pragmatism denied that there was a world which was mysteriously concealed from the active and curious mind. Yet the central agent of the self appears to be an inhabitant of that world: it has been endowed with all the trappings of an unknowable essence. Symbolic interactionism can neither assimilate such a recalcitrant and anomalous object nor oust it from its pivotal place.

The 'I' has been so constructed that it must always remain the unscrutinised subject. It is inextricably submerged in immediate experience and can never become present in consciousness. Anything that seems to represent the 'I' can be no more than a masquerading 'me', an object pretending to be subject: 'the "I" in memory is there as the spokesman of the self of the second, or minute, or day ago. As given, it is a "me", but it is a "me" which was the "I" at the earlier time'.[35] That which has been defined as perpetual subject cannot be transformed into an object unless a new, superior subject is marshalled as the final spectator. The early interactionists attempted to avoid the intellectual snares of an infinite regress of reflexive selves. They consequently refused to countenance the possibility of the 'I' ever being known. It must remain a more or less obtrusive anomaly.

Some sociologists, like Howard Becker, have acknowledged the opaque character of the 'I' by exiling it to the province of things which are considered unanalysable. They concede its existence but attend instead to those events which offer sure knowledge. In particular they examine the manner in which observed identities are shaped by social structure, preferring not to speculate about invisible processes.[36] Others have virtually abandoned the 'I', denying the existence of any personal continuity between different social contexts.[37] They are compelled to move towards the definition of self as chameleon. Yet the 'I' cannot be readily dismissed because it forms a critical stage in one of the rare interactionist arguments that demand systematic exposition. The inner transactions of the self mould and channel almost all the important processes that concern symbolic interactionism. They affect the way in which identities are maintained and transformed, meanings are constructed, and social interaction itself is conducted. Their analysis must form the preface to any discussion of the visible phenomena of social life. It is their supposedly distinct properties that justify the intellectual edifice of interactionism and they cannot be wholly neglected.

Most of the original definitions of the self are circumscribed. They reflect the restrictions that a commitment to phenomenalism must impose. Thus Simmel treated the self as another form which lends order to an otherwise inchoate content. That content is simply unknowable in its purity: its effects and quality are forever unimaginable. Similarly Peirce asserted that the self is no more than an inference: it cannot be intuited or known directly. As an inference, it is built up as all known objects are, uncertainly and incompletely.[38] Mead himself attempted to bridge the disturbing gap between a hidden mind and revealed action by emphasising the behaviouristic importance of the significant gesture.[39] The gesture is an unfolding revelation of subjectivity, chronicling what might else be totally masked. These definitions closely follow the sociology's description of the structures of knowledge. The sociologist or philosopher does not arrogate to himself powers of understanding which are forbidden to Everyman. He must proceed as Everyman does, grasping the self cautiously and deductively. If motives and attitudes are obscure to Everyman,[40] so must they be to the analyst. They must be teased out of obscurity by a functional model of the necessary phases of reflexive activity. The 'I' exists because it explains what would be otherwise inexplicable: it is the midwife of the social 'me'. By turning to the inferential reasoning of lay people, the interactionists could not only adhere to their epistemology but also reproduce the self's own evolution. The self arises out of consciousness; in turn an emulation of that consciousness will illuminate some of its constitution.

Yet the reluctance to assume extraordinary interpretative powers has tended to preserve the self's mystery. The 'I' is laid open to uncertain analytic management. It can become no more than the object of oblique reference and occasional discussion. Its blend of marginality and centrality prepares the way for diverse and sometimes discrepant definition. William James remained faithful to phenomenalism by banning the 'I' as a substance from his psychology and philosophy. Instead the 'I' became what it was sensed to be, a succession of states of consciousness: 'metaphysics or theology may prove the Soul to exist; but for psychology the hypothesis of such a substantial principle of unity is superfluous'.[41] The 'I' is the Thinker, and the Thinker is thought to which other thought is referred: 'the I or "pure ego" ... is that which at any given moment *is* conscious, whereas the Me is only one of the things which it is conscious *of*'.[42] So defined, the 'I' comes to resemble the transcendental ego of Kant, the pure reasoning subject which cannot become object. Cooley however refused to impart an arcane meaning to the 'I'. He resorted to the everyday usages of the words 'I' and 'me', avoiding the 'metaphysical discussion of the "pure ego" – whatever that may be'.[43] 'I' was translated into that which a man called his own: the sum of personal pronouns and personal territories. It embraces anything that evokes a particular sentiment of identification. Swamping over into great tracts of social terrain, it represents a unity between social objects and 'self-feeling'. It is located neither in the body of a person nor in the environment about it. Rather it is a phenomenological incision into both, arising out of an instinctive urge but given form by what is socially possible and imaginable. It is the area that lies within the self's incommunicable domain, demarcated by what is felt to be part of the biography and interests of the individual. Society thus penetrates into the inner reaches of the self, becoming merged with instinct and primitive impulse.

Mead's conception of the 'I' tends to be somewhat more complex. The 'I' projects organic drives into activity, it serves as the unorganised and spontaneous phase of the self,[44] and it looms up from the realm of indescribable and immediate existence. But it is also organising, formed and conscious. It is not to be contrasted with the social 'me' as a prereflexive or animal facet of humanity. It is, instead, a part of consciousness which arises with the emergence of language. It has been portrayed as the individual confronting his socially-situated self: the reply which a person makes to his 'me'. It is as much a rational and vocal aspect of the self as the 'me': it launches the stimuli to which the self can mediately respond in the stance of another; it answers that response; and it houses some of the most profound structures of imported social organisation. If the 'me' presents the self with the social reality of others, the 'I' itself is not socially unformed. It has been portrayed as a kind of sedimentation of social processes which fold back on the gestures and projects of the self.

In all its guises, the 'I' is taken to be unclearly distilled out of social experience and the stirrings of the organism. It seals together what no reflecting mind could ever comprehend or master. It is itself permanently elusive, escaping conscious surveillance and known only in vague caricature. Yet, although it can be no more than an object of pure speculation, its intentions and vagaries must be assimilated in any interpretation of what one is doing. Because the 'I' is epistemologically similar to the noumenon, such interpretation must be based on a version of analytic *a priori* reasoning.[45] Further, because the meanings of identity are fluid and 'stability in the self is . . . just as problematic as change',[46] there is abundant scope for definitional licence. The imputations of others may become as plausible as one's own in the effort to determine one's 'I'. Outsiders do not then only establish one's 'me', they may contribute to knowledge of what one 'essentially' *is*. Of course that knowledge can only be addressed to the phenomenal presentation of a 'me' and may be taken to be an essentialisation of the 'me'. But it also refers to the 'real person' behind all phenomena, the person who organises and takes attitudes towards his phenomenal self. It is an imputation about the concealed essence of a man.

There is a social stock of characterological types which lend clarity to the delineation of substantial selves. Klapp, for example, has discussed the parts played by heroic, villainous and foolish typifications in awarding central identities to people.[47] He has also discussed what he takes to be a major theme of expressive social movements, the search for a true identity.[48] Similarly Duster has analysed how particular phenomenal signs are commonly read as revelations of the core structures of the self.[49] In the context of such existential doubt and uncertainty, the seemingly confident assertions of an authoritative outsider might resolve what one is 'truly like'. Much work in the interactionist sociology of deviancy has accordingly focused on the ritual organisation of 'labelling', the process by which deviant selves are ceremonially conferred, donned and discarded.[50] The critical effect of such degradation work may be to expose the noumenal 'I' to the world.[51]

The consequences of such indeterminacy have become more than a mere topic for symbolic interactionism. They have influenced the analytic work of the sociology itself, leaving many conceptions incompletely defined or resolved. In particular, the cognitive status of immediacy, the significance of social participation, the effects wrought by the organism, and the uncertainly social character of the 'I' have remained unsettled and unsettling. I shall pursue these problems in chapters 5 and 6.

Being the express object of the self's own awareness, the 'me' is quite unlike the 'I'. But that consciousness of self tends merely to open up possibilities of greater knowledge, it does not assure them. There is no immanent power within the self which totally comprehends its own appearances and productions. Authorship does not necessarily confer authority. As Morris argues, 'observations never reveal the self of the observer in a different status than [sic] surrounding things or persons.'[52] Indeed the self is not closely monitored or observed at all in many transactions. It may simply be 'there' and cannot be clearly remembered or described. A special effort may have to be made to bring it into vision. When it *is* knowingly reviewed, it can confront one as a problematic and ill-defined entity. Instead of firmly understanding what he is in a particular situation and at a particular time, a person must actively solicit and learn the meanings of what he has established. Amongst the different selves that may have to be

The Self

grasped in a setting, his own also looms large: 'establishment of one's own identity to oneself is as important in interaction as to establish it for the other. One's own identity in a situation is not absolutely given but is more or less problematic'.[53] A person's surmises about his 'me' are not underwritten. He may make 'incorrect' inferences; he may not appreciate the direction or nature of changes in himself or the setting; and he may misjudge others' interpretations of his behaviour. There is thus no warrant to suppose that self-reflexive knowledge is very different from knowledge about any other phenomenon. It may well be less substanital because it lacks the material of other forms of speculation.

Certainty of meaning generally grows with social distance. Much that one does oneself is unwitting and improperly heeded. Were that not so, the flow of expression and activity would become stilted and contrived. The artful management of appearances can contradict the contents which they are supposed to convey. But no management could ever succeed in being totally comprehensive. It is impossible to gaze at all the facets of one's performances. Attention can be devoted only to a limited span at any one moment, and undue attention may actually thwart its development by transforming prereflexive fluidity into conscious mannerism. A person cannot stare at himself as he does at others because he is not visibly present as others are.

Even if he did so stare, little could be seen directly. The most alert and articulate interaction is largely buried in experiences which cannot be bared to the conscious mind. His gestures might appear reified and discrete to an outsider, but they seem stubbornly opaque, immediate and interlocked to himself. Although they can be remembered in the past or imagined in a projected future, they are elusive and fleeting in the present: 'each participant can respond so immediately to the other's tones, speech rhythms and gestures that his own response is unconscious when it is made'.[54] In sum, the 'me' must also be investigated and defined by its organising 'I'. The 'I' may be aware of its 'me', but it is an awareness that requires cultivation. Parts of any social relationship must be coaxed into clarifying what one is and what one might do.

Social action then becomes a continual process of discovery in which the two phases of mind construct one another inferentially. Just as the 'I' is a problematic object whose meanings must be sought, so the 'me' is an ambiguous entity which needs elucidation. More complexly, the 'me' occupies a dual status because it may be read as a running index of changes in the 'I'. The 'I' can become manifest only in interaction, unfolding as it orchestrates the phenomenal self. It thus 'interprets [its] own gestures as representations of the self, as appearances which can be taken as indications of [its] true identity.'[55] The symbolic interactionists construe self-consciousness as a series of acrobatic workings of mind in which a self's own products undergo contortions in order to understand themselves.

Most of those contorted movements do not furnish 'true' or authentic knowledge of the self. In the case of the 'I', at least, it is not at all clear how the truth could be recognised. It is similarly difficult to know the 'me' with any certainty. Interpretations are built up mediately through the standpoints of imagined and constructed others: they are imputations of imputations. Action can rarely proceed on the basis of sure and searching investigations of oneself and others. Instead, it must operate with a working knowledge that is prepared out of ideographic cartoons and loose interactional recipes. The most significant feature of that knowledge is not its validity but its utility and conventionality. If it serves to provide viable formulae for managing impressions, questions of truthfulness may be suspended. A common universe of expectations, descriptions and explanations allows selves to be identified and projects formulated. Communality rather than 'accuracy' tends to become the chief practical test of knowledge. Identities and acts then come to be compounded out of definitional forms. In turn, they are observed and judged with those forms. Standardised typifications organise the work of knowing the self. They flow out of a general vocabulary of situations and characters, transforming the unique and the complex into instances of recurrent and familiar occasions. The forms shape the intractable content of social life into roles, selves and acts. They symbolically order what is potentially anarchic and, having imposed order, assume a reality which is *sui generis*. As Turner argues, there is a 'basic tendency for actors to behave *as if* there were roles.'[56] Ironically, that order can be defined as perfectly authentic. If selves are the forms which awareness places on itself, the conventionality of symbolic representations does not threaten their 'real' status. In the matter of self-indications there can be no inauthenticity. The unknowable self may be made known by the collective outcasting of confusion.

Purposes and intentions also become symbolic artifacts, the emergent products of 'vocabularies of motives' which form the will and precede, succeed or accompany action: 'the key linguistic constructs which a person applies to his own conduct in a certain set of circumstances are motives; the complete process by which such verbalizations are used is motivation'.[57] It is in this fashion that thoughts are held to be the thinker, that language makes the self. There is no substance or process outside these systems of representation which can properly be called the self: representation and represented are one. Some of the more unmanageable implications of interactionist ontology are thereby emasculated. That which might have been the self's noumenon is translated into an array of phenomena alone.

The stylisation of identity is further encouraged by the manner in which others tend to be grasped pictorially. They present the only models which are available for imagining how one might appear to the outside world. What is plausible about them is likely to be held plausible about oneself. As Baldwin stated: 'my sense of myself grows by imitation of you, and my sense of yourself grows in terms of my sense of myself. Both *ego* and *alter* are thus essentially social; each is a *socius* and each is an imitative creation.'[58]

Inferences about one's unobservable 'me' are organised by a series of ideographs of others. The forms which apparently order another may be brought to work back on the self, simplifying the task of resolving what appearances should be like. Those forms are simultaneously one's own, the other's and the community's. If they were not, interaction would go seriously awry. In turn, the working representation of the other stems from a logic that one has mobilised oneself: its effects are eminently intelligible. The definition of oneself thus feeds on the definition of the other; each being extrapolated and matched to reinforce its mate, each displaying an affinity with the other which anchors the form in a taken-for-granted world.

I have argued that the impressions created by others may seem more significant and solid than one's own. They frequently take on the appearance of reasonably coherent figures whose activities are purposeful, precise and decisive. We rarely attribute to them the blankness and confusion that dominate much of our own experience. Neither do we impute our own sense that motives are diffuse and obscure. Instead we seem often to assume that others are not surprised by what they do and that they accomplish what they intend. Such a transformation of the other is a successfully fabricated 'me'. It translates him into a phenomenon that is serviceable for purposes of interaction: one that has been organised and simplified to reduce one's problems of prediction and response. The 'me' of the other is a preeminently symbolic construct, a perspective which suppresses some complexity and emphasises only that which is interactionally salient. Without that symbolic transfiguration, the distinct, unknowable and complicated individual would present overpowering difficulties of understanding. The other's 'me' is then contrived and relatively simplex. Its gestures may be treated as largely unequivocal and legible. They are held to be substantially consistent and reliable, their normal appearance not being belied by deceitful intent. In turn the 'me' cannot give off too great a multiplicity of meanings. Its expressions, physical position, style of speech, body movements and mannerisms must contribute a visible and integrated frame for each unfolding act. Each act is nicely outlined, enjoying a comparative objectivity and certainty which distinguish few of one's own works. The entire 'me' may itself be lodged within a larger environment whose use and social organisation furnish a silent commentary on intentions and behaviour.

The 'me's' which define one's own are then artificially intelligible creations. There is no reason to suppose that they are necessarily and uniformly clear. Indeed there will always be some confusion about the meanings and motives of others. The 'me's' of one's companions tend to remain problematic. But it is with those 'me's' that one must align one's self, and it is from them that principles of organisation must be drawn. Any interaction is a symbolically mediated encounter which distorts and arranges its objects. It entails the forcible imposition of clarity. People cannot address themselves and others as wholly ambiguous, convoluted and intricate entities whose actions and motives are almost inexplicable. They erect instead workable imitations of human beings which facilitate the processes of interaction. Those imitations are always likely to enjoy an uncertain correspondence with the people they portray. Any sustained relationship will revolve around miscalculations, reassessments, and falterings. Yet the simplifying typification of the 'me' is the pivot of all viable transactions.

Some stability and order are imposed on the symbolic arrangement of 'me's' by granting a history to oneself and others. Events and discoveries in the past are not lost but continue to form the present and the anticipated future. One does not need to prepare onself afresh each time one appears before others. Rather there is an assumption of relative permanence which allows most selves to become a further revelation of an established and documented identity. 'Me's' are then thought to reappear or persist: they stock a kind of dramatic repertory of the self which can be exploited in the production of specific appearances. Although each 'me' could be cast as a unique performance,[59] its affinities and connections are emphasised by the use of names and gestures. Words permit one to identify seeming similarities between various aspects of oneself. The unchanging name preserves and restrains the potentially volatile 'me'. More interestingly, actions and past selves linger in memory so that their influence can become spread over many different stagings of identity. In a sense, an act is never finished until it is completely forgotten.[60] Its depiction as 'past' is misleading because it may still provide scripts and contexts which become ever more intricate with the passage of time. Selves are then frequently re-enacted, acquiring a crescive definition which eases each successive performance. They tend to be placed within the framework of an emerging biography that explains and relates particular happenings. Since each significant social exchange illuminates something of the self, the biography is reconstituted with every important 'me'. Mead argued 'a past never was in the form in which it appears as a past. Its reality is in its interpretation of the present.'[61] Correlatively, the present is a shifting platform from which the past is interpreted. The past has no existence outside the minds of those who resurrect it. They animate and produce time as a form of consciousness which produces them. They are the mediators and mediated of an experience of themselves as objects in history. Selves can then become incremental rather than isolated accomplishments. The freedom of the 'I' to produce novel 'me's' is constrained by the possibility of an enforced autobiographical constancy. Autobiographies can change and achieve new significance, sometimes dramatically so,[62] but selfhood has its own manufactured inertia.

Selves are temporally extended. They do not consist of a series of erratic hops from one 'me' to another, but are arrayed over time as a continuous statement of evolving identity. Indeed the interactionists hold that it is a defining quality of significant thought that it projects its objects from the past and into the future. As Mead reflected:

> if we recognize that experience is a process continually passing into the future, objects exist in nature as the patterns of our actions. If we reduce the world to a fictitious instantaneous present, all objects fall to pieces. . . . no such knife-edge present exists. Even in the so-called specious present there is a passage, in which there is succession, and both past and future are there, and the present is only that section in which, from the standpoint of action, both are involved.[63]

A 'me' cannot then be regarded as some kind of existential mayfly. It is embellished with an ancestry and a life that moves out beyond the present. It has solidity and depth. Almost any 'me' has within it the potential to turn back on the self which made it as a form of more-than-life. It can become alienated and external, opposing its 'I' as an autonomous phenomenon which requires a certain deference. When asked to define who or what he is, a person might cite those constituting 'me's which seem to impose a personal tradition and organisation. A neglect or betrayal of these 'me's would represent an act of .self-abandonment. They provide a system of independent anchorage points for the self. In this sense, the 'I' realises itself in conduct, creates facts about itself, acquires illumination from those selfsame facts, and experiences them as constraining realities which must order the course of any future action. Pragmatist and interactionist accounts of the self thereby replicate Simmel's dialectic of existence as more-life and more-than-life. The 'capricious' and spontaneous 'I' generates forms which become reified and confining. Selves expand out into their environment, so framing it that their own reality is both restricted and emphasised:

> Ideas are in the present; but they refer 'beyond themselves', and in this reference beyond the immediate present of the organism the things referred to are given characters with the value of the things themselves. Thus the outcome is that the life processes produce organisms so constituted that they reach out beyond themselves; these organisms seem to require a larger environment, and they satisfy this requirement by reaching beyond their immediacy into spatial and temporal extensions which are built up and adorned by characters found in their own immediate present.[64]

The Self as a Collective Achievement

Mind creates a world of meaning for itself, progressively replacing its own subjectivity and insubstantiality by the firm structures of alienated thought. It furnishes a symbolic context which directs the selves that may plausibly emerge out of its moving present. Around the 'I' – 'me' dialogue there grows a web of realities which expands to organise and envelop life. Any decision made in that dialogue will implicate further selves,[65] and any self will implicate further decisions. That symbolic web can never be entirely private, although little may pass beyond its borders. The generating machinery of the self lies within consciousness, but consciousness itself is not a private process. The ordering discourse of the mind is mediated by collective representations. It transmutes its objects into recognisable forms and then projects them out into the visible world. Histories, selves and territorial claims emerge as candidates for public endorsement. Without that eventual endorsement the contexts and constructs surrounding an individual would shatter, imploding back into the frail subjectivity of the 'I'. No identity can attain symbolic significance and coherence unless others make it plausible. It can be secured only by rooting it in a reality which transcends the solitary representations of individual thought. An unquestioning agreement on the character of an object can transport it to a sphere where it is no longer personal and malleable but embedded in the anonymous order of things. It ceases merely to be someone's ephemeral idea but becomes a fact akin to the facts of nature itself.

The maintenance of impressions is always a fragile enterprise and even the most carefully rehearsed performances can go adrift. They depend not just on an initial acclaim but on continuing recognition in the conversation of gestures. If that conversational support wanes, identities themselves will fail. Much interaction may thus be conceived as the exchange of ceremonial courtesies which prop up the fallible pretensions of its participants. It rests on a version of the 'pious perjury', a willingness to extend benign indifference when errors and breakdowns occur. The artifice and delicacy of role-playing are such that all interaction must be buttressed by a collusive self-protection. Every identity is in jeopardy, and its survival is assured only by a readiness of others to do remedial 'face-work':

> A person's performance of face-work, extended by his tacit agreement to help others perform theirs, represents his willingness to abide by the ground rules of social interaction. Here is the hallmark of his socialization as an interactant. If he and the others were not socialized in this way, interaction in most societies and most situations would be a much more hazardous thing for feelings and faces. The person would find it impractical to be oriented to symbolically conveyed appraisals of social worth, or be possessed of feelings – that is, it would be impractical for him to be a ritually delicate object.[66]

Few selves can withstand a sustained attack of disbelief or neglect: their unpredictability and contrivance weaken control; their diffuse-ness and low visibility hamper surveillance; and their constitutive forms are largely inarticulate. Above all, selves are simplistic typifications which cannot bear excessive scrutiny. They are symbolic devices which serve as substitutes for the morass of interchanges that make up the amalgam of organism, mind and society. As stylised and partial perspectives on identity, they may be contradicted by other facets of the self, by discrepant impressions, or by failures of staging. Every 'me' is rather less than it purports to be. No man can invest himself totally in a single performance: there is always a mass of indiscreet, burdensome, irrelevant or unmanageable matter that must be censored away. His intentions and thoughts may well be concentrated elsewhere; he may take a particular 'me' to be fairly peripheral to his 'essential' self; or he may merely be engaged in the ritual preservation of others' appearances. Interaction is organised around a conventional order that must be overtly disregarded if it is to endure. The integrity of self is thus exposed to constant hazard in even the most co-operative transactions.

Yet it is difficult to discover a wholly co-operative relationship. Bonds between people are riddled with traces of conflict, competition and uncertainty. Each participant in interaction has a particular stake in the emerging activity. Each has a self whose boundaries recede or expand as action unwinds. Identities are not often set or precisely defined in America and Britain;[67] and their instabilities pose problems for any who embark on joint behaviour. A self is put at risk when it is aligned with a shifting companion.[68] The outer reaches of every 'me' may encroach on adjoining personal territory, threatening to appropriate it as its own. The nursing and prompting of another's appearances cannot then be too unstinting. An eager compliance with another's claims may merely dwarf one's own. Orderly transactions therefore tend to be disciplining processes which regulate the demands that any member can make. They entail forecasts and reviews of the tacit bargains that are struck during the course of a relationship. They consist of a running series of claims and counter-claims, patrollings and enforcement strategies. In a sense any interaction may be defined as an emerging area of social terrain which is subject to continually revised treaties. Collaborative face-work is always circumscribed and conditional.

It would therefore be misleading to depict social intercourse as an example of a simple if somewhat strained consensus. The symbolic interactionists hold that sociation is compounded out of forms which tend towards decay and renewal, negation and synthesis, destruction and creation. As Simmel observed, 'the solid organizational forms which seem to constitute society must constantly be disturbed, disbalanced, gnawed-at by individualistic, irregular forces, in order to gain their vital reaction and development through submission and resistance.' The contours of a self are established by opposition and contrast as well as by similarity and union; its definition flowing out of a dramatisation of what it is not, what it shuns, what it can overwhelm, what it denies, and what it threatens. The purity of one's self may indeed be achieved only by forcing others to be impure.[69] After all, the special quality of that self might be most lucidly advertised by conspicuously rejecting the claims of certain other people. The presence of rebuffed claimants to character underscores the definitional system of hierarchy, power and segregation. Appearances are framed in an agonistic world which is replete with possibilities of dishonour, degradation and exclusion.[70]

Founding a self clearly entails a set of demands which extend beyond a private obligation to maintain personal continuity. Indeed this is possibly the central argument of the interactionist description of selfhood. A self is a socially-accomplished process, produced by the forms and shaped by the responses of others. It is literally void without those responses. It implicates others who may stipulate particular conditions before it is recognised. Thus the tentative presentation of a 'me' may be read as an assertion of a mandate to be a certain kind of person. The acceptance of that mandate by oneself and others brings enforceable commitments in its train. One such elementary commitment is the pledge to treat one's own self with a proper degree of ceremonial respect. With acceptance, an identity ceases to be a wholly personal item which may be altered or abandoned at will. It has become a form of public property, a ritual object, in which others have acquired a stake. Their selves have also become implicated in that object, receiving definition and direction from its anticipated course. Even a frivolous 'me' must be preserved and presented with some decorum. It cannot be rudely shed in the middle of interaction, leaving the selves of others hollow and futureless. All selves change, but inexplicable and abrupt transformations are profoundly disturbing to a collective sense of personal and social order. They promote an awareness of the conventionality and precariousness of action, suggesting that seemingly sound appearances are false and arbitrary. Possible alterations of self must be announced and then gradually accomplished, permitting others to program their own responses. A 'me' must then be played through predictable stages which coalesce with the activities of those who have sponsored it. If it is not, it may well be devalued or unheeded when it appears again. Its creator will not be taken seriously: he will be thought to be one who is sometimes alienated from his performances, 'not himself', and therefore mischievous or opaque as a source of direction.

Every self should display a patterned and illustrated history because it is involved in the obligation to support the performances of others. It should not be so tailored that it presents insuperable problems of co-ordination and anticipation. Neither should it be so unregulated and expansive that it threatens to engulf the identities of others. It is part of the conversation of significant gestures that others' responses can be intelligently compressed into the production of a self. If those responses defy interpretative understanding, or if they promise to overwhelm one's own identity, significance dies. Even in the polar instance of a conflict relationship, the participants must prompt one another with prepared scripts. As Simmel and others have observed, almost all conflict is itself a form of sociation which rests on the tacit contract of mutual support.[71]

Forms are joint accomplishments but they do not reside in some spectral zone outside individual encounters. The symbolic interactionists do not subscribe to the simplistic dichotomy which has confused much orthodox sociology. They recognise no ontological chasm between the 'individual' and 'society'. Neither do they believe that an analytic focus on the individual represents an example of a failing called 'reductionism'. Rather, the individual is brought into description as a refracted microcosm of 'social organisation'. He is not a perfect condensation of all that is social but a particular emphasis or incision which renders him more than a bundle of psychological states. The self is taken to be a special importation of social process which is transformed in the conversation of gestures. It is simultaneously inside and outside society, individual and collective, unique and general. As Simmel argued, 'the "within" and the "without" between individual and society are not two unrelated definitions but define together the fully homogeneous position of man as a social animal.'[72]

The social forms, then, work in and on people as sources of integration, division and opposition. The poor, for example, are not a distinctive social group because they share a pool of intrinsic qualities. On the contrary, they appear as a discrete category because of their dialectical relation with other groups and other forms. Simmel stated,

The Self

'it is only from the moment that the poor are assisted that they become part of a group characterized by poverty. This group does not remain united by interaction amongst its members, but by the collective attitude which society as a whole adopts towards it.' Similarly the isolated individual is isolated only because he engages in a particular relationship. Paradoxically, enforced loneliness is a form of sociation which knits him irretrievably into a network of connections. He is not on his own in an autonomous and contained social world but is thrust apart from his fellows. Isolation hinges on rejection not autarky.

The presentation of self in even the most alienated conditions, then, commits a person to maintaining the forms about him. Those forms must be accepted as real and compelling despite their capacity to subjugate and belittle him. A denial of the forms represents a defection from the organising structures of society itself. Its occurrence cannot itself be formalised. The indescribable breach of convention that is caused by such symbolic mutiny has been described by Scheff as 'residual rule-breaking', *residual* because it is what remains when all specifiable transgressions have been listed.[73] The man who observes forms will then collude in his own isolation, poverty or abasement. He who does not risks identification as mad.

Forms, the Self and the Logic of Social Structure

Relatively stable clusters of forms can themselves be abstracted to compose master forms. These forms of forms may variously be identified as 'classes', 'races', 'churches', 'infrastructures', 'superstructures' and the like. Thus Blumer observed, 'social organization enters into action only to the extent to which it shapes situations in which people act, and to the extent to which it supplies fixed sets of symbols which people use in interpreting their situations.'[74] Institutions, social systems, corporations and organisations are symbolic typifications which order and amass subordinate representations. They are both 'inside' and 'outside' transactions, emerging out of sociation but taking on the character of the forms of more-than-life. An evolving bureaucracy, for example, will typically begin life as a relatively fluid system of exchanges in which hierarchy and office are understated. It will flexibly respond to problems which appear out of its dealings with the outer world, shaping its component parts into new configurations. Activity and function are identifiably rooted in the ongoing interaction between distinct people. Over time, however, that interaction will become reified. It will act back on its participants as an alien force which imposes demands.[75] The institution then tends to become independent and coercive, its forms detached from personal authorship.

Ultimately organisations are 'simply' representations which are animated and produced by the people who defer to them. They are forms of estranged consciousness. Yet, as the most alienated of all forms, they present an unusual power to intimidate. Their imputed reality may even come to dwarf that of specific people so that martyrdom and self-sacrifice may appear appropriate responses. Their obduracy and permanance combine to make them central identifying tokens for the self. Individuals define themselves by their affiliations with religious groups, occupations, geographical regions, social classes and nationalities. They are constituted by the very forms which they realise.

There is no distant and objective point of vantage from which an institution can be appraised. Every person will arrange his perspective on an organisation in a slightly different fashion, reproducing it in his own situation. His past history, setting and interactional alignments frame his reading of what an organisation is. In a sense, then, there are as many versions of an entity as there are people to construe it. A university cannot be defined as some unwavering essence: it is a phenomenon which is grasped severally by students, teachers, administrators, gardeners, cooks, porters, journalists, maintenance workers, government officials, parents and schoolchildren. None of these formulations is unequivocally or demonstrably correct. Neither is it necessarily complementary with any of the others. They are all contingent upon the conduct of practical affairs.

Of course, all conduct is made possible by the significant gestures which weave different visions together. Some working unity of forms will distinguish the university. Without it all its subordinate worlds would simply fall apart. Indeed, that is what a university *is*: an evolving master abstraction which interplays with the grounded perceptions of the form's constituent groups. That abstraction is both a specific and a generalised representation. It has significance for particular people in particular conditions and for some more anonymous population at large. Those who espouse local typifications tend to recognise their parochialism, just as they recognise that there is a wider and vaguer meaning in currency. The nebulous representation of everyone's knowledge cannot be put to sustained use unless it is partially redefined. Neither can the various groups which have some stake in the university co-exist without a commonly circulating definition. The local and generalised typifications thus continually influence one another. An interpretation of immediate surroundings will be shaped by a sense of context which is more or less firmly provided by the generalised form. But that form, in turn, is viewed from within those immediate surroundings. It furnishes the groups and the contexts in which it is manufactured.

As conflicts and coalitions develop between minor worlds, so particular and overarching definitions change. Not all are equally important in the determination of that change: the power of different groups affects their ability to mould the emerging forms. Some definitions may be upheld by force, manipulation or structural intimidation.[76] The superiority of certain groupings may indeed be so great that it can linger on after the physical death or disappearance of all their members. The founders of a form, for example, might impose a definitive shape which is resistant to modification. Those who drafted Magna Carta or the United States Constitution prestructured the interpretative debates that could follow their acts. They established the debates, the debaters and the object of debate.

Organisations cannot then be regarded as *things* unless they are the reified objects of thought. They are the processes which co-ordinate and flow out of subsidiary processes. But they can become very real in the lives of those who appear to fall under their aegis. Membership in them exacts commitments which may be more onerous than any of the petty obligations of social life. The joining of a profession, for example, is customarily held to require a special discipline. There is a sanctionable expectation that one should accede to the idealised behaviour befitting a doctor, a lawyer, a clergyman or teacher. In this, as in other areas, forms do not only supply organisation but moral demands. They can become so compelling a statement of what *is* that they are transmuted into an assertion of what *ought* to be. Of course not all forms attain such autonomy or prescriptive power. Persistence, scale and definition must precede the transformation of an area of social life into an end in itself. But all groups of forms have that potential to affirm what they outline, providing a range of apparently external perspectives on themselves and the rest of the world. If that potential is realised, the forms can become self-validating and self-constituting, subject only to the authority of higher master forms. So alienated may they appear that they seem untouched by the specific transactions which manufacture them. They can stand apart from the mundane world, creating a duality between appearance and ideal. It is in this sense that interactionism could concede an idea of social structure. The grammar of alienated forms has much of the character of the autonomous realm which orthodox macrosociologists seek to explore. It is a process which lends stability, permanence and impersonality to human affairs. Without it the world discussed by interactionists would be too fluid, fleeting and elusive to permit orderly conduct or sensible analysis.[77]

The duality between appearance and ideal generates ambiguity about organisations. On one level the forms of sociation are totally dependent on routine transactions. They are not intimations of the Absolute but scattered and transfigured depictions of themselves. Yet their autonomisation may lend them a disembodied and real character. Many institutions then come to be seen as 'themselves' and as 'more-than-themselves'. Universities are not only the uneventful places in which people make careers and pursue unremarkable research. They are also partially consecrated organisations which transmit and encapsulate high knowledge and culture. Similarly, in the instance of the occupations, Becker states that the word 'profession' is ambiguous because it embraces a structural definition and a moral claim. It runs 'afoul of the tension between an objective listing of differentia and the necessity of taking account of the layman's subjective sense that certain occupations are morally worthy of the title of professions while others are not'.[78] Indeed, professional people themselves sense that theirs is a vocation or calling which entails a subordination to a higher and nobler order. The virtually sacred character of their pursuit is preserved by outcasting those who have defiled it. It may contrast markedly with the very ordinary experiences that infuse their work, but nobility still remains.

Every institution can thus fold back on practice in a two-fold manner: as an idealised reification and as a working description of activities in the mundane world. The twin aspects of such alienated forms tend frequently to conflict. Their contradiction reflects the disparity between the one facet as a representation of mediated activity and the other as a moral reification. Thus 'law' refers simultaneously to the squalid market economy of plea-bargaining and to justice as an absolute and impersonal moral order governed by the imperative *fiat iustitia pereat mundus*. 'Medicine' can conjure up the exploitative and predatory pursuits of some doctors and the ideal realm personified by Hippocrates. Such contradictions are typically mediated by sets of ancillary forms which have been designed to reconcile disparity. Codes of practice, rule-books, structural blueprints and disciplinary procedures are often attached to organisations, feeding into the play between forms. A complex institution may then be described in at least three major ways: as a series of ongoing everyday activities; as a reified abstraction; and as an official organisational chart with specified offices, tasks, processes of induction and expulsion, and communication paths. None of those forms is complete in itself, although many sociologists of organisations have been partisan in championing the analytic supremacy of one or another of them. The forms represent interlocking realities which act on and against each other.[79]

The Self in an Environment of Forms

Each type of form offers something of a world for the self. Each is fraught by the contradictions which may be housed within the one setting. Each provides a fairly distinct perspective on the significant others whose responses could be included in gesture and identity. Thus people may be classified as competent or incompetent colleagues, trustworthy or untrustworthy associates, rivals or sponsors, congenial or uncongenial companions and the like. Those varying typifications need not meet with neat synthesis, so that the friend might be unreliable and the rival a necessary co-worker on a particular project. What one is in such a context depends critically on one's immediate reading of the situation. Fellow-members of an institutional sphere are not always aligned in a stable or unambiguous manner. They are instead capable of presenting different 'me's' to one another which will elicit very different styles of address and behaviour. As Strauss argues, 'the mode of interaction can change at any instant or phase of interaction and not remain the same throughout its duration.'[80] The forms which mediate a specific self at a particular time must be made known and heralded lest misunderstanding result. Various phases of the self are thus often punctuated by distinct signals and periods of adjustment. Time itself becomes a social construction that is divided into staged episodes which organise the appearances of people acting together. Discernible and advertised shifts of performance occur when an interview or oral examination 'starts', when a work exercise ends or an academic paper is presented. In turn, there are corresponding forms which are employed to resolve the contradictions between discrepant 'me's'.

Goffman, for instance, has discussed 'role-distance' as a ritual form of self-alienation and self-reconciliation.[81] Contrasting 'me's' may be ordered by a contrived glimpse of a counterfeit 'I'. In some circumstances people intersect in selves prepared by the most abstract definitions of identity: when soldiers parade together, when nurses and surgeons work in an operating theatre, or when public lectures are delivered. Selves then become taxing approximations of the stereotypical ideal. They impose a rigour that excludes many of the little interchanges of everyday life. But those selfsame people may also meet when they are less obviously the objects of a reified and disciplining order. It would be improper to fall back on their more alienating identities. One solution may be a resort to avoidance tactics. Indeed the physical planning of institutional space sometimes reflects the concern with caste-like conceptions of the pollution that might be inflicted by undesired contact. Separate lavatories, entrances, elevators, dining rooms, common rooms and messes may be provided to prevent the embarrassment of strained interaction. Alternatively, stress may be dissipated by ritually-compressed versions of the Saturnalia or All Fools' Day: doctors and officers often serve their inferiors at official Christmas dinners, or pantomimes may be laid on to mock the forms of hierarchy in safety. 'Role-distance' itself is a third strategy. It enables people to visibly renounce the practices which had hitherto sustained their appearances. By advertising that another, more appealing self is normally masked by formal constraints, one may acknowledge contradiction and reveal what one's 'real' unalienated self is like. However, Goffman claims that such role-distanced displays are powerful sources of reinforcement for the abstract order. They tie men together by displacing and defusing hostility. They entail the public disowning of 'me's' that may be privately cherished.

As a person moves through an institutional world, his links with the arrangement of forms will shift, providing new combinations of significant others and new perspectives. Careers are the organisationally-derived forms which order such changes. They typically plot plausible biographies and relationships, preparing one for the processes that one may undergo. The careers of a work organisation, a family, a hospital or the life-cycle itself allow selves to be rehearsed in the imagination. A string of 'me's' can be projected into the future, becoming objects in the present. A person will then incorporate his own responses into his acts, building up what he anticipates will be a consistent and manageable identity. He will curtail and expand commitments, phrasing himself so that future embarrassments are avoided and present selves are treated as capital. The institutionalised control of status passages fosters the programmed and co-ordinated evolution of motives, ideas, perspectives and relationships. It induces the appreciation that current interpretations are not timeless but provisional, that they will change to shape as yet alien selves and definitions of the situation. In turn, it tempers ambition by phasing transformations of identity and providing explanations for failure. All careers are buttressed by folk recipes and institutional accounts which mollify the unsuccessful.[82] Indeed, people are offered dual histories from the very first: one to contend with the realisation of ambition and the other to discount it. In English primary schools, for instance, schoolchildren depress the vanities of each other by a traditional stock of epithets and cautionary tales. Conspicuous accomplishment is deflated by allusions to being 'posh',[83] 'a show-off' or 'big-headed'.

Although one might see the world around one refracted into multiple images of future action, one is nevertheless armed with timetables which ease certain courses and complicate others. The reified forms of an organisation map out sequences of 'related transformations'[84] or 'patterned . . . adjustments'[85] which are extended and compartmentalised over time. Benchmarks are furnished which regulate the preparations to slough off old selves and begin acquiring the new. They orchestrate shifts in motive and attitude, eliciting dissatisfactions and promoting novel desires. Similarly, the responses of significant others will be framed by the career which is extrapolated for the self. Their meanings will systematically alter as they are read in the spectrum of contexts that are bestowed on future 'me's'. Those others will also be endowed with a range of careers which affect their present and emerging relevance for oneself. What might now seem trivial or central can assume a very different importance when it is extended in time.

The temporal scheduling of interaction is made even more complicated by the overlapping and play of different cycles. Each transaction itself is loosely phased into a beginning, middle and an end. What is said or done at the beginning may be construed differently from what takes place at the end. Meaning recedes or swells as it occurs in the varying stages of an encounter. It takes on a crescive character so that the order of utterance and performance becomes vital in the determination of significance. Further, interaction is sited in careers and in general movements of the self. What is signified by a young, unattached girl may not be at all the same as that meant by an old woman. What is stated by an august professor tends to be taken as graver than the sentiments of a new undergraduate. Indeed, the 'same' argument will change appreciably as it is offered by the ascending ranks of the academic hierarchy. Moreover complexities are redoubled because people do not move through time in company. As Strauss argues:

> Since a person is, during a crucial phase, quite literally a different person than when he was not, it is necessary that others, if they are to handle him skillfully [sic], must learn to recognize such phases. . . . the observer himself is human and therefore going through phases also. Interaction is between people who are 'in phases' — differential ones.[86]

Selves are thus time-bound objects which intermesh with other like objects. Their significant others will have histories which must be read so that responses can be located. Any 'me' must be placed in a multiplicity of co-existent personal and institutional timetables.

The planning of identity is clearly a formidable undertaking. The neophyte policeman, for example, will have to order his self not only on the basis of his 'present' situation but also on all the situations that are latent within the present. He may, like the revolutionary soldier, carry the baton in his knapsack. Any current action must then be mediated by himself as a fictive superior officer who surveys him from an immanent future. He will also have to cautiously discover the serpentine connections between the small world of his colleagues, the police station, the larger organisation, the institutions of criminal justice, and the abstract domain of law. They, too, must be granted probable futures. His first contacts could become both immensely significant and insignificant as he anticipates promotional moves away from a district or a rank. But he cannot treat them as insignificant quite immediately. They must be assessed by a tiered sequence of perspectives, each organising the rest, and each intended to come into play in its own time. If he misjudges his context or timetable, he will have donned the 'right' identity in the wrong setting. Thus Niederhoffer has chronicled how the teachings of the Police Academy are progressively transformed during the early phases of a policeman's work.[87] The officially-ratified self of a recruit becomes a 'me' that is considered improper by patrolmen on the beat. The recruit must be re-schooled into treating most obligations as only situationally binding. What holds in the Police Academy is not reflected in the everyday world of patrolmen, just as the moral claims of that world cannot be made public knowledge. Decisions about commitments and selves will flow out of the initiate's arrangement of the different formal strata, his anticipated tenure of various positions, the likely fates of his colleagues, and his ability to dissemble. A Serpico who takes the most abstract typifications of policing seriously will be penalised.[88] A corrupt policeman may also be punished. But none of the formal levels or multiple worlds of policing is ever completely sealed against the others which support, parallel or transcend it. Each represents a different emphasis on the whole rather than a separate order. No level can therefore be protected against the moral directives that flow down from above. Even the most corrupt police department is unlikely to court evil with unabashed zeal.

Careers impose some intelligibility on action, but they are no more than symbolic constructions. They depend on stability and the orderly realisation of intentions. As Hughes argues, 'in a society where major changes are taking place, the sequence of generations in an office and that of offices in the life of the person are disturbed. A generation may be lost by disorders lasting only for the few years of passage through one phase.'[89] Institutional orders may collapse or shift unexpectedly. They may promote the previously excluded (by 'affirmative action' for example) or reject the once included (as a result of the Nuremberg decrees).

Even in a predictable world of organisations the evolving biographies of people may go awry. Timetables may not be met when examinations are failed. Projected relations may dissolve. Few marriages are contracted in the firm expectation that they will end in a scandalous divorce. Physical disabilities may hinder plans. It can only be the odd adolescent who reckons seriously the possibility of early death or incapacitating disease.[90] Instead the phenomenal world of the present is typically accounted as one phase in a lifetime that will uneventfully pass into old age. Above all, there is an organising assumption of a reasonable continuity of motivation and identity. The world that now appears normal and natural is not thought to be dangerously at risk. The normality of appearances is underscored by the interwoven web of careers and forms that carries on beyond the specious present. It is also underpinned by the silent language of ritual which yields the reality and irreversibility of status passages. Marriage, birth, death, graduation and retirement are not signified as petty or arbitrary. They are made to emphasise the underlying order of social occasions. Mourning and celebration are adorned with the collective representations which they support. They stamp experience into profound forms which seem to borrow little from a capricious convention or a meaningless universe. They provide materials for the creation of selves that seem attuned to a larger flow of events.

Careers may chart a framework for the self, but they are not exhaustive. Much is left unregulated, and substantial tracts of social life appear to consist of unrelated encounters and actions. Those encounters seem neither incremental nor consequential for the future. None of this activity is unformed, but it lacks the relatively precise governance of the institutional domain. Instead of a series of formulated anticipations, resort must be made to a combination of very general typifications and minor forms of etiquette. Those typifications furnish catholic and diffuse meanings for the attributes which are awarded broad significance. Race, social class, sex, age and estate are the movable contexts of action, infusing each encounter with a loose collection of interpretations. Action in relation to them cannot be minutely specified; rather, their exact relevance emerges within the course of an interaction. Yet their very diffuse quality may bar the initiation of some transactions altogether. They cannot be readily unnoticed but colour all the exchanges which their recipients experience. These great anchoring forms cut across almost all institutional boundaries, transforming the process within so that identities are complexly redefined. It thus becomes remarkable when a Black first enters a particular police force, when a member of the working class takes a seat in the House of Lords, or an earl is discovered to be the occupant of a thoroughly ordinary job. Conventional associations are made between typifications so that a grammar of formal possibilities has arisen. Some forms are held to display affinities for one another; others are contradictory; and others are taken to be members of distinct and separate spheres. That grammar may be used to constitute the world of the self. It furnishes commentaries on experience and orders anticipations. It represents the animating logic of social understanding, the lay sociological reasoning which lends vitality to interaction. It emerges out of the organisation of a consciousness which mediates and is mediated by careers, master stereotypes, reified classifications, petty interaction and language itself. Those forms, in turn, are communicable exemplifications of its workings. If the forms are the synthetic *a priori* of social experience, they must sustain a more or less tenuous connection with the minds that produce and are produced by them.

The grammar of forms precludes some happenings as absurd and indicates that others are most probable. It makes it plausible that middle-class children will enter university and avoid crime, but that working-class children will not. It recognises the ramifications of the U.S. Presidency, of femininity and of negritude and concludes that a female Black President is an ambiguous and unlikely occurence. As Hughes argues, 'people carry in their minds a set of expectations concerning the auxiliary traits properly associated with many of the specific positions available in our society. . . . The expected or "natural" combinations of auxiliary characteristics become embodied in the stereotypes of ordinary talk, cartoons, fiction, the radio and the motion picture.'[91] In this symbolic business of objectification, opposition and synthesis, society itself is condensed and explained.

The formal orders of institutions are not contained. They act upon each other, further complicating the work of the self and the grammar of forms. Laws thus penetrate into the conduct of business organisations; capitalist organisations attempt to affect the course of law; economics enters religion, and religion economics. So complicated has this interplay become that Berger likens the churches of America to theological enterprises which compete in the provision of spiritual and social services.[92] The early metaphors of the Chicago School have been retained to supply an imagery for the working of this logic. The forms of competition, succession, accommodation and conflict are occasionally invoked to describe the relations between various groupings of institutions.

The interdependence between Voodoo and the numbers racket in some parts of urban black America is thus claimed to be symbiotic: Voodoo offers prophetic direction for the playing of numbers, whilst the numbers game makes Voodoo seem credible and useful.[93] Similarly, the links between the reputability of 'good people' and the disreputability of 'dirty work' are held to exemplify symbiosis: the tainted and unpleasant tasks of society are performed by polluted occupational castes which preserve the impeccable qualities of the pure and uninvolved.[94] The cost of remaining unbesmirched is a loss of effective control over stigmatised activities. Probity and irresponsibility are yoked together in a division of moral labour. Erikson, too, has extended Durkheim's argument to illuminate the dialectic between deviancy and convention: deviancy dramatises and chronicles all that morality is not, it provides a vital antithesis to the good.[95] In a latter-day version of *The Grumbling Hive*, deviants are held to be busily occupied with the perverse work of conserving virtue.

The interactionist logic of forms has also been employed to explain symbolic coalescence. Different facets of the social world tend to coagulate into distinct structures. As Rose argues, 'symbols . . . do not occur only in isolated bits, but often in clusters, large and complex.'[96] Clustering may be a product of the recognition or sponsorship of affinities. Thus Finestone has mapped the thematic forms of the 'cat's' life-style: different styles of dress, music, speech, drug-use and leisure were harmonised into a creative unity.[97] The tracing of such affinities may well become a focal part of a group's activity. Like the new industrialist of the nineteenth century, distinguished connections may be sought by those who attempt to advance a particular representation of themselves. The American undertaker, for example, strove to rewrite the significance of his work. Habenstein has documented how he promoted identification between funeral directing and the occupational forms of medicine and psychiatry.[98] Even nudists have tried to redefine the meaning of nakedness as a healthy and sexually-neutral phenomenon. Earnest efforts have been made to exploit the affinities between nudity and a sexually-innocent nature.[99]

The form of conflict has been explored in the interactionist period of the early Jock Young. In *The Drugtakers* he illustrates the unfolding opposition between the police and marihuana-users of Notting Hill in London.[100] Once contradictory elements became progressively integrated as the transaction developed: actions which had originally been based on an interpretative fantasy brought their objects into being; imputed social structures actually began to take shape; and the roles manufactured by mystifying typifications became concrete as a practical outcome of police activity.

In this fashion interactionism treats the self as the moving centre of society. It alone synthesises whatever order may exist. Society is ceaselessly produced in myriad exchanges which have little fixity of structure or definition. Indeed it can have no reality outside those exchanges. There is no Olympian plane to be occupied by a society which is independent of selves in interaction. Every person is the animating core of a process which furnishes a limited and often temporary organisation. As problems are confronted, so social objects are built up or destroyed. They attain form in activity, being shaped by the experience and purposes of those who confront them. In this sense, as Lafferty argued, 'facts are bits of biography'.[101] The very self of a person is constructed around provisional anticipations of his own behaviour: it is an object which is projected into the possible future of his actions.[102] Yet few activities are brought to a neat conclusion, uninterrupted by distracting or competing engagements. Lines of action may cross, projects may be abandoned, and forms become fragmented. In turn, the objects produced by conduct are themselves rarely well-formed. They must usually be lacking in detail or scope. Even selves are generally wanting. One cannot often explore all the implications and particulars of an identity. In most instances only a rough indication of one's appearance must serve.

The Generalised Other

Perhaps the most important objects for an individual are his significant others. If his performances are not to be a chain of chameleon selves which change with every performance, some universalisation of meaning and experience must occur. In constructing its objects, then, the self does not only anticipate its own responses and the responses of others who are immediately present. It also generalises itself by imputing a form of universality to social reaction. It is consequently a moving synthesis which supplies a 'generalised other' for itself, that other being a typification which forces stable significance on local and transient happenings. The generalised other is an abstract summation and embodiment of all the varied replies that have been elicited by different 'me's'. It represents a kind of condensed general will which responds to his performances. As such it may stand against or oppose any of the specific others whom a person may encounter. So independent may it become that it need not be distilled out of a person's familiar surroundings at all. Neither need it be a composite of the living.[103] Instead its construction tends to be checked only by the risk of breakdown through unintelligibility. Faced by constant disbelief or contempt, a person might be under some pressure to redraft his generalised other.

The clarity, authority and structure of the generalised other depend on the unity and connections of the groups through which a person passes. To the extent that they do display a common identity, his own typification of them will be reinforced and solid. To the extent that they do not, his sense of what is universal and consistent will itself become fragmented and contradictory.

Others are constituted by the self in a dialectical process:

> the 'other' forms the self as the self forms the 'other'. In all situations of social life, the 'other' is manifest, concretely or abstractly. And as the 'other' manifests itself, its character and

content become causally significant to the emergence of the self and *its* nature and content.[104]

Some stable dialogue between 'I', 'me' and generalised other is indispensable if erratic and disquieting transmutations of self are not to occur. Industrial societies are thickly peopled with diverse groups and conflicting existential claims. The responses of each person may be so idiosyncratic that selves may become relatively infirm. The heterogeneity of others presents problems which may be met by a number of solutions. One possible answer is to adopt a *blasé* and urbane posture, methodically discounting the force of each impression that one receives. But that may merely dull reactions rather than contend with problems of fractured identity. Many others may impinge simultaneously, demanding the accommodation of highly differentiated replies into a single objectification of the self. It might be possible to satisfy all those others by fabricating new, hybrid roles. But innovation could be theatrically difficult. Moreover, it might simply provide unwelcome or unmanageably fragile selves. A common solution is to reduce the range of significant others to those who will lend some semblance of unity to a train of 'me's'. Jarring encounters will either be avoided or treated as peripheral except in their own insulated contexts. The selection of people who are likely to reflect themes valued by the self can contribute towards a sense of order in the social world. Such a process commits a person to choose the others who constitute him:

> We are in a time when part of the very struggle to be a man is the search for one's 'others'. It takes intelligence to find the 'others' that will bring out the best in one's self, and it takes courage to follow — no, not to follow, but to walk abreast with the collective 'other', ready made or created by mutual effort — when one has found it.[105]

The generalised other is then itself isolated by a person. It is an artifact designed to feed organisation into an otherwise incoherent universe. It will act as a reservoir of supporting or correcting perspectives for one's particular definition of situations. Even Robinson Crusoe and Pincher Martin required some animated social response to retain their sense of selfhood. The generalised other becomes a permanent albeit changing, companion. Indeed, according to Miller, Mead treated his idea as a secularised version of the God who stays with one at all times.[106] The continuity of the generalised other makes it a more intimate and consequential phase of the self than many of the fleeting acquaintances which one might form.

Language makes possible broad opportunities to participate in communication. In turn, the very use of language suggests the creation of the most diffuse of all generalised others — the community of speakers of which one is a member: the most inclusive social class of humans is 'the one defined by the logical universe of discourse (or system of universally significant symbols) determined by the participation of communicative interaction of individuals.'[107] In turn, society itself can be portrayed as a constellation of diverse generalised others. It provides different arrangements of order and motivation. One person might be responsive to an amalgam which overlaps little with that of another. In this fashion society consists of a network of contexts and social groupings which take on disparate meanings for its members. The 'same' situation might remain the same only so long as one person, or others like-minded with him, continues to monopolise its interpretation. The university can then become a bastion of liberalism, reaction or radicalism according to the particular social world which one inhabits. In Britain for instance, governments are not invariably well-disposed towards the university. According to one Minister of Education, Conservatives dislike universities because they are dominated by left-wing staff. Labour Party members dislike universities because they are composed of middle-class students. If conflict and confusion are not to abound, people must undergo some measure of segregation and accommodation. For instance, special areas or times may be tacitly allotted to groups in order to prevent a clash between their varying conceptions of order. Special areas of many large cities are given over to a moral regime which would be construed as offensive elsewhere. Those areas tend to be contained, their boundaries policed and controlled, so that people are offered a choice between versions of society. That choice is often extended by systematic changes in the moral character of an area over time. A person who wanders abroad in parts of London or New York may not expect to be affronted by what he sees at midday, but he has forfeited some of his right to be shocked if he goes there at midnight. An urban territory can then undergo predictable and quite discernible cycles during the course of a day. Soho in London or 42nd Street in New York not only present contrasts with their neighbours but also with 'themselves' at different points of time. Similarly, groups may make special provision for their members. A religious policeman might not be assigned to the group of patrolmen who collect dues from brothels. The anti-Semite might be denied a post teaching in a school which has a number of Jewish pupils. More stringently, a sect may withdraw its members from all 'unnecessary' contacts with the secular world, advertising its symbolic defection by the insignia of dress, speech and deportment.

Conclusion

Symbolic interactionism thus conceives the self to be the lens through which the social world is refracted. It is the medium which realises the logic of social forms. Fundamentally, however, the self emerges *from* the forms. It is made possible only by the activities and responses of others acting in an organised manner. A self without others is inconceivable.[108] Its doings and shapes must be understood as a special mirroring and incorporation of the social process in which it is embedded. Because language and society are taken to be historically and analytically prior to mind, interactionism does not proceed by deducing social phenomena from consciousness. Neither does it assume that individuals are 'given' and therefore unproblematic. It is the self which arises in sociation, not sociation from the self. As Luckmann argued, Mead's description is characterised by 'a complete reversal of the traditional understanding of the relation between society and the individual'.[109] Anchoring analysis in the geometry and grammar of the social forms, interactionism is also able to furnish a conception of social structure which is relatively free of scientific reification.[110] Structure is animated by the everyday behaviour of people, not by an immanent and *sui generis* logic of its own.

Problematic Aspects of the Interactionist Idea of Self

In its original formulation, the interactionist model of the self offered a limited but useful description of the relations between mind, body and society. It was useful because it referred to observable and communal processes which shaped mind. It permitted a synthesis of the different phases of social and individual process into one master scheme. The model was limited because it did not pretend to embrace private, subjective experience. It was not comprehensive or phenomenological. Rather it adhered to the behaviourist principles which Mead had advanced. In that guise, there has been one other major limitation which is not commonly recognised. By focusing on one ideal-typical self as a general process, there has been a tendency to portray all selves as undifferentiated and interchangeable. Further, the organic anchorage of the self has been lost in the writings of interactionism. The self has consequently become a rational, distant observer of social scenes rather than a varied participant which alters with them. It is fundamentally outside the interpretative scope of sociology although it represents sociology's chief object. In its phenomenologically revised form, the self has also lost much of the practical utility which it once enjoyed. It has become a somewhat mysterious process whose problematic qualities are little appreciated by the revisionist interactionists. Although nothing private is excluded from analytic survey, few directions are provided to guide descriptions of the enlarged self.

roduction

[Mead] does not neglect with the traditional psychologist the social process in which human development takes place; he does not neglect with the traditional social scientist the biological level of the social process by falling back upon a mentalistic and subjective conception of society as being lived in antecedent minds. Both extremes are avoided by an appeal to an ongoing social process of interacting biological organisms. . . .[1]

Despite its central significance, the interactionist portrayal of the self is tinged with ambiguity and contradiction. The self seems to have been originally presented as a compromise between the phenomenologically faithful and the analytically possible. It was a fragile and ambitious construction, designed to unite the disparate elements of reality into one intellectual model. As I shall argue, the pragmatists did not entirely manage to achieve that unity. The disconnected components of their scheme were left to become the cores of discrepant visions in symbolic interactionism. The discrepancies were not fully acknowledged. Because the interactionists neglect their intellectual foundations and advance grounded theory, they have come to work with imagery whose precise implications are obscure. Further, the emphasis on fidelity tended to increase as interactionism developed. An analytic artifact began to be confused with a true and comprehensive description, bringing a deceptive ontology into being.

Mead and Dewey described the self as a creature of consciousness, a process of mind reflecting on itself and constituting itself as an object. The forms of that process were conversation and language, transforming the inner world of subjectivity into a mirror of objective relationships. Much is accomplished by that formulation: for all analytic purposes, the self is not taken to be qualitatively different from any of the objects that are inspected by the recognised method of empirical science. Inferences about the invisible dialogue within the inner forum could be made by extrapolating from a relatively unproblematic social psychology. Those dialogues were further cast as rational and intelligible. The mysteries of internal action and *Verstehen* were dispelled by axiom.

The self is not to be confused with experience itself. Rather, it is an organisation which its possessor and the sociologist impose on experience. The unique, private and ineffable territories of the self defy any attempt at discovery or explanation. Thus Mead stated 'I do want to insist that the self has a sort of structure . . . that is entirely distinguishable from this so-called subjective experience of . . . particular sets of objects to which the organism alone has access.'[2] Neither is the self to be confused with some versions of consciousness: 'we cannot identify the self with what is commonly called consciousness, that is, with the private or subjective thereness of the characters of objects'.[3] The self is then a process or creation which is promiscuously available to analyst, owner and outsiders alike. It has been prised away from all the intricate and hidden areas which render existence a solitary and unshareable condition.

The very phase of the self which bestows order on experience is similarly concealed and unknowable. The 'I' can become an object to itself when it is self-estranged in the past or an imagined future. In the immediacy of an ongoing situation, it is as mysterious and alien as lived experience. Indeed it may be construed as lived experience turning on itself and creating organisation. Subject can never confront subject, but must transform itself into objects which are phenomenologically distinct from itself: 'the "I" does not get into the limelight; we talk to ourselves, but do not see ourselves. . . . I cannot turn around quick enough to catch myself'.[4] The 'I' must be built up solely through inference: it constitutes that necessary functional stage of a process by which the self is realised.

The organism, too, cannot enter the self directly except in the guise of the imagery which the self provides. It prepares the conditions of existence; it describes a range of human responses and sensitivities; it provides the impulses which acquire social expression; but it is distinct from consciousness. The self can know its organic casing only as a series of environmental phenomena which are not immediately understood. There may be a unity between mind and body in the intimacy of lived experience, but consciousness reifies and objectifies bodily phenomena: 'the complete imaginative presentation of the organism is unable to present the living of the organism. It can conceivably present the conditions under which living takes place but not the unitary life-processes. The physical organism in the environment always remains a thing'.[5]

It is apparent that this version of interactionist ontology offered a simplicity of interpretation and explanation. It mapped out the self as a rational and public process containing few mysteries. As Mead argued, 'the essence of the self . . . is cognitive'[6] and it is an essence which is laid open to inspection. Yet that statement has given rise to perplexing difficulties which continue to complicate interactionist analysis. In particular there have been problems posed by attempts to apply the pragmatist conception of experience. It may have been quite feasible to assert that intelligence and knowledge were parts of nature and that activity did not generate false experience. It did not seem possible to recognise all the implications of a biological model in sociology or social psychology. The entire complex of organism, mind, self and society could not be mastered in one scheme. Instead the organism came to occupy a segregated place in the first stages of most analysis. Thereafter, it was unobtrusively neglected. Segregation was encouraged by treating substantial sectors of the mind and the self as if they were *sui generis*. Consciousness was variously analysed as independent of the body and interdependent with it. Segregation was further fostered by the sheer technical and descriptive problems of synthesis. Conventional language could not offer a series of terms or metaphors for that very special relation which the pragmatists claimed to have discovered. Thus Mead observed that there was a 'legitimate distinction' between mind and body, but it was a distinction which could be refined and transcended. There were no logical barriers to that transcending conception, 'it is merely a lack of our apparatus of knowledge'.[7] When the pragmatists asserted that the self is problematic to its own consciousness, they denied the legitimacy of direct introspection. They also denied themselves the possibility of examining the particular dialectic which informed much of their reasoning. They could neither name nor inspect the interaction between the organism and its thought.

The complex edifice of the pragmatists was thus fractured by a gulf between claims and performance. Existence was held to embrace a totality made up of an acting biological form rooted in nature and in society. But the task of pursuing that vision of reality could not be easily accomplished. A somewhat fragmented imagery of social life was passed on to be absorbed by the symbolic interactionists. Its disjointed character revealed itself into a number of relatively disparate themes. Instead of a reasonable totality, contradictory perspectives on the organic, the experiential, and the social were taken up in a piecemeal manner. Of these strands, the organic was largely discarded. It now occupies a kind of phantom role in analysis, remembered but not included. Rose, for instance, argues 'the symbolic interactionist does not exclude the influence of biogenic and psychogenic factors in behavior, even though he does not incorporate them into his argument.'[8] The physiological system is thus transformed into a suspended and unemployed appendage of the self. Once the body became redundant, and the biological matrix was dismantled, much of the integrity of a pragmatist sociology was also subverted.

The appeal of immediate experience remains to haunt some interactionists. Yet the cerebral definition of self has also been retained by others. There are interactionists who have taken over a yearning for the certainty of praxis, but it is a yearning that is denied by their conception of self. Faithfulness and authenticity are still claimed for the sociology by a number of its adherents although its central organic buttress has been removed. Manifest and latent confusion thus abounds. The symbolic interactionists had inherited a once coherent but untenable argument whose dismembered portions now lack full significance. Collectively, these unravelled strands can promote a return to the Idealism which Mead and Dewey shunned. There is an occasional leaning towards the 'objective Idealism' which Mead believed had been superseded by pragmatism. 'Objective Idealism' identified mind as:

> the sum total of reality, the subject-object relation existing not between mind and what lies outside mind but between different phases of the spiritual process of reality. The undertaking failed, for one reason, because it identified the process of reality with cognition, while experience shows that the reality which cognition seeks lies outside of cognition, was there before cognition arose, and exists in independence of cognition after knowledge has been attained. Two modern trends of thought have appeared seeking to recognize the independence of nature over against cognition and, at the same time, to return to nature that which had been placed in mind ... [One] trend, that of pragmatism, regards cognition simply as a phase of conduct, denying any awareness of immediate experience.[9]

Different strands were thus injected into interactionism. The possibility of an unchecked Idealism, in particular, was realised in the later treatment of the self. It is with these themes that the rest of the chapter will be concerned.

Interactionism and the Disembodied Self

The fragile pragmatist balance of mind and matter could be easily disturbed. Thought could be extracted from its organic housing and made sovereign and independent. Disturbance was especially likely to be created by a community of sociologists who were impatient of epistemology and anxious to establish the significance of the social dimension. It was further encouraged by the unwieldiness of the pragmatist scheme. Formulated to contend with philosophical problems, it did not lend itself to ethnographic or sociological application. Dewey and Mead did not describe various observed selves. Rather they tended to write of Mind and the Self as single, ideal-typical processes which were presumably generalisable to all empirical settings. Those unitary models were not supposed to be differentiated into a range of types: they served to explain all the operations of every rational mind. One process was made to illuminate all the nuances of human conduct. But it was also a process which was so complex and cumbersome that it could readily be dismantled.

A debate amongst the early interactionists did lead to that dismemberment. It was a debate which Faris described in terms appropriate to an exorcism. The organism came to be redefined as an entity whose influence on speculation was largely harmful. Its outcasting led to 'a final freedom from instinctivism and internal physiological determinism'.[10] Actually, so loosely constructed a sociology as interactionism does not lend itself to 'final' or comprehensive resolutions of problems. The organic emphasis lingers on in sectors of interactionism. Blumer, for instance, still adheres to many of the original perspectives of pragmatism. He depicts the sociology as an Idealist stance which is restrained by its recognition of the obdurate character of the empirical world.[11] Amongst the 'root images' of interactionism, he places the claim that 'human beings face their world as organisms with selves'.[12] Indeed the phrase, 'organisms with selves', takes on the status of a Homeric epithet for Mead and Blumer alike. In most writing however there is very little more than a genuflection before a dim recollection of pragmatist ontology. Its transparent tokenism reduces the ontology to a vapid and irrelevant conception. In the main, current interactionism celebrates a resurrected Idealism which is almost entirely unchecked. The complexities, subtleties and internal links of pragmatism have been abandoned. Interactionists have largely severed mind from body and regard the latter as a mere 'lump of flesh'.[13] Pragmatists themselves appeared unable to maintain the organic connection, and some of the early interactionists were anxious to destroy it. One of the prime agents of exhumation was Cooley: he insisted that 'persons and society must . . . be studied primarily in the imagination',[14] and enquired 'what could the most elaborate knowledge of his weights and measures, including the anatomy of his brain, tell us of the character of Napoleon?'[15]

If the part of the organism is discussed at all, the entire question is dismissed as somehow improper and indelicate. In the main, mind was liberated to become the sole source of social structure and action.[16] Such militant Idealism enabled the restoration of Kant's complete disjunction between reason and the material world. Reason is not allowed to be plotted or explained by the workings of nature: it is uncaused and free of restraint. In interactionism, the revival of the dualistic abyss has nurtured a propensity to conceive all allusions to the organic as evidence of a discreditable positivism and scientism.[17] Thus Matza[18] referred to the tyranny of the organism which can make captives of the will and the imagination, but that tyranny is a polar case whose ontological implications are distasteful: 'sociologists would do better to describe the ways in which their subjects proceed through an open process by being willing than to substitute procedures derived from a subhuman world. The first is a dynamism suited to our topic of inquiry — man; the second is an insult . . .'[19] An emphasis on will can permit a return to the neo-Hegelian world in which all minds are participants in a transcendental collective consciousness. When man's symbolic work is alone stressed, the complex totality of ideas forms the prime ontological reality. Moreover, if the thought of the knower is paramount, and if the knower is indefinitely and inseparably extended in his environment, the self becomes little more than a dialectical moment of the moving whole of a society. Idealism then afforded another prop for asserting the identical and undifferentiated character of selves. Each person is merely another glimpse of the Absolute. In Cooley's formulation:

> Society . . . in its immediate aspect, *is a relation among personal ideas*. In order to have society it is evidently necessary that persons should get together somewhere; and they get together only as personal ideas in the mind. Where else? What other possible *locus* can be assigned for the real contact of persons, or in what other form can they come in contact except as impressions of ideas formed in this common *locus?*[20]

The dismemberment of the pragmatists' biological matrix also provided a further support for the abandonment of causality. Thought and action became creatures of a self-constituting will whose limits were provided only by the limits of imagination and the materials on which imagination feeds. Indeterminacy could become integral to interactionism.[21] Indeed, extrapolated in the work of Alfred Schutz, the self appears to be so liberated that it no longer engages in collaborative world-building.[22] It generates its own universe. The interactionists who have borrowed from Schutz can relegate transactions to a minor place.

Society as Will and Imagination

Discarding the physical and the physiological, interactionism has turned to knowledge as the author of structure. If it is knowledge that builds up and constitutes the social world, then the paths which knowledge takes must be followed so that the forms of society can be understood. It is only by re-enacting or accompanying the emergent developments of knowledge that the nature of social life can be analysed. Since the primary reality of society is not the sociologist's but that of Everyman, it also holds that description must focus on Everyman's achievements. The detailed observation of small worlds is thus prompted by another imperative.

The doings of Everyman, however ideal-typical or puppet-like they may be, display an indeterminacy which does not govern the creatures who populate the models of the macrosociologists. The interactionists do not wholly reject such models, but they have maintained a fondness for the small-scale and the immediate. That particular province has long been recognised as particularly recalcitrant to disciplined analysis. Although he may be discussing homunculi which are largely of his own devising, the interactionist is committed to an especially wayward subject. The actions of the individual or a small collection of people cannot be subjected to neat prediction. Rather, they must be understood by a language employing the language of uncertainty, 'soft determinism', will and the like. W. I. Thomas remarked:

> It is ... highly important for us to realize that we do not as a matter of fact lead our lives, make our decisions, and reach our goals in everyday life either statistically or scientifically. We live by inference. I am, let us say, your guest. You do not know, you cannot determine scientifically, that I will not steal your money or your spoons. But inferentially I will not, and inferentially you have me as a guest.[23]

Problems in the Idea of the Self

Where the forms of change in knowing are traced, and those forms are chiefly distinguished by indeterminacy, there is little licence to engage in an analysis invoking the causality that once was cited in the physical sciences. Thomas himself proposed the rejection of causality as a topic and explanatory mechanism in sociology. Becker, Blumer, Matza and others have chosen to do likewise. Almost all the interactionists succeeding Thomas have discarded causality and have resorted instead to a form of Weberian explanation which delineates the subjective logic of social life.

An uncaused world can appear random and unstructured. Indeed, one that is free of all causation would defy description because the logic of analysis would be utterly independent of its object. Some interactionism veers towards such an imagery of the indescribably fluid and capricious. Erving Goffman, for instance, undertook an examination of the moral career of the mental patient. His definition of that career reflects well the developmental vision of the knowing self which I have described: 'the moral career of a person of a given social category involves a standard sequence of changes in his way of conceiving of selves, including, importantly, his own. These half-buried lines of development can be followed by studying his moral experiences — that is, happenings which mark a turning point in the way in which the person views the world . . .'[24] Apprehended from within, the career entails an unfolding series of anticipated and unanticipated occurrences, betrayals and impositions which culminate in the assumption of patient status. Apprehended from without, Goffman argues that this experiential voyage mirrors chance and a freedom from necessity: 'one could say that mental patients distinctively suffer not from mental illness, but from contingencies'.[25] So it is with Lemert's management of deviance: abounding primary deviation is filtered by contingencies to provide a limited population of secondary deviants.

Yet there *is* a logic in the interactionist world. It is not necessarily the Aristotelian logic of things following one another in determined sequence.[26] It is the occasional rationality of the action as it is construed by those who engage in it. Following Dewey and the adherents of a modified Idealism, the interactionists build their models around the reasoning employed in the problematic situations which they describe. Theirs is not the causality of a determined world that constrains people to act unwittingly. They pursue, instead, the emerging logic *in* social situations. In general, then, interactionists are committed to the principle that all action must ultimately display an intelligible rationality.²⁷ After all, interactionism attends to symbolic process whilst eschewing social structural explanation. Its peculiar territory is meaning and it cannot assert the inexplicability of major areas of that territory. There should be no experience which defies every intelligent attempt to portray it as situationally appropriate and reasonable. Even the maddest, most deviant and bizarre occurrences must eventually succumb to the work of analysis.

Max Weber claimed that some configurations of process are so far removed from rationality that they can be explored only through an examination of their external forms. Charisma, for instance, was defined by Weber as the gift of grace which was bestowed on certain authorities. It is a mode of legitimation that is discontinuous with past authority and with the conventional logics that explain and justify power. The charismatic could not become the subject of interpretative analysis because it is existentially and rationally alien to the sociologist. Interactionists are rarely given to making such comparable exceptions. Some may, but the limits of rational understanding have not been clearly described in interactionist writing. It would seem that most symbolic interactionists tacitly argue that particular phenomena may prove unusually resistant to interpretation, but all phenomena must demonstrate a communicable logic of a kind.

That claim to unrestricted scope must be inferred about symbolic interactionists. Practitioners of the sociology do not often make express disclaimers or introduce detailed qualifications when they report their work. Indeed, rather than seek out those forms of experience which have an affinity with the sociologist's own, many court research into the deviant and the strange.²⁸ In that pursuit of the marginal may be a read a proclamation of the sociologist's powers.

Pragmatist and orthodox symbolic interactionist ontology provides no warrant for such an assumption of scope. Mead had presented the cognitive forms of the self as communal and therefore publicly accessible:

> There are certain common responses which each individual has toward certain common things, and in so far as these common responses are awakened in the individual when he is affecting other persons he arouses his own self. The structure, then, on which the self is built is this response which is common to all, for one has to be a member of a community to be a self.²⁹

Similarly, Stone and Farberman remark, 'we eschew the notion that meaning is preeminently a philosophical or speculative matter. We shall regard meaning as *objective* or *behavioral* . . .'[30] The communality and objectivity of analysable forms impose two limits on sociological description: substantial tracts of the self are private and closed to observation because they are not common; and intelligible tracts are available only to those who participate in a community of shared understandings. Of course, communality may be rather diffuse. Moreover the forms which shape one world may have significance to the members of another. There are few worlds which are so alien that they prohibit all attempts at sociological description. But certainty does reside in those situations where a sociologist and his subjects share a universe of meaning. Interactionism is at its most telling when it confronts a homogeneous symbolic environment. Mead's conception of explanation was clearly not intended to embrace only the solitary man or the small group, but its potency declines as heterogeneity grows. Sociology encounters multiple symbolic communities and these too must be somehow incorporated in analysis if the discipline is not to fail.

Latter-day symbolic interactionists are committed to the exploration of social diversity. They ground explanation in reports about the manifold ways in which social reality can be constructed. Unless they are doomed to be the captives of their own parochial worlds, they must claim the competence to understand very different styles of interpretation. The degree of common response between discrete worlds will always remain problematic until ethnography has been carried out but ethnographic possibilities are themselves affected by the insistence on communality. It cannot be argued that a sociologist actually knows a process unless he scrutinises it closely. In turn that scrutiny must itself be organised by the assumption that he can decipher the alien. The 'problem of foreign worlds' is simply an extension of the 'problem of other minds' and it is no less intractable. An *a priori* assertion of communality is not supportable. Neither is it possible to infer consensus from the observation that societies appear to rest on widely circulating symbolic currencies. Men impart unlike meanings to the 'same' words and symbols. Unless that seeming uniformity is upset by knowledge which illuminates the disparate contexts and shades of meaning, a spurious sociology will emerge. As Becker and Geer observe:

> Any social group, to the extent that it is a distinctive unit, will have

to some degree a culture differing from that of other groups, a somewhat different set of common understanding around which action is organized, and these differences will find expression in a language whose nuances are peculiar to that group and fully understood only by its members . . . So, although we speak one language and share in many ways one culture, we cannot assume that we understand precisely what another person, speaking as a member of such a group, means by any particular word.[31]

Interactionists therefore deny the invariance of human responses. Their sociology addresses a differentiated world which manifests itself in differentiated gestures. It is analytically imperative to proceed as if the communal constraint could be waived. But there are also strains to disregard Mead's other, more compelling limit. Interactionist analysis has covertly attempted to rescue banished experience from its exile. The effort has been covert because it has not been the object of much discussion. Yet it is evident that there has been a continuing encroachment on the private and ineffable territories of the self.

That encroachment has been encouraged in part by the manner in which common responses have undergone progressive redefinition. No sociology can avoid dissecting and poring over the rational forms of Everyman in a fashion foreign to Everyman himself. Some of the special expertise of sociology resides in its capacity to recognise more in phenomena than common sense might allow. Sociology further treats as problematic what common sense dsmisses as trivial and natural. A sociological grasp on a phenomenon then tends to be different from that exercised by a layman. It may lead to a more graphic and intricate description which can eventually render the common most uncommon. The concern with the symbolic commerce of everyday life has produced extended expositions which must seem arcane to any but the sociologist. Components and consequences may be delineated which are not generally acknowledged. A logic and an order may be traced which are not harmonious with experience itself. Thus Dewey argued:

In speaking of 'steps' [in reflective thought] it is perhaps natural to suppose that something chronological is intended, and from that it is presumably a natural conclusion that the steps are taken in a temporal sequence in the order taken [in analyses of reflective thought]. Nothing of this sort, however, is intended. The analysis is formal, and indicates the 'logical movements' involved in an act of critical thought. It is a matter of indifference which comes first. . . . [In almost all cases there is actually a] fusion into one process of induction, deduction and experimental testing.[32]

Wholes may then be ripped apart into their necessary elements, but the elements are never experienced individually. The mapping out of symbolic processes can become so exploded that the charts prove almost unrecognisable to the outsider. David Matza's *Becoming Deviant*, for example, professed its adherence to the principle of 'naturalistic faithfulness'. It attempted to lay bare the detailed physiology of the processes which might culminate in the assumption of a deviant self. Its description of the emergent transformations of common responses is so erudite that accomplished sociologists are themselves occasionally unable to understand it. Only the most sophisticated deviant could unravel and translate that description back into phenomena familiar to him. Interpretative fidelity may, then, be forced to assume guises which make its connections with everyday life problematic and superficially tenuous. Of course, sociology would be little advanced if it merely reported common speech and common explanation. Neither should the languages of description and analysis necessarily coincide. It would be impossible to conduct intelligent sociology without transcending some of the common sense which prevails in the settings which are analysed. Yet that understanding of the purposes and methods of sociology inevitably complicates the interactionist management of communal phenomena. Those phenomena cannot be allowed to remain either very communal or very phenomenal. The meaning of a 'common symbol' becomes elastic in use.

The pragmatists had monitored the development of phenomenology in the works of Bergson and Renouvier. In the main they discarded what they conceived to be the solipsistic implications of certain forms of Idealism and adhered to their commitment to phenomenalism and praxis.[33] However, interactionism is not strictly policed and its frontiers are permeable. The successors of pragmatism were open to novel formulations and syntheses which embraced phenomenological and other elements. In the 1960s, especially, the rediscovery of the writings of Alfred Schutz propelled sociologists into the manufacture of new perspectives on the analysis of subjective order. There are abundant affinities between phenomenology and symbolic interactionism which encouraged the importation of the ideas of Schutz, Husserl and Merleau-Ponty. One intellectual wing of interactionism then merged imperceptibly with a variant of phenomenology.[34] In so doing, it recanted much that was central to the Meadian portrait of the self. It tended to retain a distaste for abstract methodological and metaphysical discourse, but it also embarked on analysis that is ontologically alien to the core traditions of interactionism. Phenomenology claims great swathes of subjective territory as its own:

> there has been a tendency to treat the subjective as 'merely' subjective or as so idiosyncratic that social science, concerned with patterns and generalities, cannot seriously study it. This overlooks the possibility of finding patterns in the subjective experiences of individuals and denies the social scientist access to human experiences. . . .[35]

Phenomenological sociology in turn adopts a methodology and an ontology which the pragmatists disowned. It urges the sociologist to turn in on himself, advocating an inward quest for existential essences. The noumenon of the self, the 'I' in immediate experience, is available to those who exercise disciplined introspection. It is not ineffable or formless:

> Phenomenological inquiry . . . represents a struggle to 'see' the phenomena as clearly as possible and as they are given in immediate experience, in one's own *consciousness of* those things . . . Immediate experience is not a 'buzzing confusion' but rather is meaningful and structured.[36]

Symbolic interactionism has thus become the resort of radically opposed thinkers. There are those, like Becker[37] and Strauss, who conserve the purity and limitations of Mead's original model of the self. There are others who verge towards the revived Idealism of phenomenology and the Eidetic reduction. Accompanying that move there is an increasing commitment to the claim that it is possible to interpret every manifestation of sociologically significant thought. Mead's contracted definition of the self has been expanded to encompass the bulk of experience.[38] Only parsimony and relevance restrict the scale and depth of much interactionist analysis.

Problems in the Idea of the Self

The Actor as an Undifferentiated and Rational Man

The redrafting of interactionism has led to a companion redefinition of its objects, and the older self of the pragmatist has grown more complex in the process. This interplay between a discipline and its objects is characteristic of all variants of sociology. Indeed it would be a curious explanation that did not impose a distinctive order that was reasonably consistent with its principal themes. Symbolic interactionism has continuously discovered social processes which offer support for its general ontology and methodology.[39] After all, its perspectives were designed to define and discover those very processes. In its construction of a particular analytic universe, interactionism merely does what any organised vision of life attempts to achieve. It would be inconceivable if a person in Parsonian analysis were to become a candidate for Lukács's proletarian consciousness; if one of the Gluecks' delinquent women revealed a dialectical imagination; if a legislator in the Schwendingers' world were disinterested;[40] or if a Marxist paradigm generated people whose activities were modulated by the pattern variables. When the figures projected into analysis are working extensions of the sociologist's mind, there must be an affinity between the situated logic of action and the logic of explanation.

Many interactionist models centre on figures constructed to illuminate facets of the social world. The rationality which they employ tends to resonate sociological intelligence. In a sense they are no more than marionettes performing the activities which their masters have programmed. Every response and every action has been constructed for them by their sociological authors. Much interactionism is consequently more complex than a simple reading might suggest. It brings people into being; endows them with a lay version of sociological competence; reports their activities as the phenomena of situated experience; and explains them by that selfsame competence.

Interactionist ontology and epistemology have structured descriptions of everyday behaviour. In particular, the emphasis on the rational and the cognitive has translated the creatures of symbolic interactionism into the wide-awake followers of a common-sense logic that might be adopted by anyone. All the diversity of human expression, style and reasoning tend to undergo an entropy in interactionist works. Goffman's mental patient, Davis's cabdriver, Gold's janitor, Matza's deviant. McCaghy's stripper and Roth's tubercular patient are all eminently rational and undifferentiated in their competence and lay methodology. Settings and biographies may vary, but they are cut through by the uniform logic of Everyman. Indeed, many explorations of the deviant and the curious eventually rediscover the same Everyman parading in a different mask and a different set of clothes. As Young observes, 'the new deviancy theorist portrays his deviant as an open-minded, calm, rational actor . . .'[41] The legacy of Idealism has conspired with the projections of the sociological imagination to produce one overwhelming strategic style for coping with the exigencies of everyday life. In revealing that style as banal, the interactionists undertake a demystification of the social world that borrows a little from their own analytic procedures.

Rationality was written into interactionism from its very inception. No description could proceed without that assumption. It is built into Mead's conception of language as the instrument which promotes reflection.[42] It is also present in his contention that sympathetic role-playing is a demonstration of rational intelligence. The self is constructed out of communal materials which are logical and intelligible.

More complexly, a universal rationality is to be discovered in the covert claim that all men are competent manipulators of symbolic forms. The suggestion is rarely made that some people are less capable than others at organising and grasping a symbolic field. The pragmatist origins of interactionism might have fostered a concern with the organic capacities of those who think and act. If the organic integrity of the subject had been preserved, the span of varying human conditions might have been fed into analyses of people's interpretative work. Some interactionists *have* preserved a residual interest in that facet of knowledge, thereby denying a conception of man as totally disembodied intelligence. Taylor, for instance, invokes incompetence as a possible source of some sexual diviance: he argues that the difficulty of mastering sexual scripts may prove excessive and encourage remedies that outrage convention.[43] Similarly, Scott pursues a substantially interactionist analysis of the blind by exploring the changes which impoverished sight can inflict on interaction and the construction of subjective worlds.[44] Yet most other interactionists methodically ignore even elementary differences in capacity. The differences are explicitly or implicitly defined as irrelevant matters of context which can have little bearing on enquiry.

The simplest relations of interdependence between mind and organism have thus been removed from analytic surveillance. The processes by which the self builds its objects are rendered obscure. There is no sense that action can be understood as the mediated impulses of the organism. Neither is there any consideration of the physical limitations which may mould social experience. 'Cripple', 'deaf', 'blind', 'dumb', 'giant' and 'dwarf' then become no more than invidious characterological labels which form the self but have little to do with the physiological underpinning of identity. All organic diversity is transferred to a plane of symbolism on which it may or may not become a matter for typification. It has thus fallen under the sway of an unfettered Idealism which cannot attend to the basic points made by Mead:

> The . . . prevalent signification of consciousness is found simply in the presence of objects in experience. With the eyes shut we can say we are no longer conscious of visual objects. If the condition of the nervous system, or certain tracts in it, cancels the relation of the individual and his environment, he may be said to lose consciousness or some portion of it; i.e., some objects or all of them pass out of experience for this individual.[45]

All this is ruled away: the mind portrayed in contemporary interactionism sometimes resembles a lidless eye which misses nothing. The freeing of thought in interactionism has worked important consequences. Conscious, purposive rationality becomes all. Thus the restrictions of sight and hearing are assigned little significance although the range and detail of observations available to a man will affect the interpretations which he can make of a situation. Put crudely, those who are inaudible and invisible are likely to exert a difference influence from others who can be seen and heard. Similarly, the near-sighted man is liable to respond to a smaller and therefore simpler circle than the far-sighted. Memory too is neglected although a man's capacity to retain and retrive complicated perspectives will shape his management of social life. Unfinished acts, past others, and early situations will fashion different structures in the present. It seems, however, that the men of interactionism, like the Bourbons, forget nothing: 'symbolic interaction theory shares with psychoanalytic theory the assumption that man never forgets anything'.[46] It is unclear why that assumption should be made or whether all interactionists do subscribe to it. It is in fact so rarely discussed that memory is another tacit 'given' in the sociology.

Physical restraints on mobility are also ignored despite their effects on the number and variety of settings which can become accessible to a person. There is a practical denial of the organic counterpoint which shapes processes of thought, symbolisation and social performance. The palpitations, flushes, fatigues, headaches and tremblings which accompany interaction have been censored away. Again, and rather particularly, the copious interactionist analyses of drug-taking typically refrain from considering the transformations which drugs induce in their users' social style and competence.[47] Goffman *does* allude to some members of this organic chorus, but he celebrates the dualism of mind and body by describing them as 'animal releases' which well up from the physiological abyss into the social world.

Other features of human existence have become equally distorted. Sentiments and affections, the 'contents' of a transaction, cannot be awarded a place in a sociology which attends to form above all else.[48] Motives are taken by the interactionists to reside only in the domain of what is articulate and symbolic.[49] Most importantly, there is little interest in the sheer ability of men to undertake the work of ordering and synthesising facets of their world. There can be no organic sources of confusion, incapacity, anxiety or intellectual incompetence.[50] All men are equally intelligent, knowledgeable and astute. The symbolic interactionists have constructed a universe which contains the utmost liberty and egalitarianism. But it is also a universe whose landscape is rather flat and colourless. None of these limitations would be very important if interactionism did not represent itself as a special kind of intellectual exercise. After all, no description can ever exhaust the possibilities of its object. Much must be neglected or simplified if coherence is to emerge. But it is the particular claim of interactionism that it can furnish faithful depictions of the social world. It pretends not to subordinate society to its procedures, but its procedures to society.

I have attributed the dominance of the interactionist version of Idealism to the overthrow of the organism, but other influences have also been at work. Some of this levelling may have stemmed from the collapsing together of two analytically distinct properties of social order. Most interactionists hold that an exploration of forms can reveal an intricate organisation which generates all the phenomena of society. It is maintained that, despite the seeming contradictions and superficialities of social life, there exists a fundamental etiquette whose rules may be described as instances of an impressive practical rationality. An appropriate intellectual incision will demonstrate how clever, complicated, purposive and subtle are even the most mundane and petty transactions. After all, if no such order existed, sociology itself would be unable to proceed. The discipline is committed to the belief that process must eventually be revealed as intelligible, meaningful and interconnected. Those who engage in that process may then be credited with the competence that 'inheres' in the rituals of everyday life. Few are completely incapable of performing those rituals, and few can escape being identified as masters of the interactional arts. When activity is presented as necessarily logical, the 'rationality' of the forms may be claimed for those who employ them.

Pragmatists would assert that people fundamentally *are* the forms; that they exist, know and emerge in socially-structured praxis. Mead certainly effected that collapse by representing language, action, reflexivity and social objects as phases of the same rational process. Although not an interactionist,[51] Garfinkel accomplishes the same merging of rational action with a situated rationality. In the opening paragraphs of *Studies in Ethnomethodology*, he asserts that his central recommendation

> is that the activities whereby members produce and manage settings of everyday organized affairs are identical with members' procedures for making those settings 'account-able'. The 'reflexive' or 'incarnate' character of accounting practices makes up the crux of that recommendation. . . . [The central topic is] the rational accountability of practical actions as an ongoing, practical accomplishment.[52]

It is not at all apparent how it is possible to make such an *a priori* identity between practical action and rational 'account-ability'. But Garfinkel and the interactionists do make it. They thereby argue that the rationality of a form provides evidence of a wide-awake reasoning. Since forms cannot be analytically distinguished by the specific character of their users, all users become further translated into the deployers of an undifferentiated rationality.

Perhaps, too, the levelling flows from insufficient attention having been paid to the extraordinarily problematic feat of taking the role of the other. Mead and the early interactionists had assigned prime importance to the progressive exchanging of perspectives which develops in any encounter. Men see themselves and their situations through the organised interpretations of others. A communality or complementarity of understanding emerges which enables the appearance of selves, projects and collective action. Man as a social being is grounded in that process. Thus Mead observed 'what we term "reason" arises when one of the organisms takes into its own response the attitude of the other organisms involved. It is possible for the organism so to assume the attitudes of the group that are involved in its own act within this whole co-operative process. When it does so, it is what we term "a rational being".'[53] The earlier, restricted definition of the self could transform *Verstehen* into a rational process of apprehending the visible forms of joint action.[54]

The redeveloped self of the later interactionists contains much that Mead's definition expressly excluded. It embraces complex phenomena and processes which can never be observed. Its comprehension has nevertheless been informed by analytic procedures which were once thought appropriate to the older and starker conception. They have relied on the authority provided by a virtually overthrown pragmatism. By anchoring the organism in a biological matrix, the pragmatists claimed that they had put the unsettling problems of conventional philosophy behind them. Other conceptions of mind had posed false perspectives which engendered false dilemmas. The early interactionists, in their turn, refused to exercise themselves with epistemological questions about the existence and character of other minds. Those minds were held to be integral parts of the natural world, no more problematic than other segments of nature. They were objects like other objects, unfolding during the course of practical activity. They were, of course, opaque and intricate, but they did not occupy a special position which defied understanding.

Yet, when the self is enlarged to include great tracts of once banished material, few assumptions can be legitimately made about the ability of one man to *understand* another. The problem of faithful interpretation is especially massive in the interactionism which has been exposed to phenomenology. Indeed it would seem to defy all solution. Thus Zaner enquires, 'how is it possible that although I cannot live in your seeing of things, cannot feel your love and hatred, cannot have an immediate and direct perception of your mental life, as it is to you – how is it possible that I can nevertheless share your thoughts, feelings, attitudes?'[55] The argument might be further put that even if such sharing did truly occur, there would be no warrant to know decisively that it *had* taken place. The most prolonged and searching questions might reveal only that there was an insuperable problem of translating one private experience into the materials of another. It is never possible to conclude that the symbolic vocabulary of one is identical to that of his fellow-man. Yet these issues have not been fully introduced into the symbolic interactionist's employment of interpretative analysis. That strategy has been advanced as if it were still adhering to the simpler and more manageable model of the self described by Mead. The complexities of *Verstehen* have been presented as an elementary methodological operation which requires only a brief recital.

Interactionist methodology preserves other pragmatist postures towards problems. It adheres to the contention that epistemological dilemmas are largely irrelevant to the sociological enterprise. It maintains an aversion to portracted philosophical disquisition. It also upholds the alleged affinity between lay and scientific reasoning. Reflective thought is not taken to be significantly different when it appears in various contexts: its constitutive practices are much the same in any guise. The emergence of the self is itself characterised as a rational event which may be rationally analysed. The self's owner, his significant others and the scientific observer can all witness and grasp the processes which produce it. They are not mysterious processes. After all, most social transactions evolve with some ease. If all men seem to be demonstrably successful at taking the role of the other, and if that work is the very prerequisite of social life, it can be asserted that the sociologist's own capacities should not be impugned. Problems of analysis are then typically attached to the consequences of role-taking, not to the activity itself.

An even stronger statement of identity between subject and object can be made by those who sponsor a revived Idealism. The sociologist is then depicted as no more than a phase in the totality of minds. He is a member of a group which bears a culture, and his membership grants him unfettered access to the inner life of his fellows. He can know *Logos* because he is an aspect of *Logos* himself. Thus Cooley argued:

> The human mind participates in social processes in a way that it does not in any other processes. It is itself a sample, a phase, of those processes, and is capable, under favorable circumstances, of so far identifying itself with the general movement of a group as to achieve a remarkably just anticipation of what the group will do. Prediction of this sort is largely intuitive rather than intellectual.[56]

The appreciation of other minds is therefore dwarfed as a problem. Instead interactionists typically associate methodological problems with the matters of avoiding reifying initial definitions of a process; of obtaining access to settings; of passing in those settings; of securing trust; and of keeping accurate records. It is certainly the case that the adequacy of interpretation is held to require demonstration: recommended procedures include monitoring the competence of the sociologist at passing as a member; resorting back to the subject; examining whether a description offers a plausible script for simulating a subject's activity, and the like. Those procedures do not appear to be used as a matter of routine. None of them poses the problem of whether other minds are fundamentally alien to the sociologist. There may be difficulties of translation, but the sociologist's analytic language is taken to be a recognisable transcription of other people's motives, accounts, symbolism and situations. By adhering to praxis and 'taking the role of the acting other . . . the sociologist [is permitted] to escape the *fallacy of objectivism*; that is, the substitution of his own perspective for that of those he is studying.'[57]

The imponderable qualities of *Verstehen* have also been belittled because the interactionists have proceeded beyond Weber's contention that a rational mind can appreciate only the rational properties of other minds. The separation of mind and body has encouraged an occasional resurrection of Kant's imagery of consciousness as autonomous and uncaused. Interactionist ontology does not uniformly subscribe to that imagery, but there is sometimes a resort to description which suggests that intelligence is ultimately a *spectator* and not a total participant in social life. An uncaused, disembodied mind cannot be wholly social. Indeed, little of its organising intelligence may be explained by social process. Although interaction, experience and discourse are mediated by forms and symbols, they are analytically distinct from their mediations. More especially, forms do not penetrate the appraising intelligence of the self. The 'I' is not quite situationally determined: it is 'something that is never entirely calculable . . . the 'I' is always something different from what the situation itself calls for'.[58] It is as if mind were constrained to employ the conventional order of signs, were lodged within an environment that is signified, but is itself free of those signifying systems. Its own procedures work *on* social materials but they are not themselves socially constituted. Standing against society there is a free, asocial and rational consciousness which is the interactionist's route to *Verstehen*. Ironically, the self of the interactionists lies outside the province of sociology.[59]

There can be no other framework for such an enterprise as

symbolic interactionism. If mind, body, self and society were closely linked to become a fused system, no sociologist could ever insert himself into another's life-world and confidently take his role. *Verstehen* becomes untenable unless there is an area of certainty which replicates the rational faculties of the sociologist and any other observer. The responses of a Samoan, a college teacher, a migrant farm-worker, a city policeman, an acrobat and a pimp must be functionally and structurally similar for imaginative acts of empathetic bridging to take place. In turn, those responses must be sufficiently free of context and biography to provide a workable similarity. The Samoan and the acrobat may be socially constructed, but they cannot be so entirely. A socially-unaffected residue must be preserved. Without that residue, the differences between them would be so enlarged that there could never be a reasonable warrant to suppose that common understanding is possible. The Samoan would not only work with 'Samoan' materials and 'Samoan' symbols, but his working consciousness would itself be thoroughly 'Samoan'. It would operate in a qualitatively distinct way, deploying a discrete logic. Some shared ground rules may bind the populations of different social areas together, but there are problematic gaps and dissimilarities between them. In a comprehensively sociological conception of the self, varying conceptions of time, space, causality and significance would structure the innermost reaches of intelligence. There would be no liberated areas which permit the sociologist to assume that all men house a core rationality founded on an unsituated logic.

Arguments centring on the socially structured limitations of *Verstehen* may be subjected to a *reductio ad absurdum*.[60] They may assert that none but a middle-aged white acrobat can make any sensible observations about a middle-aged white acrobat. All men would become the captives of the symbolic universes of their own small areas of social space. There could be no common discourse, no common understanding and no sense in the social world.[61] As Simmel argued, 'one need not be Caesar in order to understand Caesar.' Yet there is a current within symbolic interactionism which would build on Simmel's contention to assert that all men are Caesars in miniature, that the differences between Caesar and others reside only in varieties of situation and experience.

Sociology in its interactionist form is evidently sustained by contradictory proposals: it must champion the sovereignty of the social, but it must also investigate the social by imputing an unsocial, emancipated intelligence to its objects. The dramaturgical analogy has lent special emphasis to that contradiction. Those who make use of that analogy maintain that man, the role-player, presents himself in different guises and with different masks, he collaborates in staging scenes and dramas, he makes use of props and settings, and he relies on a diversity of scripts. At bottom, however, there is a knowing actor who is alienated from all the ongoing performance about him. His estranged mind cannot be completely immersed in theatrical structures. It is as remote as that of the surveying sociologist and, sharing that affinity, is open to sociological understanding. If the actor were truly absorbed, subjective interpretation would have to give way to a behaviourism of external appearances. Thus Goffman argues:

> Throughout . . . it has been implied that underneath their differences in culture, people everywhere are the same. If persons have a universal human nature, they themselves are not to be looked to for an explanation of it . . . If a particular person or group or society seems to have a unique character of its own, it is because its standard set of human-nature elements is pitched and combined in a particular way.[62]

Obviously dramaturgy was offered as analogy only. It is not to be taken as identical with its object. Goffman states, for instance, 'all the world is not a stage — certainly the theater isn't entirely.'[63] Yet, even as metaphor, it reveals grounded and necessary assumptions about what must be true of man if sociology is to become possible. Interactionism must thus engage in a modest betrayal of itself. It cannot be faithful to a phenomenon if the phenomenon is not amenable to faithful description. The sociology's objects have to be redefined so that there can be a fidelity of rendition. Interactionism is forced to exempt its central problems from its general social ontology. There must either be a reversion back to philosophical dualism or else an insistence on a comprehensive holism which dismisses all variation between men as spurious. In both guises a universal core humanity must be distinguished from the surface world of symbolism and action.

A sociology which assigns equal competence to all can tend to promote a mild anarchism. Much interactionism is concerned with the pursuit of demystification: it exposes the myths which dominate thinking about social life. In particular it systematically reveals the contradictions and reifications which precipitate the bestowing of

Problems in the Idea of the Self

alienated status. Work on mental illness, for example, suggests that madness is an imposed category which stems from distorting and unequal negotiations between the 'sick' and their managers. The incompetence and suffering connoted by madness are made thoroughly subordinate to the social transactions which organise the world of mental illness. They are denied authenticity or are endowed with an authenticity which recognises them as situationally rational. That denial is given further support by a sociology which attaches primary significance to form. There may be some substance to Gouldner's criticism of Goffman's general metaphor of the theatre: 'the dramaturgical model allows us to bear our defeats and losses, because it implies that they are not for 'real' . . . winning and losing become of lesser moment. It is only the game that counts. . . .'[64] An opposition to differential labelling may also be encountered in the writings on juvenile delinquency which have asserted a fundamental similarity between the rationalities and capacities of the young and the adult defendant.[65] The legitimating convention of *parents patriae* is cast as an obfuscating and myth-ridden device. In short, if men cannot be ranked ontologically, all discrimination is arbitrary, oppressive and unjust.

Further Analytic Foundations of the Undifferentiated Self

All analyses must rest on assumptions of *ceteris paribus*. Garfinkel identified those assumptions as 'etectera clauses' which force certain matters out to the margins of interest. It is patently impossible to attend to all the features of an area. It is also impossible to conduct an enquiry when the area is itself treated as wholly unstable, changing and problematic. Some issues must be taken on trust and stabilised. The interactionist cannot trivialise social structure because he is ontologically unprepared to subscribe to the idea of social structure.[66] As Manning observes, 'the assumption [is] that the world [is] fluid, ambiguous, at times absurd, and defined as the actor [sees] it . . .'[67] The interactionist cannot take the contents of social life to be invariant because contents are largely unavailable to him.[68] His most concrete materials are the forms of change, the emerging self and its organised interpretations of process. If those solid facts are dissolved into fluidity, little is left but an unmanageable whirligig of processes. The self is defined as moulded by the forms of change; it is virtually as extensive as the situations in which it is lodged; it is dialectically fused with its context, its past, its future and its own internal workings; it is an emergent which hinges on inner and outer transformations. The intricacy of the interactionists' conception of self is so great that further complexity might render it unanalysable. Important aspects must be mastered if description is to proceed. The central topic of interactionist writing, the self, is then tailored to permit reasonable scrutiny. It would seem that the complexity of varying competence and diverse existence would simply prove intolerable. At bottom the self must be treated as basically analogous to all other selves and to the self of the observing sociologist in particular.

That solution permeates almost all interactionist discourse. It is the largely unstated condition upon which analysis rests. The examination of any issue is conducted as if its central actors were ultimately rational, employing a logic which is the universal reasoning of all men. Thus Goffman's discussion of the mental patient is unintelligible without the invisible preface which urges that the responses of the 'mad' should be interpreted as if they were much the same as those of anyone else. Much is yielded by imposing that condition. The world of *Asylums* is profoundly illuminating despite its resort to a hidden contrivance. But it is also the case that interactionist claims to authenticity and faithfulness become rather forfeit. The identical subject-object acquires a strange guise. Thus Matza's injunction to naturalism is somewhat misleading because it furnishes a reconstituted deviant whose intelligence is that of the intellectual mind which created him. The central figure of *Becoming Deviant* has a claim to be Matza's *alter ego*, a shell which is given life by Matza's own phenomenological sensibility. In that, and other essays, the integrity of the knowing-known transaction has been partially breached.

The pragmatist strain which most importantly produces a *de facto* resolution of this problem stems from the imperative to turn to the world and ignore abstraction. Interactionism is essentially a practical enterprise, being directed at the anthropological and away from the speculative. The potentially alien quality of other minds and the complexities wrought by human diversity are managed by a fundamental neglect. It is possible to argue that the bulk of sociology represents a massive act of faith rather than a solid accomplishment built on certain knowledge. Outside propositional logic, nothing can be 'proved' once and for all. Sociology, and especially interpretative sociology, can never satisfactorily meet the problems posed by a rigorous sceptical attack. It cannot even handle the problems presented by the most basic solipsism. I take it that it was in this sense that Becker stated 'we all know that social science is, in principle,

Problems in the Idea of the Self

impossible. If it were possible, we would not do it anyway'.[69]

All sociology is an attempt to make sense of what must finally defy sense. Its analytic attacks upon the social world must ultimately be defended by pragmatic criteria which partially suspend issues of truthfulness and fidelity. It thus appears that most interactionists simply resist exploring the quagmires of uncertainty and logical regression which have attracted the sociological phenomenologists and the ethnomethodologists. After all, it was the alleged superiority of existential knowledge over abstract reasoning that fostered the development of interactionist ethnography and participant observation. The anthropological inflection affirms the sociology's conception of the self: method and theoretical justification are one. As Truzzi remarked, the interactionist concern with 'legitimizing *verstehen* has not taken the direction of trying to experimentally establish its validity. . . . The effort has been to take it out of the hands of armchair theorists and place it as a working device into the hands of those involved with the cultural meaning-structure through participant-observation.'[70] When validity is assured by treating knowledge as a matter of doing and being rather than as a state of contemplation, the contemplative support for practice can appear self-falsifying. Interactionists do not therefore seem overly concerned about the contradictions and paradoxes of this phase of their project. Too exhaustive an attempt to resolve them would merely exacerbate the problem. They consequently undertake research which is comparatively unreflexive, leaving the problematic qualities of the self unimpaired.

There is perhaps one final influence which has wrought an important impact on the interactionist description of the self. The sociology argues that the character of the social world is molested when its form and content are given an analytic structure before enquiry begins. It urges that analytic *a priori* definitions should be displaced by synthetic *a posteriori* findings.[71] The sociologist must consequently abandon much of his own modelling of the world and submit, however briefly, to the social reality which he discovers. Thus Bruyn remarked:

> . . . the social scientist who is a committed Protestant seeking to understand the culture of the Catholic world, or the Catholic sociologist who seeks to understand the Protestant world, must, as a social scientist, be willing to 'suspend disbelief'. The participant observer who seeks to understand the world of the schizophrenic

must be willing to suspend his disbelief in the hallucinations and delusions he comes to know, if he wants to understand the schizophrenic, and, in addition, learn to record this same process in his writing.[72]

Symbolic interactionism does rather little work to restore belief after it has been suspended. What can be more *real* to an interactionist than the primary reality of the Protestant's or the Catholic's world? The interactionist is not epistemologically entitled to claim that his account is more credible or truthful than that offered by his subject. He *may* have different interests, and those primary realities are not left unaltered in analysis. As Denzin argues:

> the sociologist must operate between two worlds when he engages in research – the everyday world of his subjects and the world of his own sociological perspective. Sociological explanations ultimately given for a set of behaviors are not likely to be completely understood by those studied; even if they prove understandable, subjects may not agree with or accept them . . . An irreducible conflict will always exist between the sociological perspective and the perspective of everyday life.[73]

Yet the sociological perspective does not yield more authentic knowledge. It merely serves different purposes. In all this, there is a delicate balance to be struck between a preservation of the symbolic integrity of the subject's world and the provision of a larger frame which denies its completeness and adequacy.[74]

Interactionism is comparatively little occupied with the creation of overarching intellectual schemes which neatly arrange, collate and subordinate individual observations. As I have argued, authenticity is primarily rooted in the existences and experiences of the immediate knower, not in retrospective or prospective theoretical schemes. Thus Blumer advocates the pursuit of 'investigation that is directed to a given empirical world in its natural, ongoing character instead of a simulation of such a world, or to an abstraction from it . . . or to a substitute for the world in the form of a preset image of it.'[75] Although theorising is necessary, it occupies a somewhat discredited place in any interactionist epistemology.

Those who adhere to the more orthodox interactionist style tend to disregard content and the prepredicative as matters lying beyond intellectual reach. They hold that the forms can alone be assembled and assessed. The conservers of that starker sociology cannot usefully incorporate the invisible and inarticulate in their work. Indeed, like Mead, they veer towards a radically modified behaviourism which attempts to knit empiricism and a limited *Verstehen* together. Their prime materials are the organising forms which shape and transcend content. In that sociology of Becker, Hughes and Davis, no claims are made for immediacy or the phenomenological. The intuitive appreciation of symbolic universes is replaced by a disciplined concentration upon the universal properties of interaction. The language is typically one of 'career', 'socialisation', 'profession', 'institution' and the like. It is a language seemingly designed to subordinate the particular and the embedded to a larger grammar of social relations. Any focus upon the superficially distinctive contents of settings will ignore the possibility of comparative work and formal analysis. At some points, then, the phenomenologically salient will become petty or distracting to the classical interactionist. For instance, Everett Hughes remarked 'the comparative student of man's work learns about doctors by studying plumbers; and about prostitutes by studying psychiatrists.'[76] That statement would be intellectually upsetting to the phenomenologist and appalling to some ethnomethodologists. Such formalism dissipates utterance and attends to grammar, ignores colour and matter and examines geometry. It neglects most mundane similarities by an abstracting methodology. So constituted, symbolic interactionism can somehow overlook all the differences that are conventionally assigned to men. The prostitute and the psychiatrist both confront clients, problems of confidentiality, the business of working in a largely dyadic relationship, the unexpected effects of catharsis, and the issue of organising an occupational career. At bottom, the interactionist who leans on Simmel will purposefully bracket the phenomena which separate the two people. Bracketing, indeed, becomes a methodological imperative. It was Hughes again who argued 'we need to rid ourselves of any concepts which keep us from seeing that the essential problems of men at work are the same . . . Unless we can find a point of view and concepts which will enable us to make comparison between the junk peddler and the professor without intent to debunk the one and patronize the other, we cannot do our best in this field.'[77] It is apparent that formalism is a great leveller. When a piece of research has been completed and analysis proceeds, the appreciably unique and differentiating nature of men and their settings is subjected to a descriptive style which searches for what is abstract.

Contrasts may be discovered, but they are not contrasts between the special properties and capacities of organisms with selves.

Other interactionists have absorbed some measure of phenomenological method.[78] They too are disinclined to match, rank or compare selves. Having stressed the validity of immediacy, they turn towards intuition and unalloyed appreciation as the nearest approximation to truth. Their chief object is content that has been seized by the imagination. For instance, Bruyn does not dismiss analytic reasoning but he does maintain 'analysis at certain stages may prove to be a barrier to [the researcher's] understanding. The researcher seeks a certain kind of communion with the observed and in any efforts to comment descriptively about the situation keeps himself outside it. There is no place for either rational or emotional comments at the point of intuitive contact.'[79] There is an implication in much that is written by the phenomenological interactionists that such a 'point of intuitive contact' is the existential site for an authentic grasp on reality. As distance from that site grows, so sociology becomes analytically possible and intellectually unsound. When immediacy is paramount, little is invested in the building of a rationally conceived hierarchy of truths. Indeed all such abstract system become suspect.

The outcome is the production of a relativism with political leanings towards anarchism. One of the chief tasks of the sociologist is to present and order the social realities which he discovers. But his presentation cannot be ontologically or even analytically superior to those realities; it cannot reconstruct existence as it seems to be experienced. Its sole justification is that it performs a service which is not otherwise available. When intellectual schemes are devalued and there is no central hierarchy, it is difficult to achieve comparisons of realities.[80] Immediate knowledge cannot be ranked against immediate knowledge. They may simply be different and closed to the making of sensible contrasts. In consequence both the formalist and the phenomenological interactionists tend to subscribe to what Gellner has called 'The Principle of Universal Charity',[81] a principle that urges the ultimate intelligibility and propriety of all action. Every interactionist world is either a *nonpareil* or a vein to be mined and left barren. Morally, the abandonment of truth and discrimination has left only one social group supremely culpable. When any discriminatory definition is invidious, definers alone attract sustained criticism.[82] That principle has received special prominence in the debates about the legitimacy of social regulation. In *Victimless Crimes*, for instance, Schur maintains that all paternalistic legislation is misconceived: arguing with Bedau, a moral philosopher, he states:

> I find nothing in Professor Bedau's discussion that persuades me 'moral philosophy' uniquely enables us to surmount [the] difficulties [attending the selection of defensible criminal laws].... No matter how convinced we may be that the judgment we make in a particular instance is called for by our overarching scheme of general principles, there is no getting around the fact that it is a *judgment*, and indeed that it is a judgment based on *our* scheme of principles.[83]

A sociology which does not defer to the idea of precisely articulated strata of truth cannot happily compare Protestantism with Catholicism, schizophrenia with sanity. Indeed in many analyses there is no larger purpose which demands that those worlds be arranged in an order of competence, truthfulness or morality. Faithful rendition or analytic abstraction is often the sole goal. Interactionism disowns the claim that there is one master reality which permits or encourages such judgment. It is only when the sociologist aligns his work with an independent and suprapersonal reality that consciousness may be true or false, perceptions 'reality-based' or 'unrealistic', desires genuine or sublimating, accounts rationalising or authentic. The interactionism that was grounded in formalism and pragmatism would reject all such dualities, and it eschews their accompanying ideas. The interactionism wedded to Schutz, but not to Scheler or Husserl, would do likewise. It has thus come about that selves are generally taken to be situationally adequate and comparable for all the purposes that can be envisaged by the interactionist. Symbolic interactionism dwells on the ritual play of forms and, as Goffman observes, the person who enters analysis 'must have within him something of the balance of characteristics required of a usable participant in any ritually organised system of social activity'.[84]

6 Participant Observation

Participant observation is perhaps the pivotal strategy of interactionism. It is a concrete demonstration of the pragmatist emphasis on practice. The methodology uses the self of the sociologist as a tool to explore social process. It directs the sociologist to place himself in the scenes which he wishes to analyse, requiring him to observe and participate at the same time. Its justification stems from the definition of knowledge as an ongoing practical activity; from the argument that sociologists cannot know by introspection or surmise; and from an injunction to respect the reality of appearances. Its pursuit generates paradox for any who choose to discuss it. It is made up of contradictory imperatives, conflicting postures and seemingly insuperable problems. Those paradoxes are largely resolved by the exaltation of practice and the discrediting of abstract methodological treatises. Dilemmas are held to be soluble *in situ*, a matter for management by the prereflexive mind. Like all normal science, anomalies and absurdities are overwhelmed by neglect. Participant observation mirrors other pragmatist processes because it turns to praxis and away from speculation.

Introduction

Participant observation is not an untrammelled technique which can be adapted to serve any of the dominant forms of sociology. It brings in its train a series of intellectual commitments which are uncongenial to much academic thinking. As a sociological device, it has become chiefly associated with the programme of symbolic interactionism. It has been used to put pragmatist epistemology to work, withdrawing the sociologist from a contemplative stance and encouraging him to engage in a special version of praxis. In effect it has become a condensation of the interactionist thesis, and one that is awarded little authority by the bulk of those working in the discipline. Some sociologists are prepared to allot it a minor place as a strategy which can pursue certain limited problems.[1] Others are occupied with conceptions of sociology which render fieldwork unmanageable or trivial. Sociology must be phrased in a particular way before it becomes receptive to the claims of participant observation.[2] It would thus be misleading to discuss the method without tracing its wider connotations.

Participant Observation and Sociological Methodology

The division of intellectual labour has produced a corresponding separation of technical and pictorial styles. American economics, sociology and social psychology are more than the focused reflections of an undifferentiated society: they furnish an economic America and a sociological America and an America of the psychologists. An academic discipline may, then, be understood as a series of landscaping possibilities which chart and fabricate analytic areas for purposes of investigation. Once established, its materials tend to reproduce themselves. The discipline organises its scientific objects out of a selected imagery, logic and metaphor. The organisation will then justify and elicit the intellectual forms which were first used to construct it. A mathematicising stance describes the world in a manner that can promote little but further mathematicisation. An analytic style which leans on literary rhetoric will create and discover phenomena that must be explored by extensions of the rhetoric. Distinct formal and substantive concerns thereby manufacture perspectives which fold back on the discipline to define form and substance, transmuting analytic worlds into somewhat isolated spheres. Intellectual work is stabilised by the seeming autonomy and facticity of its own constructions.

The social landscapes which disciplines prepare do not always complement one another. They are rarely compared or merged: sociologists do not commonly look to economics for much of their understanding about social life, and economists seem to disregard sociology. Indeed sociologists who draw from psychology and economics have been castigated for reductionism or vulgar 'economism'. There is also a range of graphic styles within each discipline and they too veer towards closure and self-sufficiency. Functionalists do not extract many themes from the writings of the sociological phenomenologists. The interactionists borrow little from mathematical sociology. Most theses would have to undergo appreciable redrafting and transcription before they could be exported from one sphere to another.

In a sense the distinctive methodologies of economics, sociology and social psychology are both arbitrary and necessary. They are arbitrary because there is little that is innate in their character which would make it mandatory to resort to any one methodology above all others. *A priori*, the advantages of particular schemes are not so self-evident that they commend themselves as superior to every rival. But some unifying order must be imposed on an otherwise incoherent field so that work can proceed. The contours and contents of the discipline's world demand definition; there must be some elucidation of the methodologist's problems, purposes and position; it is necessary to suggest appropriate ways of moving in that world; and the apparent consequences of such manoeuvring require interpretation. Intellectual coherence, exchange and collaboration hinge on the acceptance of the common methods which foster recognition of common phenomena. Methodologies impose order, but there are many possible methodologies and many types of order. When commitment has been made to a scheme, however, the claims of competitors will be systematically invalidated. Intellectual technologies establish criteria of relevance, plausibility and demonstration which discredit pretenders to dominance. They thereby dispel the confusion wrought by unsettled disputes and limitless choice.

There is often some superficial affinity between a methodology and its object. When Adam Smith ceased observing the workings of a pin factory, few economists undertook detailed ethnographies of the worlds of production, distribution and exchange. Instead they became increasingly engaged in mathematical and statistical simulations of economic process. In part, economics has tended to be numerate because a monetary and productive system lends itself to quantitative manipulation. Yet numeracy does not exhaust the intellectual possibilities of the field and much has been neglected. By contrast, social anthropology adopted fieldwork and participant observation as its central strategy. Alien worlds encourage slow and tentative reconstruction because there can be no sure transposition from the familiar to what may be wholly unfamiliar. The anthropologist often maps previously unexplored societies. He may have intelligent anticipations about their composition, but he is rarely entitled to proceed with abstract or firmly structured schemes which might conceal their distinctive features.

Sociology has sporadically flirted with participant observation, yet the thrust for such work has usually come from positions on or without the frontiers of the discipline. Occasionally, intellectual outsiders have produced studies which have been absorbed by sociology.[3] Participant observation has typically dominated community studies, for instance.[4] Within sociology itself, symbolic interactionism has resorted extensively to fieldwork. But interactionism is a peripheral segment of sociology, and participant observation has not received general emphasis as a pivotal methodology.[5]

The fieldwork strategy generates and flows from a special conception of sociology and society. It rests upon a peculiar interpretation of the world which is resisted by all but a narrow span of the discipline's styles. The epistemological and ontological connotations of the strategy jar markedly with the principal axioms of much sociology. In the main, sociology is wedded to versions of truth and understanding which render ethnography unnecessary: it denies that scholarly knowledge is uncertain, that embedded meanings are analytically important, that small social scenes house sufficient materials for adequate explanation, that phenomenal appearances are *sui generis*, or that reason and natural science are inappropriate interpretative media.

The devaluation of fieldwork has been accelerated by the development of 'methodology' as a virtually autonomous sub-discipline of sociology. In America and elsewhere there has been a tendency for 'theory' and its history to have become strangely divorced from the organisation of sociological methods. They have been transformed into distinct enterprises within the university, taught and pursued by different groups of sociologists who are somewhat wary of one another.[6] What passes for sociological technique has been appropriated by a separate faction within the profession. That faction has imposed its own conception of authoritative order and reasoning on teaching and on many pieces of research. It is a conception which withdraws legitimacy from the interactionist conduct of fieldwork. Methodologists have ostensibly eschewed metaphysics, promoting instead a deracinated intellectual technology. They cannot readily assimilate participant observation because it is so entangled with interactionism's idiosyncratic versions of the sociology and philosophy of knowledge. Fieldwork cannot lend support to the tacit assumption that ontology and method are separable. Accordingly it is not an appropriate subject for fragmentation and dissection within an increasing division of academic labour. No discussion of fieldwork can be confined to the neat boundaries which are appearing about sociology's sub-disciplines. Questions are posed and uncertainties retained which translate ethnography into more than a set of instructions for 'methods' alone. Thus Douglas, who espouses ethnography, claims that 'methodology' 'has largely separated "research methods" from the basic questions of epistemology, of truth . . . [It] has separated research methods very largely from the general nature of the social world, from the concrete subjects of study, and from the personal experience of the persons writing about research methods.'[7]

The methodologists' search for parsimony, lucidity and precision has impelled them to define themes within interactionism as obfuscating and unscientific. The core assumptions of interactionism and 'methodology' are frequently in contradiction. The interactionists assert that methodologists have replaced the proper concerns of sociology by a tyranny of mechanical operations which flow from uninspected definitions of man, society and knowledge. Blumer, for example, argues 'instead of going to the empirical social world in the first and last instances, resort is made instead to a priori theoretical schemes, to sets of unverified concepts, and to canonized protocols of research procedure.'[8] In their turn the methodologists maintain that such practices as fieldwork are loose, inconclusive and scientifically primitive. Borgatta states, 'possibly this era is passing, but there is still a visible presence of and insistence on procedures that seem to state that the "real" data of sociology are those that are either directly experienced as insights from the contact with the natives or are the analysis of the myriad unmeasured variables in a complex and underdetermined system.'[9] 'Methodologists' and 'theorists' are growing apart, working with different analytic languages and different visions of the sociological terrain. The former veer towards a concern with the determinate, the causal, the numerate, the specifiable and the discrete. They have borrowed liberally from other disciplines whose contents are not those of sociology.[10] Their work is beginning to represent an independent realm of reasoning about thought and its possibilities.[11] By contrast the interactionists not only subscribe to a radically different understanding of sociology, but they also stress that the activity of research is itself a proper object of sociological enquiry. Research is not taken to be a disembodied agent of pure logic, but a social encounter.

More importantly, participant observation is not a process which can be transmuted into the materials of teaching and formal discourse.

An emanation of pragmatism, it defies exact explication. Indeed its ineffability is its prime justification: the interactionists would argue that fieldwork becomes unnecessary if tactics for grasping the world could be expounded. Participant observation centres on an interpretation of knowledge as praxis, not as an analytic *a priori*. Sociological understanding cannot be acquired by means of explicit programmes and directives: it is an emergent quality of being in the world. Interactionists tend to claim that the construction of a sociological explanation cannot be reduced to *a priori* ratiocination. By doubting the validity of logico-deductive work, they would question the assumption that methodology can be distilled into formulae or recipes. Indeed the use of such formulae mars work by prematurely warping its product. Humphreys, for example, argued 'hypotheses should develop *out of* . . . ethnographic work, rather than provide restrictions and distortions from its inception.'[12] Similarly Becker states that fieldworkers 'assume they do not know enough about [an area] *a priori* to identify relevant problems and hypotheses and that they must discover these in the course of the research.'[13] Polsky flatly observes that any methodological preparation is a handicap: 'the problem for many a sociologist today – the result of curricula containing as much scientism as science – is that [human] capacities, far from being trained in him, have been trained out of him.'[14] The salient concerns of the sociological methodologists are thus dismissed as epistemologically naïve. If understanding flows from an ongoing exploration of society, it cannot be engendered by fixed schemes and carefully manufactured hypotheses. There is little to discuss in the seminar or the research briefing or the manual.

For the interactionist, too, authentic knowledge is not furnished by scientific method but by immediate experience. Immediacy so alters understanding that it cannot be translated into a communicable system of analysis. Symbolic interactionism is at the very margins of science: its methods and interpretations are barely intelligible to the uninitiated. The content of the sociology is most appropriately conveyed by imitating the actions of its adherents, not by reading or discussing their works. Thus Znaniecki remarked, 'when I wish to obtain first-hand information about a certain object, I try to experience it. There is only one way of experiencing an activity; it is to perform it personally.'[15] Knowledge inheres in doing or being, it is a quality of the knowing-known transaction. Any programmatic methodology is a pallid and corrupting substitute for the truth derived from a return to the natural phenomena of the social world.

Indeed some sociologists who have aligned themselves with interactionism have felt constrained to apologise for the abstractions which compose part of their analyses. Goffman stated for example that his essay on frame analysis 'is too bookish, too general, too removed from fieldwork to have a good chance of being anything more than another mentalistic adumbration'.[16]

Thus conceived, participant observation affords the interactionist his sole method of grasping social reality. It is a valid phase of that reality itself. It is pursued because it has significance as a way of being *in* truth. But such a state is also pursued because any other appropriation of the truth is false, including schematic descriptions of the state itself. Authenticity is betrayed when it is made the object of a methodological agenda. Hence Bruyn referred to the purest stage of participant observation as the mobilisation of intuition: the participant observer 'assumes that there exists in human feelings, a capacity to reveal knowledge which is independent [of] (as well as interdependent with) the rational-empirical sources of knowledge'.[17] He denied the legitimacy of conceptual operationalisation, claiming that it deforms phenomena.[18] Similarly Dalton maintained that his research was ordered by an understanding which could not be made explicit or analysable: 'possibly from our wish to say all and the inability to do so with a definition of science that excludes such stopgap terms as "insight" or "intuition", we are led to elaborate on the need of being explicit. . . . Our pluperfect definition of science prevents us . . . from falling back on resource words suggestive of the method of art to fill in our demonstrations.'[19] In short, the existential yield of participant observation is an unscriptable[20] access to truth, its cost is the ineffability of understanding. Interactionists undertake fieldwork, in part, because they conceive it to be a vehicle for entering reality; in part, because no abstract exposition can ever replace it.

In turn, fieldwork cannot become a topic for extensive teaching and examination. Those who are sympathetic towards it are unable to relay it fully. Those who are antipathetic are awarded few materials or themes for purposes of discussion. Participant observation has not become a subject for dissemination by methodologists. Instead they turn to tactics and procedures which are open to lucid and detailed argument. The methods which reveal an affinity with axiomatic logic, mathematics or statistics are available to such argument. Methodology must, after all, be an activity which men can talk about. What passes for sociological technology is then preponderantly systematic, communicable and logical. Consider the contents of a special issue of one journal which was turned over to 'Continuities in Methodological Research': 'Forming Composite Scales and Estimating their Validity through Factor Analysis'; 'The Duality of Persons and Groups'; 'Testing Theoretical Hypotheses: A *Pre* Statistic'; 'On Interpreting Ordinal Analogies to Multiple Regression and Path Analysis'; 'Analysis of Partial Rank Correlation Measures based on the Product-Moment Model'; 'Continuities in Ordinal Path Analysis' and 'The Use of Ordinal Statistics in Causal Analysis of Correlations'.[21] An inspection of a series of volumes on sociological methodology, officially sponsored by the American Sociological Association, reveals much the same conception of the nature of analytic technique.[22]

'Theoretical Sociology' and Participant Observation

A sociology need not be committed to the American construction of methodology before it discards the assumptions which support fieldwork. Most forms of the discipline are radically unsympathetic to observational strategies. Subjective Idealism, realism and historical materialism, for instance, grasp society principally by means of reason or intuition. Social appearances are read as little more than epiphenomenal deceits which fetter the unschooled mind. Analytic meaning fully resides in deep structures which must be reached by special techniques. Observations of surface phenomena cannot yield authentic understanding because science transcends such alienated and reified reflection. Sociologies embedded in Marxism, ethnomethodology, structuralism, psycho-analysis, demography and structural-functionalism methodically discount the phenomenal. When the surface is presented as a series of mirages or shadows, there can be no incentive to peruse it closely. Neither can it ever become problematic enough to prompt inspection: its seemingly contradictory and inexplicable eddies are of no intellectual consequence. Those who address them have merely halted their analytic work at an inappropriate level. Thus Adorno reproved Mannheim for becoming befuddled by the gratuitously perplexing world of individual 'facts':

> ... social reality has, prior to every theoretical ordering glance, a highly 'articulated' structure upon which the scientific subject and the data of his experience depend. ... The social scientist's experience does not give him undifferentiated, chaotic material to

be organized; rather, the material of his experience is the social order, more emphatically a 'system' than any ever conceived by philosophy. What decides whether his concepts are right or wrong is neither their generality nor, on the other hand, their approximation to 'pure' fact, but rather the adequacy with which they grasp the real laws of movement of society and thereby render stubborn facts transparent.[23]

The sociologist is thus aligned with his objects in a context of preexisting and obdurate reality. Unlike the pragmatist, Adorno's social scientist discovers truth and does not produce it. Discovery, moreover, deploys techniques which are epistemologically prior to any universe of facts: reality must first be mapped out before 'facts' can be properly appreciated. So conceived, fieldwork can never generate the material of sociology. The facts which it unearths are without significance until they are lodged within a scheme that can be articulated independently of them. Participant observation attends primarily to a visible world which is radically devalued in all schemes that stress the stratified nature of social reality. It can flourish only when interaction is defined as an order which is *sui generis*, not simply as the vehicle for the manifestation of the sovereign and deep structures of society. Symbolic interactionists confront that order as an autonomous language of forms which cannot be reduced down to more fundamental elements. Having discarded philosophical dualism, they pursue a phenomenalism which maintains that the observable *is* the ongoing reality of the sociological object. By extension, the observable must be the prime resort of the sociologist himself. That which can be seen and heard does not simply mediate or stand for other, intangible truths: it has its own facticity and organising power. Thus Blumer argued that much sociology interprets social interaction:

> merely as the arena in which . . . determining factors work themselves out into human action. These approaches grossly ignore the fact that social interaction is a formative process in its own right – that people in interaction are not merely giving expression to such determining factors . . . but are directing, checking, bending, and transforming their lines of action in the light of what they encounter in the actions of others.[24]

Interactionism stems from that narrow band of sociologies which cannot translate the immediate into an array of indices, trends, epiphenomena or instances of a more profound social order. It may have some occasional dealings with the ideas of latent function or social stratification, but they engender the possibility of strain and inconsistency in the scheme. Interactionism espouses participant observation because it is based on an epistemology that describes immediate experience as an irreducible reality.

In turn, an advocacy of observational techniques is likely to flow out of a restrained Idealism. There has been fieldwork void of all Idealism,[25] but the very idea of participation conjures up the methodological authority of communion with truth, a state of being which is radically Idealist. Florence Kluckhohn's description of the strategy appears to have become accepted as the standard definition for American sociology. She stated that participant observation is the 'conscious and systematic sharing, in so far as circumstances permit, in the life activities, and on occasion, in the interests and affects of a group of persons.'[26] Strains within symbolic interactionism have extended that definition to refer to a virtual communion between the sociologist and his objects. By inserting himself into the reality of social life, the sociologist can transmute himself into the identical subject-object. Thus Bruyn argued 'the aim of the participant observer is to take part in the socialization process just as the other participants do, to the point where his own inner experience can reflect the unity and structure of the whole.'[27] Similarly, Schwartz and Merten claim, 'in participant observation, the ordinary distinction between the social scientist's status as the "knower" and his informant's status as the "known" . . . usually dissolves partially . . .'[28] Not all interactionists would wholly subscribe to Bruyn's adaptation of Cooley's Idealism, but they are necessarily implicated in an epistemology which recommends some union of the sociologist with the symbolic reality of the observed world.

The opponents of Idealism would discard that union as immaterial or illusory. The analytically significant currents of social life are independent of men's imagination of society. Consciousness represents a specious and distracting realm which cannot bear on the explanation of social dynamics. At most, it simply consists of lay understandings, rationalisations, myths, false consciousness, manifest functions and sublimations. The scientist systematically supersedes such superficial reasoning. Hence Marx, although anything but unequivocal about the relations between consciousness and social reality, could assert in *The German Ideology*, 'life is not determined by consciousness, but consciousness by life', and 'the phantoms formed in the human brain are . . . sublimates of material life processes'. Again, in the *Critique of Political Economy*, he argued 'just as our opinion of an individual is not based on what he thinks of himself, so we cannot judge of . . . a period of transformation by its own consciousness, this consciousness must rather be explained from the contradictions of material life.'

If the sociologist 'surrenders' to the ongoing reality of his subjects,[29] the antagonist of Idealism would contend that he has merely surrendered his critical capacity, his objectivity and his scientific stance. The participant observer is then cast as a participant in alienated consciousness, epiphenomenal ideology and mystification. The functionalist who severs manifest from latent function, the psycho-analyst who distinguishes the thought of projection and transference from ideas governed by the reality-principle, and the demographer who prises objective trends from subjective accounts are all committed to their own analogues of Marx's false consciousness. That consciousness is an unprofitable field of study unless it is expressly denied authenticity.

Unchecked Idealists themselves, however, are under no methodological compulsion to undertake participant observation. They are offered such direct access to truth that they cannot and need not manage any facet of the world as strange or alien. The identification of an area of reality as external suggests merely that the analyst has not yet transcended contradiction. Proper understanding reveals the entire topography of ideas as an immediately intelligible field. Blocks to interpretation stem from faulty reasoning, not from deficiencies of technique which must be remedied by direct inspection of the lifeworld of others. The sociologist is a phase of truth himself: he has only to redefine and inspect his own consciousness to have and be truth. Hegel was the principal architect of most sociological Idealism. He argued:

> . . . consciousness is, on the one hand, consciousness of the object, on the other, consciousness of itself; consciousness of what to it is true, and consciousness of its knowledge of that truth. Since both are for the same consciousness, it is itself their comparison; it is the same consciousness that decides and knows whether its knowledge of the object corresponds with this object or not.[30]

An unproblematic communion with truth does not propel the

sociologist out into the work of observation. That work may be performed in a less adulterated fashion by disciplined introspection, by phenomenological reduction, or by a searching for essences. It requires no commerce with mundane events. Indeed that commerce might simply introduce muddle and obscurity into the process of search. When contemplation can wrest meaning from life, the Idealist may find everyday occurrences inferior points of access to the broad themes which infuse culture and history. Thus the early Lukács and Goldmann turned to the literature and art of critical periods for understanding. Art was held to offer an immediate appreciation of the *Zeitgeist*.

Reality can contradict the phenomena in which it becomes manifest. Appearance and essence need not coincide. Any preoccupation with appearance can estrange thought from the truth which it seeks. In particular, when reality is conceived as a monad, a totality, analysis tends to disfigure as well as alienate truth. Lukács for example dismissed all empiricism as an ontology which explodes reality: 'its own concrete underlying reality, lies, methodologically and in principle, beyond its grasp'. The inner structures of the world must be divined by reason and trained intuition. Participant observation is then again construed as an alienated activity which explores alienated reality. As Lichtheim argued, 'in asserting the possibility of privileged insight into the logic of history, Lukács by implication affirmed that philosophical conclusions were independent of the findings available to empirical sociologists, economists or political theorists.'[31] Unalloyed Idealism thus renders the observational strategy inconsequential.

Some adherents of participant observation have championed an epistemology which verges on such Idealism. They have presented the method as a vehicle for entering the cultural reality of a world.[32] It is only their sometimes vestigial retention of themes from pragmatism and formalism that supports their commitment to observation. Those themes defined appearance as real enough in itself, as an immediate phrasing of 'truth'. The innumerable scenes which compose society must be regarded as faces of reality which cannot be ignored. Phenomenalism is a vital constituent of most fieldwork.

A claim that phenomena are ontologically authentic cannot alone ward off a move towards speculative Idealism. There must be an express denial of the authority of analytic *a priori* reasoning. Phenomena must not only be real, they must be the *sole* reality for all explanatory purposes. They are not ordered by essences which await the sociologist's embrace. The sociologist can never utterly participate because there is no totality or noumenon to absorb him. The assertion of essence is necessarily accompanied by the implication that an observer might bypass phenomena and proceed directly to truth. Only when appearance is all will observation become obligatory. Committed to observation, symbolic interactionism is a research tradition. Its adherents tend to regard other postures as various examples of contemplative philosophy. As Becker remarked:

> I really don't think of many of the positions you describe as co-ordinate with symbolic interactionism as being sociology at all, but rather as a sort of philosophizing . . . on the ground . . . that they rely on some sort of supra-human revealed truth and thus do not really need research at all. In contrast, symbolic interactionism is largely a *research* tradition, the main materials consist not of theoretical expositions but of reports of research . . . In fact, to be provocative, I'll put the point more strongly: symbolic interactionism is the only one of the positions you mention (I'll except the Mertonian version of structural-functionalism) that is an empirical science at all. It's just some sort of academic accident that many of those people end up in sociology departments, not a result of some deep logical connection between the questions they concern themselves with and the ones that I, for instance, or Hughes . . . concern ourselves with.[33]

It is this denial of supra-human revelation that sustains research. In turn, appearances must be simultaneously intelligible and irrevocably alien. No sustained exercise of intuition or reason can ever completely reduce their externality. The participant observer must always observe. He is condemned to marginality, barred from total immersion in his object. Thus Vidich argued, 'his own experiences, though genuine, are at best vicarious approximations of those of his respondents; he never completely enters their world . . .'[34] In a sense, too, the respondents themselves are not completely masters of their own world. It must be uncertain and problematic to them, unfolding as their transactions proceed. It lacks total transparency. Interactionism is subservient to an imagery of men being at once inside and outside all symbolic domains.
the empirical world is an important but fragile stage in the case for an symbols which have some indeterminate independence. The intuitive yield of participation must be transformed into a language which

destroys its status as a direct statement of reality. Any introspection, reflection or retrospection alienates the participant from his experience. In particular, other minds can never be reflexively available to the observer in the manner afforded by intuitive communion: they must be translated into a set of descriptive forms which are relatively inauthentic. If, as Cooley had maintained, the human mind is a privileged spectator because it is itself a phase of its objects, it is nevertheless unable to report its comprehension without analytic molestation. The truths flowing from participation can never be an unmediated revelation. When those truths are made serviceable to sociology, an even greater distance is achieved between subject and object.

The fundamental pathos of pragmatist epistemology is therefore preserved in the buttressing assumptions of participant observation. Man is taken to be part of nature, and his knowledge is not unnatural. Yet intellectual work undoes the processes by which truth is grasped. Analytic understanding wrenches apart the organic unity of experience. Thus much play is made with the terminology of nature when participant observation is discussed. That language suggests more than the unrehearsed and spontaneous, it signifies an unfeigned authenticity. Reiss, for instance, writes of 'natural social phenomena'.[35] Douglas, too, argues 'direct observation of things in their natural state (in the natural unscientified situation) is the ultimate basis of most thought.'[36] Similarly, Schwarz and Schwarz offer a definition which smacks of a radical Idealism. They claim, 'the observer is in a face-to-face relationship with the observed, and, by participating with them in their natural life setting, he gathers data. Thus, the observer is part of the context being observed . . .'[37] The contention that the observer 'is part' of the natural setting is redolent of the search for the identical subject-object of Hegel and the pragmatists. Indeed that union is apparently accomplished: 'in the course of an investigation the observer and observed become important to each other, and it is the background of their past experiences together, merging with and reflecting itself in a present situation, which determines the nature of their reciprocity.'[38] Observer and observed can become a fused totality, a symbolic whole, which guarantees the emergent sociology of the observer. Yet any sociological product is also depicted as contrived and artificial, a construction which is both more and less than the lived experience of the encounter itself: 'participant observation becomes, in part, *a process of registering, interpreting, and recording*'.[39] As a style of understanding, it is more substantial than ephemeral experience, but it is also qualitatively different from that experience. The setting becomes alien. If that claim were not made, observation would become redundant. Paradoxically, the epistemological vulnerability of participant observation makes the method imperative. The estranged quality of formal knowledge renders it inaccessible to reason alone. The analyst cannot submit to a comprehensive Idealism because his objects will always remain somewhat alien. Reality and reason are not isomorphic. As Blumer argued:

> The traditional position of Idealism is that the 'world of reality' exists only in human experience and that it appears only in the form in which human beings 'see' that world. I think that this position is incontestable . . . However, this does not shift 'reality', as so many conclude, from the empirical world to the realm of imagery and conception. . . . Such a solipsistic position is untenable and would make empirical science impossible. The position is untenable because of the fact that the empirical world can 'talk back' to our pictures of it or assertions about it — talk back in the sense of challenging and resisting, or not bending to, our images or conceptions of it.[40]

The underlying assumptions of participant observation are therefore frail and sociologically unorthodox. They revolve around a seemingly unsullied phenomenalism coupled with a claim of phenomenological possibilities; an assertion of the obduracy and indissoluble reality of appearances married to a limited Idealism. Any further drift into positivism would generate the neo-behaviourism of the 'Iowa School' of interactionism,[41] a neo-behaviourism which shuns the vagueness and unscientific properties of phenomenological work. A drift into a more pronounced Idealism would critically depress the value of observational strategies.[42] Interactionism is then involved in a delicate balancing of epistemological styles. A focused analytic assault on the problems which they raise might endanger the entire enterprise.

For instance, Blumer's insistence on the ontological autonomy of the empirical world is an important but fragile stage in the case for an interactionist methodology. It is based on some insensitivity to the manner in which symbolically-mediated anomalies can do damage to a symbolic system. Their very representation in symbolic form emasculates their capacity to threaten a symbolic scheme.[43] They are necessarily couched in a language which disarms them. As Berger states, 'the meta-empirical cannot be conceived of as a kind of enclave within the empirical world.'[44] There have indeed been severe cases of symbolic erosion,[45] but they do not perhaps constitute so much a crisis for Idealism as for the peculiar forms which ideas assumed at a particular time. Similarly, the vital but mute denial of essence and absolutes in interactionist thought makes any analysis of generalities, process or structure a most difficult enterprise. The discovery of an order that lies 'behind' or 'beneath' appearances would seem to be proscribed. Such discovery is nevertheless the chief pursuit of all sociology, dominating the character of interactionism itself. Analysis may be defended as metaphor or useful contrivance,[46] but it enjoys an ambiguous existence in the interactionist scheme.

It is apparent that participant observation rests on rather unusual foundations. Some sociologists dismiss it as positivist,[47] others as unscientific and subjectivist.[48] Indeed, Reynolds and Meltzer claim that interactionists themselves do not universally subscribe to the method.[49] Yet fieldwork flows quite coherently out of my fabricated version of interactionism. It forms a necessary extension of the sociology as I have reconstructed it, permitting the sociologist to proceed into the social world. The very indeterminacy which encourages diversity within interactionist methodology is the base of participant observation.

Symbolic Interactionism and Fieldwork

Participant observation emerged directly out of the central concerns of symbolic interactionism. It transforms the sociology into a particular kind of praxis, refracting and condensing the special vision of knowledge which was prepared by the formalist and the pragmatist. There are no 'data' in that vision. Materials do not simply await discovery by the social scientist. Instead, facts are principally produced in the symbolic work of social encounters. They are not 'given' but created. As Lafferty argued, 'objects are social achievements.'[50] In this sense any sociological practice is itself creative. Methodology neither mirrors nor mines reality, it works towards its manufacture. The rejection of metaphysical dualism moved many of the interactionists into a changed relationship with the social world. Doing active research, they build up the very objects which they study. If they abstain from such activity, they are left without a tenable grasp on what they discuss.

Research reveals phenomena which are shaped by the social forms. It must establish what those forms are and how their logic operates. The structures of everyday meaning are held to represent the only reality which a sociologist can describe. They are 'central in their own right',[51] organising the selves, processes and institutions which people confront. But they are also properties of nature. Compared with them, all other kinds of knowledge are ultimately metaphysical and vacuous. They are fused with biological and physical processes, alone constituting a sure social realm.

So defined, social forms exact a special deference and a special practice. They can be charted neither by the application of reason nor by sets of organised hypotheses. The pragmatist cannot but immerse himself in social life and permit meaning to emerge out of his transactions with an object. Blumer stated, 'inspection is not preset, routinized or prescribed; it only becomes such when we know what [an object] is and thus can resort to a specific test . . . inspection is flexible, imaginative, creative, and free to take new directions.'[52] It is the penalty of abstract knowledge that it poses a specious alternative to understanding derived from direct experience. The interactionists tend to believe that such knowledge enforces separations, establishes boundaries and blocks useful access to phenomena. By contrast, direct experience yields authentic interpretation, and it is produced by attaining some semblance of identity between subject and object. As the knowing-known transaction proceeds, so the participant-observer is expected to merge with his materials and return to a nature where thought is not alien or speculative. Praxis, emergence and union therefore represent the chief components of fieldwork.

No science or philosophy can rely solely on a celebration of immediate knowledge. The pragmatist strand within interactionism recommends a subtle oscillation between the immediate and the mediated. According to Dewey, mediated knowledge becomes:

> knowledge in the complete sense of the word only when the indication or signifying is borne out, verified in something directly present, or immediately *experienced* – not immediately known. The object has to be 'reached' eventually in order to get verification or invalidation, and when so reached, it is immediately present. Its cognitive status, however, is *mediated* . . .[53]

Prepredicative experience is defined as a final reality to which all speculation must return. It constitutes the social world before it has been alienated, warped and ruptured by analytic thought. Grounded in nature and emerging in evolution, such experience provides an assurance that the problems of philosophical dualism are soluble. It cannot stand alone, and sociology cannot refrain from transforming it, but it presents a solid foundation which must have only the lightest analytic superstructure built on it. The procedures of rational science, however, are taken to be a recent and unwarranted imposition on truth. They recast reality in their own image, conveying a meretricious impression of lucidity and precision. The sociologist who looks to immediate understanding will shed 'scientism'. He seeks to explain the common-sense world of his fellows in the language which most nearly approximates its forms. Rather than invoke the alien logic of science, he centres his descriptions around common sense: common sense becoming both problem and explanation. As Rose observes, the selection of problematic objects in interactionist methodology is performed 'on the level of common experience with them'.[54] One aim of ethnography is, then, the *reproduction* of 'natural' processes of reasoning. The sociologist need have few dealings with axiomatic logic in order to achieve that reproduction, and his practices may appear scientifically illogical. Fully extended, that conception of truth can lead to a veneration of everyday thought. It may be argued that such thought is the fount of wisdom, an ancient and tried reservoir of interpretations, which transcends any of the technical methods of sociology:

> The human mind has evolved over the eons in direct relation to the natural world in which we live. The ideas of truth we have about the world have grown out of all that concrete experience. Those ideas of truth work for man most of the time. Let us begin with these commonsense forms of truth and truth seeking and try to improve them, to build upon them rather than sweeping them aside and imposing some bright new asserted model.[55]

The assumptions of participant observation, then, stem from a complex and precarious reconciliation of Hegel, Kant and Darwin. Unfolding mind is taken to conspire with natural evolution to mould reality into a tested, emergent and intuitively comprehended whole. Man can understand himself by replicating the peculiar animating logic that has made him. Intuition, phenomenology and a jettisoning of conventional science underpin much of interactionist methodology.[56]

Yet it is the paradox of symbolic interactionism (and other, allied sociologies) that its own analytic activity is the principal barrier to successful interpretation. Sociology both specifies the answers to epistemological issues and denies their usefulness. A creative interplay may develop between analytic and immediate knowledge, but sociology must necessarily estrange and falsify itself. An appraising observer destroys true understanding by fracturing the unity of object and subject. He stands apart from his object, condemning himself to a foreign appreciation of the inner life of society. As sociologist, the observer is an external and excluded monitor whose knowledge is not guaranteed by nature. He may not be irrevocably exiled from the world of natural social phenomena, but he can return only by discarding the trappings of the analyst. As a member of the natural social order, he cannot transcribe his experience without loss and violation. In their confrontation with a common problem, the orthodox and the phenomenological interactionists are thus joined. The classical interactionist can trace his mandate back to Dewey and Mead. Neither of those pragmatists denied the existence of immediate experience: indeed, their epistemology was principally organised around it. Such experience however should not be confused with consciousnes and could never become usefully available to consciousness. By contrast, the phenomenological interactionists have retained some major commitment to phenomenalism and a rejection of rationalism. No phenomenological sociologist need undertake ethnography unless he refuses to accept all the implications of the Eidetic reduction. His very involvement in participant observation underscores his doubts about the transparency or givenness of immediate experience. In that sense he remains an interactionist, albeit marginally so.

Fieldworkers have delineated a spectrum of possible role for the ethnographer: they range from 'complete participant' to 'complete observer'.[57] Not all would advocate the heuristic utility of complete participation, neither would they subscribe to a committed Idealism. Phenomenalism is a prerequisite of any ethnography. Yet there is a persistent series of references to the problem of 'going native', of becoming so immersed in the immediate and the natural that reflection is obstructed.[58] Thus Gold claims the fieldworker 'may "go native" . . . achieve self-expression in the role but find that he has so violated his observer role that he is almost unable to report his findings.'[59] 'Going native' at once underwrites interpretations and imprisons them. The sociologist becomes his object but, ceasing to be a practising sociologist, confronts the impossibility of faithful reporting. Methodological artifice prevents full identification with a social world.

Characteristically, then, the process of participant observation is taken by many ethnographers to be almost indescribable. Like other facets of interactionism, it drifts into the inexplicable and the anti-rational. That process is a phase of lived experience which cannot be summarised or publicised without radical distortion. Even a modest degree of analytic interpretation is disruptive of the intimacy of the knowing-known transaction. If formal argument does emerge, it typically wells up from the realm of inarticulate and unselfconscious existence. Dalton, for instance, recalled that his research underwent systematic shifts of emphasis, but 'to include all . . . changes of outlook and to report them as explicit hypotheses formulated, tested, and dropped when the process never attained such clarity seemed to me false and pedantic and, even if true, as entries that might be thought to encumber more than they would enlighten the report.'[60]

Three stages of interactionist methodology are consequently closed to detailed scrutiny: the articulation of expectations in advance of research; the minute features of working in the field itself; and the invention and development of analytic ideas. Although fieldwork *is* organised, and its structural forms have been examined, the existential contents of the process are as ineffable as all other contents. Yet it is those contents which are held to constitute the fundamental source and validation of ideas. As Douglas states, 'we begin with direct experience and all else builds on that, whether we know it and recognize it or deny it.'[61] What is laid open to discussion is no more than a phenomenologically denuded shell. The fragile amalgam of phenomenalism and Idealism permits neither full confidence in subjective appreciation nor an abandonment of the quest for intuitive understanding.

The business of ethnography is presented as comparatively hostile to rehearsal. Much of it is described as if it entailed the artless projection of the sociologist's self into the natural setting. Such artlessness is both the prerequisite and the unavoidable companion of effective communion. No amount of laboured understudying can ever guarantee the authenticity of the sociologist's dramatic performance. Some preparation may be undertaken, but the success or failure of a piece of fieldwork cannot be rigorously programmed.[62] Even overt, undisguised participant observation encounters transactional complications which can be solved only by the native competence of the sociologist. Interactionist fieldwork is designed to capture and foster prepredicative experience. It is axiomatic of the methodology that such experience can never be adequately described by words: it occupies realms which are *sui generis*. Full comprehension can stem only from engaging in the experience itself. Were that not so, participation would become unnecessary and effective analysis could be based on the exercise of observation and reason alone. It follows that the ethnographer's presentation of self must be grounded in a prepredicative appreciation of a setting's ground rules. Conscious simulation of those rules is likely to appear false and jarring; and an over-zealous remodelling of self has caused embarrassment and awkwardness in some instances of fieldwork.[63] William Foote Whyte, for example, modified his clothing and speech when entering Cornerville, but he was reproved for attempting to adopt its local slang: 'you're not supposed to talk like that. That doesn't sound like you.'[64]

Moreover, to the extent that the sociologist brings scripts into play or consciously engineers his performance, he will become detached from the flow which makes behaviour unobtrusive and plausible. Some limited dressing and tailoring of the self may take place. On occasion, quite elaborate cosmetic preparations have been employed to ease entry. One group indeed resorted to plastic surgery and dramatic coaching.[65] But it seems that the core of fieldwork must be sheer 'naturalness', an experience of being in the world which is not contradicted by obvious contrivance. Thus Erikson observed of the group that had made use of plastic surgery:

> Perhaps the most important responsibility of any sociologist is to appreciate how little he really knows about his intricate and elusive subject-matter. We have at best a poor understanding of the human mind, of the communication signals that link one mind to another, or the social structures that emerge from those linkages — and it is the most arrant kind of over-simplification for us to think that we can assess the effect which a clever costume or a few studied gestures have on the social setting.[66]

Artlessness is also inevitable because the ethnographer lacks the command to be accomplished. The underlying claim for fieldwork strategies is that they are the necessary product of a discipline which is dominated by mere knowledge about its objects. Such knowledge can be transformed into knowledge of intimacy only by conducting a detailed and responsive exploration of a problem. It is incapable of providing the procedural guidance which the fieldworker requires as he prepares to move into a setting. Perversely, too, an excessive reliance on procedural instructions would vitiate ethnography. The demand that knowledge be an emergent property of enquiry cannot be met if the research firmly prestructures what may be known. Participant observation must rest on an overt recognition of initial incompetence. The process of acquiring competence is itself the end of research. If the observer knew enough to dissemble or behave inconspicuously, his mastery of the forms in a problematic situation would be sufficient to dispel the urgency of the entire ethnographic enterprise. Fieldwork is demanded precisely when the sociologist is least equipped to perform it.

Of course, the ethnographer is armed with very general understandings about how to relate to others. There are few groups whose ground rules are so esoteric that they may not be approached by the person who employs the anonymous etiquette of public life. It is however doubtful that such diffuse guidance offers the ethnographer an opportunity to move beyond civil interaction into the intimate acquaintance demanded by participant observation. Typically, the worlds mapped by the observer are strange enough to require substantially more than such general understandings. If the research is to be successfully carried beyond a stage of simple acquaintance, those understandings will fail. As Weinberg and Williams argue, there is 'an unstructured situation: the subjects generally have no clear rules for interacting with the researcher, and the researcher has no specific rules for guiding interaction with his subjects, as methodology texts do not discuss the specific problems that he confronts.'[67] They suggest that ethnography characteristically evolves in a dialectic between the sociological subject and his objects, an evolution which is founded on opening stages in which the sociologist is serially viewed by his subjects as an interloper, novice and then probationer and by himself as salesman, stranger and initiate.[68]

Some sociologists have maintained that such incapacity may be usefully exploited. The fieldworker can become *faux naif*, presenting himself as an interested incompetent who needs toleration and remedial instruction.[69] Further, an unproblematic absorption by a group might precipitate the wrong form of artlessness, a state in which intelligent reflection is impossible. When an observer enters a role effortlessly, there may be no stimulation from the provocative awkwardness which can attend being marginal. Thus two observers of audience behaviour at an evangelistic crusade meeting were converted and ceased their observations.[70] Similarly, Reiss noticed that his study of the police was complicated by the ease with which sociologists could take the role of 'plainclothesman' accompanying detectives on patrol. His associates became detectives themselves.[71] As Vidich remarks:

> If the participant observer seeks genuine experiences, unqualifiedly immersing and committing himself in the group he is studying, it may become impossible for him to objectify his own experiences for research purposes . . . Anthropologists who have 'gone native' are cases in point; some of them stop publishing entirely.[72]

Ineptness is, then, a palpable and perhaps necessary feature of the methodology. The Idealist and phenomenalist strands of interactionism clash in their advocacy of irreconcilable imperatives. Not all participant observers expressly espouse Idealism, but their activity is inextricably enmeshed with its themes. The fieldworker is enjoined to unite with his objects but is offered little instruction and some assurance that such unity is unattainable. The varying strands of interactionism issue different perspectives on the problem. The strict phenomenalist would claim that the essence of a social world or culture cannot be grasped in research and that participation can entail little more than aping or miming the outward appearances of a phenomenon. The sociologist's self will never be more than a passable facsimile of the selves of people about him. An Idealist might counter that reproduction is available to any of the fellow inhabitants of a symbolic universe; that the sociologist is himself a part of culture. But there is evident contradiction in the interactionist scheme. The dissolution of barriers between subject and object must always be problematic.

Fusion is partially obstructed by the marginality and duplicity of the ethnographer. Marginality is imposed because the participant observer makes use of scenes in ways that are foreign to most people in everyday life. Revealed or concealed, his observations are based on a pretence of intimacy which is necessarily somewhat calculated and meretricious. He cannot engage in ongoing activity in a naïve fashion because he is continuously transforming it into a problematic object and a resource for explaining itself. His display of self is irremediably alienated from his experience. He must point to and survey his sensations instead of simply living them. Thus, however appealing a group may be, his relationship is appraising and distant. As Manning argues: 'the scientist in general . . . plays a stranger-role because he suspends his usual system of personal relevances as well as suspending the personal relevances of those he observes . . . The stranger can be objective. Objective rationality is rare in social life and therefore suspect.'[73] Sociological and lay styles of reasoning diverge in significant ways. Acting as sociologist, the observer then brings an alien rationality to bear which produces understanding and misunderstanding, intimacy and distance.

Social materials acquire a changed significance in ethnography. Friendship can become transformed into capital, personal revelation into data, and conflict into illumination. Indeed, Becker would cultivate the forms of civility in an effort to:

> coerce many interviewees into being considerably more frank than they had originally intended. I was quite aggressive, often expressing open disbelief in the face of statements that seemed evasive, implausible, or inconsistent with what had already been said . . . It is certain that such tactics, used in just this way, would not work with all kinds of people. Some of the success attained with schoolteachers must be attributed to the professional politeness and courtesy they felt obliged to extend to me.[74]

Marginality then flows from the predatory character of fieldwork. The sociologist takes on the trapping of amiability and interest in order to tap interaction for its analytic yield. Whether his research role is disguised or undisguised, he makes use of conventional appearances for unconventional ends. Those ends, moreover, may never have been sought or anticipated by his subjects. His actions and front will seem to reproduce those of people around him, but he cannot fully embrace them as his own. There is an underlying disengagement which makes his visible preoccupations hollow. The business of participant observation has been defined by Gans as 'the taking of a formal participatory role in a social situation without the emotional involvement that normally accompanies participation . . .'[75]

If disengagement falters and appearances become real enough to seduce the ethnographer, there is a betrayal of the purposes of his research. Thus Miller has warned of the interference that may arise from the assumption of commitments to one sector of a studied population.[76] Parochial allegiance can bar the asking of certain questions and the surveillance of certain facets of a world. Normal social propriety may begin to bind the sociologist himself: he is no longer so emancipated that he can define courtesy solely as a useful constraint on others. It may prompt him to offer self-disclosures and unwilling admissions too. A thorough subordination to the reality of appearances may actually come to be seen as more compelling than the acceptance of ideas which pervade the university: 'if [cultural anthropologists] 'go native' *cognitively* . . . they will no longer be able to do cultural anthropology. They will have dropped out of the universe of discourse in which such an enterprise is meaningful or even real'.[77] Some ethnographers accordingly practise a strategy of withdrawal and return in order to neuter the grip of lay social realities. They oscillate between the roles of insider and outsider, attempting to avoid disabling experiences of attachment.[78]

When the sociologist's appearances are wholly counterfeit, however, he betrays the trust which links people together. Trust is a taken-for-granted property of much social life, especially within the bounded social worlds which the participant observer seeks to penetrate. There is a faith in the integrity of appearances, a natural attitude, which maintains that what seems normal could not be otherwise. As Simmel argues:

> Our modern life is based to a larger extent than is usually realized upon the faith in the honesty of the other. Examples are our economy, which becomes more and more a credit economy, or our science, in which most scholars must use innumerable results of other scientists which they cannot examine. We base our gravest decisions on a complex system of conceptions, most of which presuppose the confidence that we will not be betrayed. Under modern conditions, the lie, therefore, becomes something much more devastating than it was earlier, something which questions the very foundations of our life.[79]

Social reality is built up in an ongoing conversation between people. That conversation lends concreteness and facticity to an eminently human construction. If support wanes, reality is itself afflicted: its contrived and precarious nature can become revealed. Covert ethnography is a systematic exploitation of the natural attitude and it may prove disruptive.[80] It is based on the lie. Even overt observation exploits. For example, sociologists of deviance are particularly prone to play the part of spy, however disinterested or innocent their pretences may be.[81]

Dorothy Douglas remarks that participant observation is centred on joining a group and that such membership demands a show of loyalty. Ethnography is then represented as a staging of performances, a problem of managing fronts which should extract much with the minimum of commitment. The sociologist is likely to be systematically tested by those whom he studies, and his presentation of self should be appropriately organised to pass such tests. The observed are often beset by anxieties about the intentions of the sociologist, fearing that some form of espionage is being practised: 'it seems that the recruit must develop a *stake* in the reality such that he can be trusted to preserve those aspects of the situation that [a protective] front was initially designed to protect'.[82] Any stake acquired by the participant observer, however, must be no more than a lure and a deceit designed to promote his secret purposes: 'it might be better for the study if the researcher only *appears* to develop such a stake, unless he can be co-opted to such an extent that he in a real sense ceases to be a researcher'.[83] Any transactions with research subjects are mere phenomena of 'front production'. They are treated wholly instrumentally: 'the point here is not the truth or falsity of his representations to the people from whom he hopes to obtain data but rather his ability to selectively present himself as possessing this or that set of attributes'.[84] In Douglas's account, at least, the sociologist plays with trust in an entirely amoral or immoral fashion. He manipulates the natural attitude for concealed ends, lying and dissembling at will.

Even if there is some semblance of integrity in research, the consequences of ethnogrpahy would rarely seem to benefit its subjects. Humpreys's revelations about homosexual transactions in public lavatories, Skolnick's work on the police,[85] and my own limited study of debt-collection[86] cannot but multiply the difficulties of people whose lives are problematic enough without sociological interference. Davis reflects:

> ... the sociologist often experiences a certain guilt, a sense of having betrayed, a stench of disreputability about himself; these despite the covers, pseudonyms, and eletions with which he clothes his subjects ... I would hold that it is just and fitting that he be made to squirm so, because in having exploited his non-scientific self ... for ends other than those immediately apprehended by his

subjects he has in some significant sense violated the collective conscience of the community, if not that of the profession.[87]

A subject may have given consent to being studied, but informed agreement requires a detailed understanding of the practices of sociology in general and of the relevant project in particular.[88] Sociologists themselves have often flagrantly betrayed confidence, undoing all the work of 'covers, pseudonyms, and eletions'. There can be few professional sociologists who do not know the identity of 'Middletown' for instance. For some participant observers, duplicity is encouraged as a matter of course: 'this sounds insidious and even unethical or somewhat immoral, but everyone employs this technique to some degree in everyday life'.[89] Indeed, whatever its humanistic protestations may be, sociology is neither a benign nor a scrupulous discipline. Its special competence is held to inhere in its capacity to upset common sense by revealing irony, absurdity, deep structure, latent function, contradiction or unsuspected order. Even interactionism belies some of its phenomenalism by awarding a central place to the distinction between Everyman's knowledge 'about' process and its own scientific 'knowledge of intimacy'. Sociology would forfeit its authority if it merely replicated the materials of common-sense reasoning. It is devoted to affronting that reasoning and invalidating the logic which produces consent.[90] As Berger remarks, sociology is an 'intrinsically debunking discipline',[91] debunking the very idea of informed consent.

The sociologists' subjects are translated into means which service the goals of research. Since many relationships are decked with the assumption that people should be ends to one another, the participant observer must always be indifferent to at least one set of moral claims. He acts in bad faith, and the quality of his interpretations is correspondingly affected. His participation is mediated by definitions and ambitions which are not communally given and which may indeed subvert community.[92] Far from entering into an unsullied union with his objects, he is forced to grasp reality through the complex and ramifying perspectives of a false self. Thus Gold has contended that the complete participant observer is necessarily a *poseur*: 'instead of being himself in the pretended role, all he can be is a "not self", in the sense of perceiving that his actions are meaningful in a contrived role'.[93] As *poseur*, the nature of his immediate experience becomes suspect, especially if it is alleged that the experience reproduces the social reality of his respondents. He is the representative of *Gesellschaft* attempting to understanding *Gemeinschaft*.

The overt participant observer may indeed be recognised as a spy by members of the world which he studies. Scott, for example, was greeted with the cry 'Oh, Oh! Cheese it, the cops!'[94] Again, in an ethnographic study of a town, there was a prevalent local assumption that a man behaving as the sociologist behaved could only be an agent of the F.B.I. or similar body.[95] Similarly an examination of work practices may, quite sensibly, be regarded as an investigation conducted to serve management.

However much mistrust there may be, uncertainty will always exist about the observer's significance and intentions. An appreciable amount of the sociologist's work will be initially occupied with allaying anxieties and restoring normal appearances. In particular it will be devoted to furnishing a definition of self which will be least intolerable in the situation.[96] In learning what that definition might be, and in attempting to produce it, effective fieldwork becomes an educational process for observer and observed alike. Layman and sociologist coach one another in ways that are not at all dissimilar to the forms of conventional interaction. It is in this sense perhaps that the Idealist aim of a universe of shared understanding is realised. Positions can be clarified, suspicions dispelled, joint histories developed, and a common world established. Throughout that process, unifying identities are progressively built up. Knowledge is acquired in those identities and turned back to give structure to the further evolution of interaction. It works on and through the observer-observed relationship, swinging between intimacy and distance. The transformations of self which accompany participant observation are data, the media of data, and sources of ideas for explaining data.

Viable fieldwork rests on a continuing conversation which takes relationships through sequences of different forms. In such conversation the observer must defer to the others' portrayal of reality, contaminating it as little as he can. He must also refrain from obviously inhibiting it through the display of indifference or disbelief. Yet, covertly, he also employs a sociological rationality which provides a secondary context for the interpretation of all that he sees.[97] He should not surrender his own understanding of the sociologically plausible.

Fieldwork may then be conceived as the organisation of a particular career for the sociologist and the field which is about him. His own identity, his interests, and those of his subjects will emerge together in a complicated interplay. It is not an evenly scheduled career: its phases are variably spaced and paced, and its component parts need not move in unison. The competence, understanding and role of the sociologist can lag behind or anticipate the changing organisation of other segments. Typically, any prolonged ethnography is made complex by its shifting objects and interpretations. Its order might be grasped *in situ*, but it can easily become forgotten or altered in retrospect. There is thus a greater dialogue which involves the sociologist in the field attempting to maintain conversational contact with himself. Firstly, he must recall how he phrased his ambitions before he embarked on research. It is quite easy to lose sight of plans and problems when one is immersed in the flow of particular events. Secondly, he must leave intelligible materials for himself when he has withdrawn from observation. What might seem obvious and unnecessarily simple at one stage may well become indistinct later. There must be an active imagination of the sociologist as he will be in the future, stripped of all the surrounding detail which now envelops him. The participant observer is therefore required not only to apprehend what is happening and who he is becoming, but how he can align himself with his own past and future selves. What is lucid in the immediacy of research can be opaque in recollection. More broadly, he has to preserve his relationships with others who are outside the research process altogether. Unless he is a social anthropologist who is remote from home, he will face the necessity of keeping some parts of his world 'stable' whilst others change. He must retain the ability to take the role of his 'normal' self.

Often stretching over considerable periods of time, the career of an investigation can become tiered into relatively distinct phases. Each phase tends to define a different aspect of the sociologist's self. Each presents some possibilities and suppresses others. As Weinberg and Williams observe:

> [There is] a gamelike attempt, usually by both parties, to work out the various stages of their relationship. In so doing, each casts the other into different roles as the research enters different phases: it is the demands of these roles that structure the nature of the relationships that are part and parcel of the fieldwork experience . . . These various social processes affect what knowledge is obtained and published by the researcher.[98]

Each stage of the emergent process may permit the emphasis of a new aspect of the sociologist's work, eliciting certain foci and epistemological perspectives. Questions arise or recede, sensitivities are alerted or dimmed, and stances come to be seen as appropriate or inappropriate. Viewed from without, those gyrations and changes can appear as further signs of the contradictory and confused quality of the fieldwork enterprise. Viewed from within, however, participant observation can be experienced as a series of distinct episodes that are adequate in themselves although not necessarily harmonious with their neighbours. Although reality itself would seem to shift as the research unfolds, it does so in a reasonably manageable fashion. The discontinuities between episodes need not appear at all disquieting in the field. On the contrary they may be taken as persuasive evidence that important interpretative gains have occurred. New analyses are not always simply incremental: they may involve a major reorganisation of perspectives in which nothing retains quite the same significance. In fact an expectation of surprise and discovery is built into the very fabric of research. The interactionists, in particular, hold that enquiry is somehow authenticated when it produces a novelty which could never have been the object of preparation.

When research is portrayed in this manner, it is possible to unearth a practical resolution to some of the problems that are associated with interactionist methodology. That resolution might appear casuistical and inconclusive if the project is surveyed as a whole because contradiction remains. Yet interactionists could argue that no project *should* be surveyed as a whole. An analytic review of research tends to be very different from the problem-solving experiences which are encountered in the field. Reviews impose an artificial and deceptive organisation on a process which can never be subject to neat programmes and orderly progressions. Moreover what are subsequently described as discrepancies and anomalies need not have seemed untoward at the time. Each of the diverse fieldwork experiences is real enough in itself although it might have been negated by its predecessors and successors. What may be dismissed as a confused and poorly integrated scheme can then resolve itself into a series of interconnected and internally coherent stages. Interactionism stresses immediacy and the importance of a responsiveness which stems from vague and imprecise thought. It deflects concern away from those dilemmas which are thought to be foreign to the more direct experience of praxis. It can thus emphasise participant observation as a process which strings discrete phases together in a pragmatically satisfactory way. There is no great urgency attending the demand that all those phases should be reconciled in one consistent scheme.

Interactionism rests on other defences of inconsistency. By rejecting absolutes and the idea of a fixed, extra-personal truth, it allows itself to entertain seemingly opposed ontologies and epistemologies. The clash between such contrasting theses may be held to occur only in some abstract metaphysical realm where all is methodologically insubstantial. When truth is depicted as the negotiated outcome of evolving transactions with the world, different realities can become equally true. The interactionist supports a vision of a pluralistic universe in which no master truth reigns. As Lafferty argues:

> Following the pragmatic doctrine, we are attempting to 'put' reality into the perspectives of the perceptual world and to see what it becomes in the process. We find that we must state the perceptual world in terms of things . . . that get their reality in the manipulatory area. As far as the distant thing lies beyond our reach — beyond the manipulatory area — it is hypothetical. If what it promises is not born [sic] out in the manipulatory area, it is illusory.[99]

Research then becomes a progression through possibly disparate but equally tenable realities — a practical demonstration of what Dewey advanced as 'pluralistic realism'.[100] Lacking a transcendental or absolute measure of truth which stands outside experience, the sociologist is not constrained to choose between the realities. His commitment to the irreducibility of phenomena and experience allows him to refuse to reject all but one stage of research as inauthentic. Like Ranke, he might claim that every phase is immediate to God. Logical inconsistency is not itself lauded, but the discrete strands of an inconsistent scheme may become valid and appropriate in their own place and time. As Stone and Farberman argued, 'we agree that *concrete reality is really inexhaustible*; that the question is at the center of our inquiries; that different accounts of human conduct are generated by the different questions that are asked.'[101] The cautious phenomenalism of many interactionists disowns the attempt to create general analytic categories or explanations which encompass all the situated detail of empirical events.[102] Phenomena are not taken to be constant or independently available to inspection. They shift as actions and purposes change. 'The world as relative occurs in the perspective of the individual. But one does not surround his own perspective by an absolute world when he relates it to another.'[103] Objects are so grounded in existence and context that propositions about them need not be generic. They are not instances of some autonomous thing-in-itself outside all experience, and the truth of one is not the truth of all.[104] The ultimate task of formal sociological analysis may impose set criteria for the evaluation and ordering of ideas,[105] but the reality of ethnography and research is changeable.[106] Thus Becker remarked 'where people do get into research, ... theoretical differences are much less daunting.'[107] Similarly Bruyn argued that seeming polarities and antitheses in theory may find reconciliation in practice. The crude dichotomies of sociological thought tend to evaporate and lose significance when the sociologist actually enters the field.[108]

The abandonment of *a priori* reasoning brings in its wake an abandonment of the need to impose coherence and harmony on the opening stages of the quest for knowledge. Some disunity and illogicality can be countenanced before and during research because the greatest emphasis is laid on a flexible accommodation with the research experience itself.[109] After all, the social life which research explains is not always understood as a clear and organised process at all. A phenomenalist sociology must reflect some of the incoherence and confusion which characterises its objects. System and interconnections may be discovered, but they lie in some strange realm *behind* or *beneath* phenomena and are not necessarily more true than contradiction and muddle.

What seems in conventional methodology to be disorderly research may then be quite tolerable in symbolic interactionism. Indeed the appearance of disorder is somewhat misleading because there is an underpinning system in much interactionist work. Interactionists do not undertake fieldwork in a haphazard or disorganised fashion. But their system does not chart results and strategies with great clarity. Rather it lays out a general procedure whose details and contents cannot be anticipated in advance. That system consists of a series of 'feedback loops operating all the way through the research process, instead of at a few specified points'.[110] The multiplicity of loops, and the abundance of checks which they produce, complicate the preparation of exact plans. Further, those loops do no more than impose a structure on experiences which cannot be easily described or predicted. The planned and the unplanned then play with one another:

analysis is carried on *sequentially*, important parts of the analysis being made while the researcher is still gathering data. This has two obvious consequences: further data gathering takes its direction from provisional analyses; and the amount and kind of provisional analysis carried on is limited by the exigencies of the field work situation, so that final comprehensive analyses may not be possible until the field work is completed.[111]

The analytic forms that are on bestowed on analysis are necessarily *a posteriori*. They are different from those that constituted the process as it evolved. It follows that the occasionally absurd and problematic quality of ethnographic assumptions is often descriptively obliterated after fieldwork has been performed. There is a 'tidying-up', as it were, which allows a marriage to take place between analytic organisation and methodological disorganisation. In turn the act of obliteration perpetuates the methodological disorganisation of participant observation. It bars the retrieval of items from the history of the research project.

Such historical reconstruction does not only take place when the research has reached some apparent conclusion. The work of recasting is continuous. Order emerges constantly during the evolution of research, reformulating or expunging what had elapsed at the pre-analytic level of understanding. As Schwarz and Schwarz remark, 'a certain amount of . . . retrospective reworking (and it is difficult to estimate how much) goes on without the observer being aware of it. Rather than finding a simple and direct connection between the occurrence of the event and its representation as data, we discovered that our observation began to expand the longer we thought about it.'[112] There is thus a complicated process of interchange between the immediate and the mediated which refashions the significance of experience and phenomena *in situ*.

Fieldwork strategies are tenable because they are deployed over time. Unlike the questionnaire survey, they can be staggered to form a fugue-like pattern in which the various segments of interactionist ontology are explored.

The ethnographer may attack explanation with different perspectives, employing each to check the problematic features of the others. Wedded to the idea of dialectic, however, he does not manage that fugue as a simple progression of discrete and opposing stances. There is no methodological tally kept of clear advantages scored by any of the contradictory positions. Rather, understanding is held to emerge out of the interrelations within contradiction. In this sense the interactionists have extracted arguments from pragmatist and formalist alike. Truth is taken to flow from specific praxis, and there are as many truths as there are forms of practical acquaintance with knowledge. In synthesis and balancing may be discovered the possibility of intellectual progress. The very conflict between participation and observation, marginality and 'going native', Idealism and phenomenalism, analysis and intuition, carries the research on from stage to stage. Thus Hughes argues:

> The unending dialectic between the role of member (participant) and stranger (observer and reporter) is essential to the very concept of fieldwork, and this all participant-observers have in common: they must develop a dialectic relationship between being researchers and being participants.[113]

The term 'participant-observer' itself conveys a sense of paradox. Ethnography becomes virtually impossible if there is a full commitment of self to the role of participation or the role of observation. Yet the two are antithetical. Marginality suspends the sociologist's natural attitude and renders the reality of others strange and interesting. It enables him to appreciate the problematic quality of social life in a manner alien to all complete participants. As marginal man, the sociologist may experience what Goffman has described as 'stumbling into awareness'. The sheer taken-for-granted nature of a social world may collapse, leaving the observer alert to its sociological possibilities. But marginality also exiles the sociologist from the critical domain of meaning and symbolic process. He may infer connections, unities and salient themes without any warrant. He must himself share the natural attitude and, in so doing, is likely to dismiss the very problems that once engaged him. Whyte's comments on *Street Corner Society* are most revealing:

> as I began my Cornerville study, everything I saw and heard was new and strange and all sorts of questions arose in my mind. But at this point I did not know enough or have enough data to ask good questions and get any answers. As I became part of the community, the richness of the data increased manyfold; and yet I found in myself a constant tendency to take for granted the sort of behavior that is taken for granted by the people I was observing.[114]

The dilemmas of fieldwork are solved by three major strategies. The sociologist may move back and forth between the two roles or epistemological universes, exploiting each in turn, and allowing one to feed on the other. He may practise withdrawal and return, periodically retreating to the margins so that his sociological sensibility is renewed. Such a procedure may be reinforced by a resort to colleagues who are able to restore him to the natural attitude of science itself. The oscillation between roles can be more minute, a small series of eddies between distance and intimacy which are seized on for eventual analytic dissection.[115] Alternatively, the entire history of the research episode may be cast as a progress from immediacy to formal theory. Bruyn for instance offers a procedural guide for gradually transcribing the concrete into the analytic language of sociology.[116] He emasculates the more perplexing implications of his Idealism by wedding them to a contrasting intellectual style. Distance is carefully built up, each stage constructed out of its predecessor. An ethnographic project is then conceived as a traversing of the epistemological spectrum, each band playing its part in a division of interpretative labour.

The solution to contradiction may be built into the very structure of the world that is investigated. Much interactionist ethnography has been devoted to exploring deviant groups which are lodged within the larger and more familiar societies of America and Britain.[117] Marginality is assured by the strangeness of deviancy. Even those sociologists who are not strangers to some forms of deviance cannot know all deviant worlds well. As Blumer remarks, 'almost by definition the research scholar does not have a firsthand acquaintance with the sphere of social life he proposes to study. He is rarely a participant in that sphere and usually is not in close touch with the actions and experiences of the people who are involved in that sphere.'[118] The juxtaposition of familiarity with unfamiliarity may furnish a proper combination of phenomenological distance with interpretability. Deviant worlds are rarely so isolated that there is no common symbolic currency between them and the outside. They provide significant refractions of meaning which are both strange and intelligible. The courting of deviancy by many interactionists may lie in that unusually provocative quality of the rule-breaking episode. As Gouldner has usefully observed, it is the grotesque which lends itself to the Romantic imagination and style of interactionism. He stresses the central part played by Kenneth Burke's 'perspective by incongruity', arguing that it is the 'pragmatic routinization of the

Romantics' concept of the grotesque — that is, it is the Americanization of the grotesque'.[119] An examination of the activities and roles that are discussed by the interactionist writers on deviance would suggest that the phenomenon is constituted solely by its phenomenological appeal to the sociologist. There is little else that unites the stripper, dwarves, prostitutes, cheque forgers, the maimed, the blind, the stuttering and the thief. What is 'deviant' reflects an opportunity to reconcile participation with observation. All other explanations appear less convincing.

More commonly, however, the paradox is handled on a prepredicative plane. The contradictions of an articulate argument about research procedure are bypassed by managing them before they become distinct. After all, interactionism does not extoll the importance of analytic and reasoned arguments to methodological problems. It portrays the world as a mass of shifting boundaries and changing qualities which cannot be mastered by fine categories of logic. It is in the immediate response to that world that solutions may arise. Whyte, for example, refused to accept the tactic which segregates phases of the ethnographic task. He alluded instead to solutions which are grasped prereflexively:

> Probably most of our learning in [the] field is not on a conscious level. We often have flashes of insight that come to us when we are not consciously thinking about a research problem at all. These insights are more likely to come to the man who is absorbed in the field situation than to the one who is always going in and coming out in order to maintain his perspective.[120]

The opposition between mediated and immediate thought is stilled by a dependence on the hidden workings of immediacy. An abstract conflict is dissipated in praxis. Whyte's solution mirrors a larger argument contained in some branches of the philosophy of science. In *The Foundations of Science*, for example, Poincaré observed that there is always an infinite number of hypotheses which might be employed to explain an event.[121] In the early stages of enquiry, one cannot choose between those conjectures on the basis of some rational principle. The selection of possible rules must be guided by criteria which are *felt* to be appropriate. Those criteria cannot be strictly formulated. Neither can they be effectively defended. Poincaré described the phase of consciousness which applies them as the 'subliminal self'. It is a self which works prepredicatively and appreciatively, and its activities cannot be subjected to the scrutiny of reason. The aesthetic sensibility of the subliminal self is 'a true . . . feeling which all mathematicians know but of which the profane are so ignorant as often to be tempted to smile'. The recognition of connections and explanations is then unavailable to rational control. It is moulded by an intuition of form which renders standard methodological recipes incomplete. That sensibility is certainly manifest in Crick and Watson's description of the discovery of the double helix.[122] Their research was impelled by a conviction that the structure of DNA must be simple and pleasing. Whyte's claim for the prereflexive strategy is thus echoed by men working in other areas.

If ethnography rests on the cultivation of an indescribable sensitivity, it follows that the training of participant observers should be conducted in the field: 'I feel that the field worker needs only a minimum of theoretical orientation before he begins his observations. . . . he may be positively handicapped if he postpones his field work until he feels that he has a thorough grounding in theory'.[123] He thus joins with the pragmatist in the elevation of experience over ratiocination, allowing research directives to emerge out of the process of knowing. That delegation of guidance to the developing knowing-known transaction leaves the novice singularly unprepared.

When there are no scripts for the performance of the ethnographic role, competence must be entrusted to the native skills of the sociologist. He is best able to chart those areas in which he is already an accredited member. The dialectic between participation and observation will remain problematic, but the issue of simulation may become subdued. For example, Becker's own biography made it possible to study the occupational life of the jazz musician;[124] Roth could study a ward for tuberculosis patients when he was himself a patient;[125] and Polsky's career as a pool player enabled him to observe the hustler.[126] Many interactionists have, then, capitalised on their non-academic selves for purposes of analysis.

If no such self is available in the research field, complementary roles are typically sought. A sociologist will attempt to find or adapt an innocuous place in the social setting which he seeks to explore. Laud Humphreys became a *voyeur*-lookout in the public lavatories which housed homosexual encounters; Whyte became secretary to a Cornerville association;[127] Herbert Gans was a resident of Levittown;[128] and Florence Kluckhohn became a shopkeeper in a

Mexican village.[129] Farberman's work on car sales was eased by his own past experience as assistant to car dealers.[130] Again, Liebow had known Blacks well throughout his childhood and claimed that he had encountered no barriers in his research for *Tally's Corner*.[131] As native or companion, the sociologist must carry off performances without undue self-consciousness. Attention to their properties would only impair their flow.[132] Anxieties corrupt smooth role-playing[133] and detachment destroys intuitive understanding.

Required to establish an artlessly displayed self, the participant observer confronts a task which would seem to be either wholly untenable or wholly unproblematic. More generally, its salient qualities are entrusted to the innate capabilities which all sociologists are supposed to possess as active members of a society. The dilemmas and hazards of *Verstehen* are legislated out of existence.[134] In common with most other problems of pragmatism, solutions flow from a return to the natural world, not from exercising reason alone. Contemplation and practice do not oppose one another as discrete alternatives. Rather, they play with one another so that reason informs practice, and practice stimulates reason. But reason cannot be the sole guide to research problems. Thus Becker quite properly observed of my discussion of contradiction in fieldwork: 'many of your criticisms are those a certain kind of philosopher might make of almost any working scientist (e.g . . . physics has gone right along in the face of contradictions that turn philosophers pale.)'[135] Fieldwork is accomplished chiefly in action, it cannot be mastered by speculation.[136]

Such ethnography is a fitting part of the interactionist enterprise because it is withdrawn from substantial analytic review, being presented as a component of the natural investigation of the social. It cannot be properly taught or explicated. In the apprenticeship structures of interactionism, fieldwork is communicated principally by emulation and the organisation of practice. 'It is, more than other methods of study, itself a practice, consciously undertaken, in sociology itself – in the perceiving and predicting of social roles, both one's own and those of others.'[137] Although the transmission of interactionist methodology has become a matter of routine, much is communicated non-verbally. For instance, Gans recalled his own training:

> When I was a graduate student at the University of Chicago just after World War II, no one talked much about participant-

observation; we just did it. Like many of my fellow sociology students, I enrolled in Everett Hughes' course 'Introduction to Field Work', and like them, I found it a traumatic introduction; we were sent to a census tract in nearby Hyde Park and asked to do a small participant-observation study. Everett Hughes gave us some words of introduction and of instruction, but . . . he quickly pushed us out of the nest and told us to fly on our own.[138]

7 Conclusion

Symbolic Interactionism has been subject to sporadic attacks by exponents of orthodox sociology. In the main those attacks have taken an *ad hominem* guise, representing the alleged weakness of the sociology as the consequence of intellectual infirmity or bias. Interactionism has been held to neglect a variety of important analytic concerns. Its tendency to shun references to history, social totalities and macrosociological entities has been portrayed as a sign of intellectual myopia, timidity or omission. Such criticisms flow from a particular conception of sociology and society which is regarded as unproblematic. Those who do not recognise that conception are accordingly thought to be flawed in some fashion. In contrast to the *ad hominem* critique, a case can be made that interactionism constitutes an alternative sociology. It is not merely a defective sociology. As an alternative, it denies the credibility or utility of much macrosociological reasoning. Its arguments stem from a substantial philosophical tradition, and they deserve careful attention. In particular they entitle interactionism to occupy a legitimate place in the spectrum of sociological styles.

My argument so far has reviewed and criticised some of the epistemological and methodological foundations of symbolic interactionism. It has not itself been representative of interactionist style or procedure: for instance, my concern has been with exposition rather than focused enquiry, schematising what has been held to defy systematisation; I have retrieved intellectual supports for a stance which is professedly hostile to intellectual disquisition; and I have been relatively distant in my appraisal of a rhetoric which attempts to faithfully mirror the animated and fluid character of its objects. As I remarked at the very beginning of this book, a description such as mine might be regarded as a betrayal of the interactionist vision. Like Alexander, the symbolic interactionists prefer to act rather than reason in their dealings with problems. By contrast I have merely brooded about the intricacy of the Gordian knot.

Yet that reflection may serve to confirm what is an obvious but often unnoticed property of interactionism. The sociology is unobtrusively framed by an intellectual context which is considerably more substantial than its critics have apparently supposed. In the main, that frame has been ignored and interactionism has been treated as the runt of the sociological litter. The sociology's departure from conventional analytic practices has generally been explained as the effect of conceptual infirmity, not as the result of conceptual difference. It is as if some basic revisions would restore interactionism to sociological competence. Thus critics have been fond of reproving it for not attending to those matters which other sociologies have always considered important. It is this attribution of a simpleton status which may be partially dispelled by invoking the pragmatist and formalist buttresses of the sociology. If they are not invoked, interactionism is translated into a sociology which is inexplicably naïve in its failure to incorporate what many take to be commonplace ideas.

Attacks on interactionism have acquired the appearance of corrective rebukes administered by those who possess a sure sociological authority. But that authority is not completely established, and it is far from firmly based. Neither is symbolic interactionism quite the sociological idiot child which it is sometimes made to seem. Many criticisms of the approach may actually be understood as part of the continuing debate about the fundamental scope, mandate and nature of sociology. They have chiefly emanated from those who would disown Weber's and Simmel's application of Kantian epistemology and its accompanying limitations. Marxists, positivists and conflict theorists form the bulk of assailants. In this sense the debate is considerably more ramifying than a superficial reading might suggest. There are major unresolved questions which cannot be settled by critical *fiat*. In particular the debate is not to be terminated by a number of reminders about the importance of 'social structure', 'history' and the like. Those concepts are not so devoid of ambiguity or difficulty that they may be recognised as instantly binding. Their very legitimacy is still part of the open dispute between the champions of phenomenalism and essentialism.

Hostile judgments on interactionism typically proceed from tacit or overt assertions about the character of the real world. It is interactionism's inability to confront that world that is principally lambasted. The world is held to be variously constituted by social structure and social class, by history and institutions, by social organisation and conflicts. Although there may be running disputes about the precise significance of these organising entities, they are nevertheless assumed to have an unproblematic existence. Thus forces termed 'history' and 'class conflict' are thought to unquestionably shape the interplay between men. Lichtman, for instance, claims that symbolic interactionism 'lacks an awareness of historical concreteness, is naive in its account of mutual typification and ultimately abandons the sense of human beings in a struggle against an alien reality which they both master and to which they are subordinate.'[1] It is of course the case that symbolic interactionism *is* built around the Simmelian dialectic of alienation, and that Lichtman does not seem to appreciate its significance. In fact pragmatist and formalist alike reveal a preoccupation with alienation. But the companion charge is representative of the essentialising strand in the onslaught against interactionism. 'Historical concreteness' is a member of a class of ideas which are taken to be self-evidently compelling. Allied with it are Gouldner's 'overpowering social structures'[2] and Smith's 'social and historical conditions'.[3] Any tendency to neglect such allegedly real features of social order is interpreted as evidence of a simple failure in perception. If they do exist, as the critics largely maintain, then the interactionist must be unusually obtuse in refusing to award them a prominent place. Orthodox sociologists are quite obviously bemused by the reluctance of interactionists to defer to 'totalities', 'systems' and 'structures'.

Even the proponents of interactionism are themselves occasionally puzzled by this kind of elementary omission. I have argued that the boundaries around the sociology are permeable and that interactionism lends itself to fusion with other, competing styles of thought. Such possibilities of amalgamation have been reinforced by the reluctance of interactionists to systematically champion their own vision of interpretation and procedure. Hostile critics have therefore been sometimes accorded legitimacy. The arguments of a phenomenalist sociology have given way to an essentialist onslaught. For instance, Meltzer *et al.* summarise a study by stating 'a large majority of the symbolic interactionists in [the] sample lack an appreciation of social organization, either confusing it with culture or subsuming it under the larger rubric of culture as "simply one of culture's parts".[4] Similarly Farberman extended some authority to attacks made by orthodox sociologists. In his introduction to a symposium on interactionism, he observed:

Intellectually, both advocates and adversaries criticize symbolic interactionism along at least four lines: (1) it is allegedly a conservative, non-critical orientation confined either to nifty descriptions of exotic marginals, or gentlemanly inspections of middle-level gatekeepers . . .; (2) it is unscientific, since, by and large, its practitioners shun the a priori (logico-theoretic) deductive method and prefer the a posteriori (grounded-emergent) inductive method; (3) it pays insufficient attention to the formal or deeper lying processes which condition how ordinary people construct their everyday lives; and (4) it lacks sufficient appreciation of the dark, demonic, subterranean side of life. Although the symposium organizers did not ask participants to take these charges into account, they were, nevertheless, 'in the air' and their influence can be seen.[5]

In the main, I would urge that it is not necessary to take these charges into account. They proceed from a competitive version of sociology, not from the only permissible description of social reality. In assessing the merits of these competing accounts, it is important to try to construct an interactionist rebuttal. The 'confusion' to which Meltzer *et al.* allude is not really so confused. Neither are the interactionists alone in such confusion. Other sociologists have also suffered from it. They too have been unsure whether a precise demarcation can exist between culture and social organisation, or whether an autonomous realm of structure exists. Thus Raymond Aron was not entirely persuaded by Marx's distinction between infrastructure and superstructure.[6] He observed that the two levels of social reality could well be mistaken for one another. Unless an *a priori* adjudication is accepted, it is difficult to know why a bank, a mine or a factory should not be treated as a constellation of eminently symbolic phenomena. Durkheim and Levi-Strauss, too, could sometimes be described as confused sociologists. They were not always prepared to sever social structure from its system of collective representations, arguing that the two are instances of the same language.[7] Indeed, there is a host of such allegedly muddled thinkers. Muddle should actually be redefined as an allegiance to a divergent approach. It is not the outcrop of rank incomprehension.

It is clear that it is not very illuminating to depict the interactionists as simply befuddled. There is more than misunderstanding in their refusal to fully acknowledge two different kinds of sociological substance. Greater profit is gained by recognising that their thought is based on a distinct ontology. Interactionists would assert that social organisation is not what the macrosociologists believe it to be. They would further assert that the separation of social organisation and culture is a perilous and probably absurd exercise. After all, a culturally uncontaminated example of social organisation would be a most implausible entity. To the Martian, all social life would be equally baffling. It would not happily resolve itself into an opaque culture and an intelligible structure. Rather, both would be in need of symbolic decoding. There can be no easy devaluation of interactionist ontology as a mere lack of appreciation. Neither can problems be met by appeals for greater clarity or conformity.

The attacks flow from a difficult epistemology which suggests that there are three distinct realms of knowledge. One realm is knowledge about society as it is available to all men of honesty and intelligence. Another is sociology itself. Sociology may be compared with knowledge about society and found more or less wanting in its description. That comparison is made possible by a third system of knowing which transcends the other two. It is alleged that even the adherents of a false sociology can eventually admit the disparity between their portrait and the reality which is portrayed. Reality itself is somehow immutable, visible, unquestionable and independent of science. There can be no fundamental disagreement about society because it is to be discovered outside the particular vantage points of organised knowledge.

Of course, few who entertain this epistemology actually concur about the nature of social life. Structural-functionalists vie with Marxists, phenomenologists, neo-positivists, conflict theorists and mathematical sociologists in their promotion of special truths. But each separate branch of the critical wing would claim that society and its component segments do indubitably exist. In turn, different sociologies are held to depict reality with ascertainable degrees of fidelity. Disagreements about the composition of that reality must be explained by an opponent's lapse into error or misunderstanding.

Interactionism is patently inept in its management of all macrosociological issues. It infrequently touches on them, refraining from detailed discussions of social class, major institutions and other features of that undoubted but disputed phenomenon called society. Macrostructure *does* form part of the interactionist's common-sense appreciation of social life, and it does provide a rough context for analysis. But it is taken to have little scientific substance. The occasional macrosociological excursions of the interactionists tend to be handled with an atypical diffidence of style. On the whole, the tripartite epistemology is rejected. Interactionists would argue that intellectual objects are not independent of the intellect that conceived them. Analytic ideas are rooted in the perspectives that are provided by specific sociologies and the penumbral concepts that surround them. There is no way in which 'reality' can be grasped outside some active process of knowing. To be sure, it is not confined only to one set of ideas. A multiplicity of definitions may bear on the same situation. But it is not possible to pretend that social structure exists, that symbolic interactionism exists, and that the method of contrasting the two is itself autonomous and above all dispute.

However, critics have been so impressed by the concreteness and certainty of their own visions of the world that they have cast the interactionist as a creature of weak understanding. Any who reject some variant of those approved visions are thought to be estranged from the community of rational men. It is as if the failures of interactionism must be explained only by deficient reason, not by the effects of relying upon an alternative interpretation of sociological possibilities. This distinctive tack of the debate about interactionism is encouraged by a particular tradition that attempts to account for the lacunae and insufficiencies of competitive schemes of thought. That tradition, identified as the sociology of knowledge, emerged as an analytic strategy for elucidating the grounds of divergent reasoning. Before its universalisation by Mannheim and the sociological phenomenologists, it was largely employed as a weapon by those who sought to discredit their intellectual competitors. The sociology of knowledge presented its own sphere of ideas as emancipated and absolute, effectively free of the parochial bonds of time and place. By contrast, rival spheres were the creations of local and ephemeral ideologies which could be exposed by describing their particular anchorage in society and history. The universe of the sociologists of knowledge was not pluralistic but simplex, being compounded out of truths and falsehoods. When Karl Mannheim turned the sociology on itself, relativising the relativisers,[8] he was upbraided for defying the possibility of absolute truth. Adorno, for instance, identified him as the emasculator of the intellectuals.[9]

In orthodox hands, however, the sociology of knowledge has always possessed its aggressive character as a tool to bludgeon the unenlightened. The Marxists wielded it against bourgeois ideologists, the Paretians against Marxists, the French rationalists against clerics, the neo-Hegelians against positivists, and the positivists against radicals. In all this contentious work, one principle was clear. The rationality of the sociologist of knowledge was held to be unimpaired and free. It alone offered a correct understanding of social life. Any who dissented from that understanding were unable to attain a proper grasp on the world of ideas. Their thoughts were not to be dissected as if they displayed an instructive logic of their own. Indeed those thoughts were merely the irrational and epiphenomenal manifestations of underlying social processes. They did not merit serious consideration in their own right. Thus the business of criticism was designed to lay bare social and psychological sources of intellectual disability. It was implicitly argued that the truth is so evident that malfunction or prejudice can alone prevent its general acceptance. By extension, differences were ascribed principally to socially-structured distortions. For example, the consciousness of the proletariat was well-founded, but bourgeois knowledge constituted ideology. Similarly Marxism was revealed to be a mere derivation of a non-logical residue, but Pareto's work was science. The Encyclopaedists were masters of reason, but the priesthood were propagators of lies and superstition. All conflicting schemes were undermined by attending to the social origins of illusion, not to their manifest arguments. Indeed, Werner Stark even refused to concede a social origin to ideology, casting it as an outgrowth of psychological incapacity.

Much criticism of symbolic interactionism has also adopted some version of the *ad hominem* mode of address. It flows from those very sociological traditions which gave birth to the unreformed sociology of knowledge. Interactionist ideas are taken to be so slight and so misconceived that they may best be represented as errors. In turn, their explanation must look to the character of their authors. Interactionists have been exposed to accusation that they are 'ideologists',[10] the unwitting or knowing apologists of late capitalism,[11] the celebrators of a new bourgeois order,[12] 'naïve',[13] 'biased',[14] evasive,[15] and manipulative.[16] All the differences between the sociology and its opponents are referred to faults of character, mind or social position. Such imputations contribute nothing to the logical or empirical invalidation of an argument, but they do focus attention on to phenomena that are supposed to incite its rejection.

That form of attack has been clearly exemplified by Gouldner's claim that the sociology of Howard Becker should be understood as an offshoot of intellectual timidity.[17] Gouldner alleges that the interactionist sociology of deviance neglects macrostructural matters because such a focus would pose a threat to established conceptions of social order. A redirection of analysis would prevent the sociologist from ingratiating himself with powerful sources of sponsorship and funds. Apart from their boorishness, Gouldner's contentions are multiply misconceived. They assault a style of sociology which is remarkably independent of the central agencies of the state. The interactionist requires little more than time and a reasonable memory because his research is generally conducted in libraries and solitary ethnographic expeditions. It is not taken up with organising survey work, computational exercises or phalanxes of research assistants. It is perhaps the least costly of all sociological methodologies, resting on very meagre financial foundations. The restrictions imposed by official patronage are thus comparatively slight.

More importantly, macrosociological analysis is not necessarily shunned because it is imprudent or impolitic. As I have argued throughout this book, there are reasoned ontological objections to that conception of sociology. Although Gouldner might imagine that macrostructural work is utterly compelling, the interactionists discard it for reasons which have little to do with pusillanimity. In fact Becker proves to be an altogether poor target for Gouldner's particular attribution of ideological bias. His politics are actually irrelevant to the cogency of his argument, but it is possible to discern a mild anarchism as the prevalent drift of his writing.[18] Anarchism and interactionism are united by an elective affinity which is more consequential than any trepidation about upsetting authority. Anarchism is an implausible candidate for state co-optation. Indeed it probably resists absorption more vigorously than any of the other political stances.

Above all, the elaborate recitation of supposed social pressures are not germane to matters of proof or disproof. Whatever they may be, the practical effects and origins of an analytic scheme have no bearing on its tenability. If those effects are demonstrably uncongenial, there may be an understandable reluctance to espouse the scheme. But the scheme cannot itself be dismissed as *wrong*. All that has taken place is a demonstration of its unpalatability. Those who reject it may do so for honourable reasons, but they have also committed themselves to an attractive illusion and not to science. Distaste does not achieve refutations. Neither are the biography and social location of an author material to the viability of his ideas. The condition and history of a Marx, Veblen, W. I. Thomas, Malinowski, Smith or Comte are interesting matters for exegesis, but they are completely tangential to

Conclusion 225

the logicality and appropriateness of his written thought. Any other assumption would be based on some form of sympathetic magic, the like-causes-like fallacy, which proposes that creditable people issue creditable ideas whilst discreditable people do not.

In contrast to the assumptions of their critics, symbolic interactionists would claim that men are not empowered to stand outside their systems of thought and inspect the real world in its raw state. They hold that the world is *produced* by the very intellectual forms that examine it. There can be no formless examination. The pitting of one complex of ideas against another cannot therefore be settled by *ex cathedra* pronouncements about the nature of social reality. Thus, although Meltzer *et al.* argue that 'symbolic interactionism's microsociological concerns blind it to macrosociological matters',[19] the ascription of blindness can be justified only after it has been demonstrated that there *is* an intelligible world of macrosociological matters for all to see. The statement that blindness is caused by excessive attention to one realm of phenomena presupposes the presence of other realms which could be equally visible. But that attention is not merely a product of sociologists becoming engrossed. As I have tried to show, more than simple oversight is entailed in interactionist ontology. Indeed interactionists might assert that, like phlogiston and the black choler, structural processes may be less scientifically acceptable than their proponents have believed. Their character must be independently established, not created by pontifical verdict.

Interactionist epistemology is itself so delicate that it does not provide a clear countering approach to the sociology of its critics. If the interactionists were committed to an unqualified Idealism, they would be involved in a parallel commitment to treat the social reality of their subjects with complete seriousness. Holding that the social world is constituted by symbolism, they would be constrained to argue that any substantial consensus about the designation of phenomena would make those phenomena true for all reasonable purposes. People who act as if class and structure were solid facts would create a world which must be explained by those selfsame facts. Like Minerva, the fruits of mind would be entirely real. Yet interactionists have only a conditional allegiance to Idealism. They do not treat consciousness as wholly sovereign. Instead, they make a tacit but critical distinction between social structure as an analytic *a priori* and social structure as a synthetic *a priori*.

Of course, these two forms are liable to a confusion which can muddle ontology. In practice they merge and meld with one another so that the differences between them rest on context and situation rather than any clear and categorical principle. In explaining the conduct of a group of Marxists, for instance, the symbolic interactionist would treat the Marxist analytic *a priori* of social class as a consequential representation which orders their behaviour. But social class attains a radically different significance when it is offered as a rival scholarly explanation. It then becomes proper to put questions about its validity and verity. It need not be simply accepted as a constituent of symbolic order. In that altered guise, social structure is regarded by the interactionist as a deceptive metaphor which purports to make sense of what is unobservable, unknowable and therefore non-existent for all sensible purposes. Its seeming coercive power is existentially important but it cannot be described as a proof of its analytic adequacy. Conviction in one area of experience should not be carried over to another. Acceptance of such proof has been termed the 'fallacy of misplaced concreteness' by one and 'a disease of language' by another:

> . . . ascribing myths to a disease of language, by which words with forgotten meanings become personal or proper names . . . a thousand . . . important superstitions spring from that most pernicious disease, . . . 'realism', by which a general name becomes the name of a reality, different from the objects or the qualities which it denotes in common. It is in this way that 'society' has appeared to have claims which the individuals that compose it do not have; and thus a reform in logic becomes necessary for the overthrow of many social and religious superstitions.[20]

Common sense may confirm a sense of social structure. The interactionist phrasing of science does not. Instead it claims that macrosociology proffers arguments about processes which are beyond the reach of any disciplined interpretative procedure. There is no external and elevated platform which provides a decisive overview of an entity called society. There is no way in which the nature of society 'as a whole' can be seen, induced, deduced or charted. That nature can only be abstracted from lay forms or intuited by procedures which are not completely sure. For all its commonsense facticity, society is an imaginative construction which is built up inferentially. Its supposed structures principally reflect the workings of its interpreters' minds. Thus, divergences between Marxists, functionalists, conflict theorists and structuralists stem as much from varying interpretative styles as from detailed observations of the social world. Indeed it is unclear how such observation could ever generate a description of social structure itself.

At most, observations might reveal glimpses of piecemeal phenomena which lack intrinsic order or coherence. The totalities which they are thought to subtend remain speculative. Between those phenomena and sociological theory there is a disquieting gap which is bridged chiefly by covert appeals to lay sensations. In a rigorous scheme, it is impossible to derive a totality from the partial and ambiguous fragments which are alone available to observational science. Any derivation implies an imaginative leap whose credibility depends solely on a kind of ontological sympathy with the leaper. Without that sympathy, there is no warrant to assume that autonomous structures *do* exist. Reference to them may make analysis easier, they may add to the pictorial effectiveness of a sociology's imagery, but they are irrevocably suppositional. The Simmelian and pragmatist insist that, outside the order imposed by a rationalistic logic, there is nothing that can lend substance to the argument that there is a social system. They might, with Cooley, assert that society is an amalgam of a collective imagination and the objects of that imagination. However, they would not hold that those objects are 'real', self-engendering or self-sustaining. 'Wholes', 'systems', 'structures' and the like are at best analytic contrivances which enable descriptions to emerge. At worst they are mystifying reifications which pretend to explain that which defies all explanation. They may in effect be estranged forms of consciousness parading as processes outside thought.

It follows that the interactionist entertains a dual conception of society. He may have a common-sense intuition of structure which affects his life in the same manner as it does others. But he also maintains that there can be no firm sociological knowledge of society *per se*. The character of society is so obscure that scientific attempts to discuss it are generally absurd. Although loose working definitions might be used to guide analysis, it is misleading to assume that the larger systems of society can ever be mapped. Indeed it is not entirely reasonable to suppose that society and its 'structures' are organised. If they are, they can be known only to analytic *a priori* conjectures which are forever uncertain or to synthetic *a priori* understanding which is utterly unscientific. The sociologist therefore hesitates to write of 'society' as a viable analytic topic at all. When he does so, it may only be to represent it as a shapeless conglomeration of fluid exchanges.

There is another sense in which society can enter the sociologist's analytic field. Society is real enough as a form which is employed in everyday explanations of social life. People do take that form to have a definite character which folds back on their activities. It is both an organisation of ideas in consciousness and a reified imagery which appears to work on consciousness. Macrosociological objects become proper matters for attention when they are experienced as the autonomous facts of social existence. They are both data and the concepts which mediate data. They must be studied, observed and explained. That study does not assume that they are parts of an order which is *sui generis*. Their invocation does not compel the sociologist to believe in all the ramifications of lay thought. On the contrary, they are taken to be collective representations, not things which are real in themselves. In describing class, therefore, the interactionist is not required to proceed as if it supplied all the materials of a satisfactory analysis. Rather it is a mediated social form which must be recognised and incorporated in some stages of his explanation. That form could just as well be witchcraft, the miasma theory of disease, historical totalities or deviance. All such organising social facts must be treated with equal deference.[21]

This position necessarily leads to a complicated relatioship between interactionism and conventional sociology. If interactionism treats the concrete facts of that sociology as a series of wraiths, it runs counter to every orthodoxy. It pursues different objectives with different perspectives. There is no neat overarching canopy which gives definition to all the phenomena of interactionism. Neither is there an assumption of inevitable order, connection or meaning in social life. The limited logic of Simmel's forms may be traced to yield a slight and atypical conception of structure. Interactionists may trace links between segments of the scientific mosaic so that description embraces a number of worlds simultaneously and systematically.[22] But the sociology does not provide a timeless and unconditional predictive scheme which is animated by its own logic. Most macrosociological matters thereby become insecure and mysterious, and interactionists translate them into two kinds of object, neither bearing much resemblance to its author's intentions. One is a highly articulate transcription of common sense, a transcription which may have an immediate utility because it organises what is often nebulous and incoherent. The other is the product of an unanchored commentary whose contentions are internally consistent but remote from any defensible observations about social process. Of course, any sociology must make occasional reference to larger typifications which cannot be grounded in confident analysis. All interactionists frame their work in a context of macrosociological ideas. But that context is usually offered with a covert apology and it is often allowed to recede as soon as possible. It is not generally taken to refer to real and ascertainable *things* in themselves.

Propositional schemes have all the appearance of grave scholarship. Compared with the faltering and unsystematic work of symbolic interactionism, orthodox sociology fosters an impression of serious purpose, rigorous procedure and solid advance. It seems to possess an intellectual authority which overshadows any of the claims made by interactionists. It is therefore unremarkable that the proponents of that sociology should feel themselves entitled to rebuke interactionism for its modest accomplishments. In their defence interactionists could repeat what Karl Marx observed in his attack on the ideology of the metaphysical Idealists. They could maintain that they are attempting to ascend from the earth of social practice to the heaven of theory, not descend from heaven to earth. Ascent is a more difficult feat and it does not always lead to conspicuous success. It is far easier to adopt the Aristotelian course of systematic classification, comparison and syllogism. That course is productive of copious theory, but theorising is not the principal constituent of science. As Poincaré remarked of mathematics, there is an infinite choice of definitions and hypotheses which might serve as the basis of an axiomatic scheme. The major problem for sociology is not the proper manipulation of its logic. It is the search for sound propositions to feed that logic. If this problem is neglected, the outcome is an anarchy of competing theories whose ranking must be decided by aesthetic criteria. Each theory would tend to be more or less internally integrated, yet each tends to be tangential to its competitors. The interactionist might conclude that the grand debates of sociology largely centre on a commerce between conflicting visions of Utopia.[23] He might also conclude, as Mannheim did, that such conflict is partly counterfeit because none of the visions is exhaustive.

Instead of establishing methods and ideas which best address a series of problems, interactionists typically set themselves problems which can be tackled by reasonable methodologies. They consequently reverse the traditional priorities of sociology, refusing to summon answers in a peremptory fashion. They are prompted to reject the imperious sociological stance which tolerates infirm and suspect procedure. When the ends of a discipline are held to be of overwhelming importance, there is a tendency for makeshift methodologies and ontologies to appear. By contrast, the interactionists tailor their ends to meet what they consider to be the possibilities of sociology. Their limited ambitions are not commonly shared by their colleagues. Most sociology was founded in a deep concern about the fate and quality of the industrialising societies of the West. Spencer, Marx, Durkheim and Tönnies variously conceived sociology to be an instrument which might elucidate the terrifying processes of alienation, social disorganisation and oppression. The principles of sociology were ordered by its redemptive function rather than by its proven intellectual capacities.[24] They were forced to generate ideas which could solve major problems. Sociology has subsequently been characterized by an excess of desire over performance. That desire has continued to goad sociology on. It has not ceased to impose tasks and establish criteria which are extremely taxing. Any who query those canons are open to accusation that they are intellectually timid or politically reactionary. Their doubts are not thought to be symptomatic of any trait but an unbecoming want of ambition.

Criticisms of symbolic interactionism have been profoundly affected by that early conception of sociology's mandate. They have urged interactionism to undertake teleological work in the high tradition of sociology. For instance, Meltzer *et al.* state it is 'overdue for interactionists to begin dealing more fully and on a large scale with problems of economic, political and historical import.'[25] Similarly Huber argues, 'for the researcher to spell out in advance and in detail what is expected is more work than transcribing events with the atheoretical simplicity of a blank mind. But such preliminary spadework would help to integrate the findings into a larger body of work, and hence make them more meaningful.'[26] The substantive and the methodological criticisms reflect the same definition of sociology: the discipline must be designed to furnish lucid answers to fundamental questions; a failure to be programmatic is evidence of inattention or laziness; and a failure to appreciate those problems suggests myopia or a perverse scheduling of effort. Lucidity and consequentiality are thought to be so momentous that all sociological work must be subordinated to those ends. They are made to become *a priori* imperatives. Many sociologists would be unwilling to concede that the determined pursuit of such goals may have a baleful influence on their enterprise. Their quest occasionally resembles that of the alchemists who sought to transmute the base metals, the evolutionists who tried to discover the primordial forms of social organisation, or the early biologists who enquired after the inner meaning of life. It is an important and worthy quest, but there is no evidence that sociology is yet strong enough to guide it. For all its aspirations, sociology has produced no stock of universal principles or laws which permit sure prediction or analysis. It is perhaps for this reason that the discipline has been so preoccupied with analytic form and so little engaged in substantive description. The sheer muddle of the social world has been deserted for the beguiling domain of the abstract model. Rationalists and essentialists would nevertheless claim that model and world are one. Their jettisoning of the impure and murky universe of phenomena impels them to upbraid the interactionist for his lack of achievement.

In another context Zinsser remarked, 'the tragedy of man is that he has developed an intelligence eager to uncover mysteries, but not strong enough to penetrate them . . . we are tortured with precocious desires to pose questions which we are sometimes capable of asking, but rarely are able to answer.'[27] Symbolic interactionism was also sired by those who looked for grand answers to grand questions. John Dewey, for instance, attempted to produce formulae for democracy. But the sociology has evolved into a relatively modest project whose humility is not quite recognised by the proponents of other schools. It does not seek to capture the essence or spirit of society; it does not claim to master the basic logic of social life; it does not pretend to address issues of majesty; and it does not assume that it has complete competence to manage the simpler work which it has adopted as its own. It merely tries to cast some light on those tracts of sociation which might yield tenable knowledge. Those tracts have been small and analytic advance has been slow and indecisive. Moreover, interactionism's commitment to phenomenalism and a restricted focus has rendered it incapable of discovering massive contradictions and ironies. The sociology cannot generate those feelings of awe which others have produced. It does not uncover a great clockwork of the social universe or reveal surprising disparities between the world of reality and the world of appearance. Its demystifying powers are slight, and it is those powers which have been cited as critical in establishing the significance of sociological observation. Davis, for example, has argued that the momentousness of sociology is construed as dependent on its ability to amaze or shock.[28] Interactionism lacks that ability. Whilst it would be philistine to contend that all is common sense, it would be mischievous to pretend that all is very different from common sense. The interactionists generally have adhered more closely to lay reasoning than have their competitors. They have not arrogated vastly superior understanding to themselves, and the contrasts between their assertions and those of everyday life are relatively slight in consequence. If their sociology does not amount to much, it may well be that no sociology is capable of very much. The interactionists have largely discarded the assumption that answers will be invariably forthcoming to questions or that those answers will be always opposed to conventional thought.

The modesty of interactionist achievements has encouraged many to grow impatient of the sociology. They have turned to other, more comprehensive sociologies. The interactionists may not have attempted to interpret the underlying order of social life, but they have fostered detailed ethnographies of the small worlds that compose American society. They have also explored the problematic practices that made those ethnographies possible. There is some reason to claim that interactionism is entitled to a place in the division of sociological labour. It could be defined as one of a number of complementary and usefully conflicting perspectives on social conduct. At the very least it presents an alternative to the great system-weavers which hover uncertainly at various points between abstract metaphysics and abstracted empiricism. It harbours a sympathetic and humane approach which characterises few of the other sociologies. The interactionist would probably be content to occupy that place. Simmel, Weber, Dewey and James acknowledged that social reality can never be saturated by a single theory or even by a galaxy of theories. They did not claim a monopoly on truth. All perspectives bear interpretative costs. The 'pluralistic realist' would have to argue that profit is gained by matching and setting ideas against one another, not by magisterially dismissing rivals as victims of unreason. He is himself the inhabitant of a particular sector of intellectual and social space, and he cannot promiscuously award authority to every other stance. It is difficult to subscribe to one stance and recognise diversity simultaneously. It is also difficult to support a scheme without proselytisation. Those who do so are forced to become a kind of sociological Jewry, condemned both to marginality and to the missionary activity of others. The interactionist is occasionally beset by his own world's equivalent of the Society for the Promotion of the Gospel Amongst the Jews.

Symbolic interactionism will continue to be a significant perspective if its adherents resist the blandishments of those who would transform it. Attempts to drastically enlarge its sphere, attempts to foist a systematic form on its reasoning, and attempts to encompass the idea of social structure will not enhance the sociology. On the contrary there will simply be a drift towards academic entropy and a loss of much that is valuable. What may conventionally appear to be barriers to the development of interactionism should actually be appreciated as its major supports. Those barriers mark the special integrity of the approach. They derive from the modesty, peculiar focus and particular openness of the sociology. Those who would synthesise or amend the sociology will do it little kindness. A commitment to interactionism entails acknowledging the limited scope of human understanding. The reforming efforts which pose grand goals for enquiry might tend only to corrupt it. Instead of outlining the paths which serviceable knowledge might take, they ensure that sociology will remain a latter-day version of the Children's Crusade.

I have argued that the crusading cast to sociology was first established by its founders. It has been perpetuated in the various contexts which reproduce the discipline. Sociology is a creature of the classroom and the textbook. It is discussed in settings which impose no useful checks on ambition and no restraints on the limits of speculation. What, after all, can restrict such analysis? There are no practical imperatives to rein disquisition. Instead, unfettered reasoning must be pursued to the very ends of the intellectually possible: it must forever hover around final questions about the nature of social life and the powers of mind. Symbolic interactionism has abstained from that style of proceeding for some time. It answered metaphysical questions by urging a return to the social world. It is thus patently at odds with the tenor of most academic discourse. In turn, it cannot satisfy the demands that are created by that discourse. It will be condemned or dismissed as a sociology which does not satisfactorily deal with basic problems. Fully exposed, it reveals anomalies and absurdities of thought. Those difficulties should not be slighted. They do plague the sociology, and I have tried to illuminate the entanglements which they produce. Yet no other sociology is free of paradox or unmanageable complexity. Each is constrained to maintain certain articles of faith which cannot stand close scrutiny. It is perhaps the peculiar quality of interactionism that it acknowledges the contrary nature of its task. It does not deny contradiction by removing thought to a conveniently exalted plane where confusion is dispelled by axiom. By remaining close to an analysis of the observable, it has accomplished two seemingly opposed results. Firstly, it has preserved the puzzling and internally warring character of explanation. Difficulties have not been erased by a return to the analytic *a priori*. Interactionism thereby stays muddled. Secondly, it has evolved a number of practical and expedient solutions to the problems that are raised by empirical investigation. The sociology comes into its own in the ethnographic setting. It has become a technique for riddling out specific problems of explanation. Few sociologies are as well equipped to master the intricate details of concrete puzzles. Most falter when they are required to address the contradictions between their own schemes and the common-sense world of Everyman. Salvation is attained only by denouncing the objects of sociology. Everyman is presented as one who is incapable of understanding his own artifacts and his own world. The truth of the sociologist is proclaimed superior to the truths of everyone else. It may not be acclaimed, but its validation is now dependent only on the sociologist's approval. When common sense cannot be accommodated in a sociological scheme, it is castigated as 'false consciousness' or 'rationalisation' or 'epiphenomenal' or an outcrop of manifest functions. It is not taken seriously, and the sociologist's system can be saved.

The answer to contradiction is thus frequently discovered in the recipe which asserts that the apparent inappropriateness of an explanation must be due to faults in the explained. For instance, when Durkheim was once challenged about the inappositeness of one of his theories, he argued that the facts themselves were wrong. So it is with much contemporary sociology. When the social world proves too recalcitrant, the scholar turns away from it. The phenomenologist moves to an introspective reading of his own consciousness; the Marxists, such as Poulantzas and Althusser, return to exegesis; and others become wholly occupied in the business of criticism. In their adopted realms, these sociologists are sovereign. The interactionist would maintain, however, that those realms float like Laputa at an uncertain distance from the earth. It is not difficult to construct a world which is rid of perplexing and obstructive disunities. It is difficult to reconcile that manufactured vision with the common experience of those who are supposed to live in the world.

The superficially problematic features of interactionism may not then prove important sources of disqualification. The sociology will never be capable of furnishing definitive analyses of human conduct. Its pretensions may never become more than humble. It may never produce any but highly focused studies. But it performs its chosen tasks quite adequately and in so doing it retains a sense of awe and bafflement. Any proposals to inject radical changes in the sociology are likely to harm it. It would be better to accept that interactionism is inherently contradictory and that improvements are no reforms. Rather, interactionists would do well to maintain their traditions. They should persist as ethnographers and detailed analysts. Other sociologists have neglected that work altogether, and their discipline would be bankrupt without it.

Summary

This book has been designed to lay bare some of the constituent arguments of symbolic interactionism. The sociology represents one complex attempt to settle the problems which flow from analysing the social world. It is an amalgam of different perspectives which were joined in the University of Chicago and subsequently modified and supplemented. Each of the separate perspectives, and the compound which they form together, is riddled with minor inconsistencies and anomalies. It would be difficult to claim that interactionism is an entirely satisfactory answer to perplexing questions about philosophical dualism, the acquisition of certain knowledge and adequate interpretation. Yet it does incorporate some interesting and detailed theses about how that answer might be framed. It extracts from Simmel a set of assumptions about the nature of sociological knowledge and social life. Robert Park, Albion Small and others imported formalism and grafted it on to the indigenous pragmatism of Chicago. Formalism urged that social objects and processes should be viewed as constructed phenomena which take their character from the structures of collaborative thinking. There can be no sure analysis of the contents of society. Rather, attention must be paid to the appearances which those contents achieve. Sociology is an abstracting activity which examines the constitution and use of forms. Its own practices are similar to those which it is intended to explore. That affinity between sociology and social processes provides a limited guarantee of the reliability of formalist thinking.

More significant was the influence of pragmatism. Pragmatism is a special adaptation of Hegelian retorts to Kant and the rationalists. It embodies an emphasis upon the fundamental unity of life, the part played by consciousness in forming existence, and the irrelevance of axiomatic logic to social enquiry. Modified by Darwinian conceptions of evolution and nature, pragmatism further stressed the emergent and integrated character of experience, the natural and unalienated properties of practical reasoning, and the central role of the organism. Scholarly thought was directed at the procedures employed by the knowing self. Society was cast as an accomplishment of conscious thought, the working product of different organisms which engaged in continual interpretation of themselves and their environment.

Fused together, formalism and pragmatism became a special vehicle of thought. They portrayed the social as a fluid and changeable series of transformations which could not be described in the language of structure and statics. Life was lent an evolving shape by patterns of dialectical thought. That thought was both public and private, simultaneously an expression of spontaneous subjectivity and alienated objectivity. It was organised by the forms which it was devised to usurp. Social life could then be read as a process built on contradiction and synthesis, opposition and affinity. It was not to be discovered outside the selves which realised it. Sociology was accordingly transformed into a limited abstracting discipline which was incapable of substantial generalisation, propositional thinking or metaphysical analysis. It must dwell on the world of the self and the grammar which sustained that world. When interactionism turned away from conventional explanation, it also cut itself off from the philosophical tradition which had created it. Its intellectual past was disowned, forcing many critical arguments to become tacit. Academic exposition was replaced by emulation, the apprenticeship and a coaching in the practical experience of research. An oral tradition emerged to serve as substitute for methodological and metaphysical argument. Much interactionism is consequently dependent on an unstated context which is assumed to be familiar to bearers of the oral tradition.

The self has become the chief focus of interactionism. It is treated as the author and product of forms of consciousness, the medium in which society is created. Selves arise when language enables men to reflect on themselves and see themselves as if they were strange and problematic. They are grounded in an internal dialogue between consciousness as subject and consciousness as object. That dialogue is ordered by conversation, and discourse has become a model for the analysis of all interaction. Unlike the self of the phenomenologists, the interactionist self is not open to intuitive or direct understanding. It is as foreign and uncertain as any other social object, and its appearances and qualities must be established in a continuous process of enquiry. That process is structured by common conventions of style and interpretation. It is collective, resting on the affirmation and support of others. As it is pursued, so facts about the self, the self's environment, and the past, present and future of objects are established. A world is manufactured, and the principles of its production reflect the forms of thought.

The self was once conceived to be a phase or moment in a complicated interaction between mind, organism and society. Authentic knowledge was held be underwritten when all the components of that interaction were secured in an explanatory scheme. However, a sociology which was impatient with metaphysics and forgetful of its past could not retain that scheme in its original guise. It also inherited a conception of the self as a single, ideal-typical process rather than one varied member of a collection of heterogeneous processes. Interactionism eventually transformed the self into something akin to pure reason, an unfettered and undifferentiated rationality which was apart from society. The central object of sociology was thus defined as an inappropriate topic for analysis.

The importance of the self may also be revealed by a discussion of the distinctive methodology of symbolic interactionism. Participant observation inserts the self of the sociologist into a research setting, permitting him to record and experience events as they unfold. It rests upon an admonition to practice two discrete and somewhat contradictory roles. As observer, the sociologist must survey social life from without, treating it in a fashion which is unfamiliar and disturbing to ordinary experience. As participant, he must attempt to merge with the world about him. Merging and distant appraisal are irreconcilable. Excessive reliance on either state is held to impede research, but the two cannot be synthesised. In the main, that tension is resolved by formulating ideas and explanations *in situ*. Although there do not seem to be any methodological recipes for undertaking participant observation, problems are dispelled before their complexities become analytically distinct. In common with answers to many other problems of interactionism, the dilemmas of participant observation are resolved in practice and not in speculation.

As a whole, I have tried to depict interactionism as one rather difficult solution to the problems which plague sociology. It is not a completely compelling solution, but it does address issues which other sociologies ignore. There is no reason to suppose that any alternative sociology is less troubled with inconsistency or uncertainty. It is the virtue of interactionism that it has focused explicitly on some of the more intractable matters which confront the discipline. It has acknowledged complexity and dismissed contemplative or axiomatic reasoning as a proper escape. Instead of repairing the faults of theory by more theory, it has turned to an extensive exploration of the social world. It is taken to be justified by its ethnography rather than by its formal statements about the nature of reasoning.

Those who have chosen to criticise it have generally tended to misread its purpose and nature. Interactionism discards most macro-sociological thought as an unsure and over-ambitious metaphysics. It claims that the realm described by macrosociology is not accessible to intelligent examination. It is a realm of the imagination whose structures mirror those of reason alone. Critics who castigate interactionism assert the sovereignty of that realm, failing to understand any who deny its existence. Symbolic interactionism is not merely an inept or undeveloped version of orthodox sociology. It is an unorthodox sociology which offers its own particular vision.

Notes

PREFACE

1. Stanley Cohen and Jock Young, for instance, furnished important ideas which merged Wilkins's thesis of deviancy amplification with conventional interactionist descriptions of labelling processes. Cf. S. Cohen, *Folk Devils and Moral Panics* (MacGibbon and Kee, London, 1972) and J. Young, *The Drugtakers* (MacGibbon and Kee, 1971).
2. For a fuller description of this process, see S. Cohen; 'Criminology and the Sociology of Deviance in Britain', in P. Rock and M. McIntosh (eds.), *Deviance and Social Control* (Tavistock, London, 1974).
3. A Small, 'Scholarship and Social Agitation', *American Journal of Sociology*, 1 5 (Mar. 1896) p. 581.
4. C. Peirce, quoted in C. Wright Mills, *Sociology and Pragmatism* (Paine-Whitman, New York, 1964) p. 126.
5. Private communication.

CHAPTER I

1. For commentaries on that oligopoly, and for claims which have been made for its members, see: A. Giddens, *Capitalism and Modern Social Theory* (Cambridge University Press, London, 1971); H. Hughes, *Consciousness and Society* (MacGibbon and Kee, London, 1959); R. Aron, *Main Currents in Sociological Thought* (Penguin, Harmondsworth, 1968); R. Nisbet, *The Sociological Tradition* (Basic Books, New York, 1966); R. Aron, *La Sociologie allemande contemporaine* (Presses Universitaires de France, Paris, 1966).
2. *The Shorter Oxford English Dictionary* defines 'epistemology' as 'the theory or science of the method or grounds of knowledge'.
3. Private communication.
4. I am grateful to Howard Becker for this point.
5. Private communication.
6. It is of course the case that the University of Chicago was also marked by conflict and a lack of co-operation. Members left or quarrelled with one another. Some seemed not to have alluded to one another in their writings despite the apparent affinities between their ideas. It is further the case that the Chicago departments were anything but homogeneous. They contained people who could not be properly identified with the developing Chicago 'school'. Yet there was nevertheless an unusual working co-operation between the early staff of the university, and it was a most fertile co-operation. For one description of that important early period, see D. Miller, *George Herbert Mead: Self, Language and the World* (University of Texas Press,

Austin, 1973) especially the introduction. On p. xxiii Miller quotes William James: 'I have had all sorts of outside things shoved upon me since my return a month ago to Cambridge . . . The best of the lot was reading up the output of the "Chicago School of Thought" . . . It is splendid stuff, and Dewey is a hero. A real school and real thought. At Harvard we have plenty of thought but no school. At Yale and Cornell, the other way about.'

7. S. Kirson Weinberg, 'Varying Interpretations and Issues in Symbolic Interaction Theory', unpublished paper, p. 1.

8. L. Broom, introduction to *Chicago Sociology 1920–1932* by R. Faris (Chandler Publishing, San Francisco, 1967) p. ix.

9. Cf. T. Vaughan and L. Reynolds, 'The Sociology of Symbolic Interactionism', *American Sociologist* (Aug. 1968).

10. L. Reynolds *et al.*, 'The "Self" and Symbolic Interaction Theory: An Examination of the Social Sources of Conceptual Diversity', in L. Reynolds and J. Reynolds (eds.), *The Sociology of Sociology* (David McKay, New York, 1970).

11. 'Dialogue with Howard S. Becker', *Issues in Criminology*, V 2 (Summer 1970) p. 160.

12. Ibid. p. 161.

13. Ibid. p. 162. It ought perhaps to be stressed that not all the members of the group named by Becker did actually evolve into committed interactionists. Freidson may certainly be cited as a symbolic interactionist. Goffman's work often turns towards interactionism. Gold has written recognisably interactionist pieces. But Kornhauser and Short could not properly be described as adherents.

14. Private communication.

15. H. Blumer, 'What is Wrong with Social Theory?', in *Symbolic Interactionism*, (Prentice-Hall, N. J., 1969) p. 148.

16. Cf. E. Lemert, Human Deviance, *Social Problems and Social Control*, 2nd ed. (Prentice-Hall, 1972) Ch. 1.

17. Cf. H. Becker, 'Labelling Theory Reconsidered', in *Outsiders*, 2nd ed. (Free Press, New York, 1973).

18. Cf. J. Manis and B. Meltzer (eds.), *Symbolic Interaction* (Allyn and Bacon, Boston, 1967) pp. 495–6; J. Manis, 'Assessing the Seriousness of Social Problems', *Social Problems*, 22 (1974).

19. In the case of the interactionist approach to the study of deviancy, see I. Taylor, P. Walton and J. Young, *The New Criminology* (Routledge and Kegan Paul, London, 1973); A. Gouldner, 'The Sociologist as Partisan', *American Sociologist* (May 1968); R. Akers 'Problems in the Sociology of Deviance', *Social Forces*, June 1968, Vol. 46, and A Liazos, 'The Poverty of the Sociology of Deviance', *Social Problems*, 20 (Winter 1972); M. Mankoff, 'Societal Reaction and Career Deviance: A Critical Analysis', *Sociological Quarterly*, 12 (1971). All revolve around fundamental misinterpretations of symbolic interactionism.

20. For instance a work which expounds one perspective on symbolic interactionism puts forward the argument that interactionists are confused and unappreciative in their neglect of macrostructural process; see B. Meltzer *et al.*, *Symbolic Interactionism* (Routledge and Kegan Paul, London, 1975) p. 117. It can be asserted however that such neglect flows from a reasoned ontology which is not based on myopia and incompetence alone.

21. Private communication.

22. Cf. K. Mannheim, 'A Sociological Theory of Culture and its Knowability:

Conjunctive and Communicative Thought', in P. Kecskemeti (ed.), *Essays on the Sociology of Knowledge* (O. U. P., New York, 1952).

23. J. Huber; 'Symbolic Interaction as a Pragmatic Perspective: The Bias of Emergent Theory', *American Sociological Review*, XXXVIII 2 (Apr. 1973) p. 275.

24. R. Schmitt, 'SI and Emergent Theory: A Reexamination'. *American Sociological Review*, XXXIX 3 (June 1974) p. 453. Of course interactionists do not all maintain that the perspective is difficult to reproduce in teaching or writing. Neither is interactionism the only sociological perspective which is reliant upon an oral tradition. But interactionism does seem to be rather importantly affected by the qualities which I have described. Although it would be misleading to suggest that they are peculiar to interactionism, they do form a necessary part of any description of the perspective's development and diffusion.

25. By 'reflexiveness' I mean a turning-back of the mind on itself.

26. Cf. T. Kuhn, *The Structure of Scientific Revolutions* (University of Chicago Press, Chicago, 1962).

27. The problem is exacerbated in the social sciences because those disciplines explore themes which have deeply embedded metaphysical roots. In an organised confrontation between representatives of phenomenology* and behaviourism**, for example, one phenomenologist observed: '. . . I shall urge that [behaviourism] has outlived whatever usefulness [it] might once have had. If you expect me to support this statement via a final and crushing refutation of behaviorist epistemology, you will be disappointed. I suspect that there is a class of positions that are wrong but not refutable and that behaviorism may be in such a class. For many methodological proposals and for certain positions of metaphysical or even empirical import, I am not even sure what a "refutation" would mean.' (S. Koch; 'Psychology and Emerging Conceptions of Knowledge as Unitary', in T. Wann (ed.), *Behaviorism and Phenomenology* (University of Chicago Press, 1964, p. 6.). *Phenomenology may be taken to refer to the study of the composition of phenomena. It generally denies the utility of studying essences or noumena. **Behaviourism is that style of enquiry which focuses on the 'objective properties' of behaviour.

28. *The Shorter Oxford English Dictionary* defines the Hegelian version of the dialectic as 'the process of thought by which . . . contradictions are seen to merge themselves in a higher truth that comprehends them'.

29. 'Idealism' may be defined as the doctrine which maintains that objects and processes in the world are ideas of some collective, single or supra-individual mind.

30. 'Materialism' is the stance that maintains the supremacy or sole existence of matter and its movement.

31. Cf. P. Berger and T. Luckmann, *The Social Construction of Reality* (Doubleday, Garden City, 1966).

32. Thus Rose asserts 'perhaps half the sociologists of the United States were nurtured, directly or indirectly, on its conceptions and approaches to research'. A. Rose, preface to A. Rose (ed.), *Human Behavior and Social Processes* (Houghton Mifflin, Boston, 1962) p. vii. However, it is important to add that few European sociologists would have been nurtured on interactionism.

33. Kenneth Plummer has observed that interactionism is not only marginal to sociology, it is also thought to be a peripheral social psychology.

34. Howard Becker has pointed out that many sociologies considered important in Europe are barely represented in America. Thus Althusser, Lukács and others do not exercise an appreciable influence over the development of American sociology –

they are not significant others in the university world. This is undoubtedly so, and it may have been misleading to make intellectual phantoms so substantial. Yet my argument is not addressed only to America, and these ignored thinkers are significant despite their spectral status in the United States. I shall continue to allude to them, appreciating that their arguments are not entertained in the concrete debates about interactionism. The intellectual importance of thinkers is not always identical to their actual importance in the settings which produce ideas. There must be some confusing movement backwards and forwards between a fictitious realm of ideas and a concrete realm of thinking.

35. I am indebted to Kenneth Plummer for this point.

36. For a discussion of the romantic character and connections of interactionism, see A. Gouldner, 'Romanticism and Classicism: Deep structures in social science', in *For Sociology* (Pelican Books, Middlesex, 1975).

37. See my introduction to *Drugs and Politics* (Transaction, N. J., forthcoming).

38. J. Lofland; 'Interactionist Imagery and Analytic Interruptus', in T. Shibutani (ed.), *Human Nature and Collective Behavior* (Prentice-Hall, N. J., 1970).

39. Cf. B. Glaser and A. Strauss, *The Discovery of Grounded Theory* (Aldine, Chicago, 1967). (No interactionist would claim that a complete absence of presuppositions is either desirable or possible.)

40. Cf. N. Denzin, 'Symbolic Interactionism and Ethnomethodology: A Proposed Synthesis', *American Sociological Review*, XXXIV 6 (Dec. 1969).

41. Cf. P. Singelmann; 'Exchange as Symbolic Interaction', *American Sociological Review*, XXXVII (Aug. 1972), pp. 414–24.

42. S. Kirson Weinberg, 'Varying Interpretations and Issues in Symbolic Interaction Theory', unpublished paper, p. 1

43. Cf. I. Taylor, P. Walton and J. Young, *The New Criminology* (Routledge and Kegan Paul, London, 1973); J. Young, 'Working-Class Criminology', in I. Taylor, P. Walton and J. Young, *Critical Criminology* (Routledge and Kegan Paul, 1975).

44. Notably A. Rose; 'A Systematic Summary of Symbolic Interaction Theory', in A. Rose (ed.), *Human Behavior and Social Processes*; H. Blumer, 'The Methodological Position of Symbolic Interactionism' and 'Society as Symbolic Interaction' in *Symbolic Interactionism*.

45. B. Meltzer *et al.*, *Symbolic Interactionism*, may be an exception but it is not lengthy and it does reflect one rather particular conception of the sociology.

46. R. Merton, *Social Theory and Social Structure* (Free Press, Ill., 1957).

47. G. Stone *et al.*, 'On Methodology and Craftsmanship in the Criticism of Sociological Perspectives', *American Sociological Review*, XXXIX 3 (June 1974) pp. 456–7.

48. Cf. H. Blumer, 'The Methodological Position of Symbolic Interactionism' in *Symbolic Interactionism* and *Critiques of Research in the Social Sciences: An Appraisal of Thomas and Znaniecki's 'The Polish Peasant in Europe and America'* (Social Science Research Council, New York, 1939).

49. Everett Hughes has employed diverse techniques in the course of his research. He has methodically adhered to certain strategies and shunned others, but he also appears to reject particular styles on temperamental and not epistemological grounds. For instance, he stated in a survey of the study of occupations: 'I leave to others the task of counting the occupations in industrial economies and the changing numbers of people engaged in each of them, and the tiresome business of fitting the many occupations into a small enough number of categories to permit crowding them into

tables. I can think of no set of categories that has been given such heavy sociological work to do . . . as those of occupations in census tables.' E. Hughes; 'The Study of Occupations', in *The Sociological Eye* (Aldine-Atherton, Chicago, 1971) p. 284.
50. B. Glaser and A. Strauss, *The Discovery of Grounded Theory*, p. 230.
51. S. Bruyn, *The Human Perspective in Sociology*, (Prentice-Hall, N. J., 1966) pp. 28, 29.
52. A. Strauss, *Mirrors and Masks* (Free Press, Ill., 1959) p. 11.
53. M. Dalton, *Men Who Manage* (John Wiley, New York, 1959). (Significantly, perhaps, the book's subtitle is 'Fusions of Feeling and Theory in Administration'.)
54. M. Dalton, 'Preconceptions and Methods in *Men Who Manage*', in P. Hammond (ed.), *Sociologists at Work: Essays on the Craft of Social Research* (Basic Books, New York, 1964) p. 56.
55. Cf. A. Rose, preface to A. Rose, preface to A. Rose (ed.), *Human Behavior and Social Processes*, (Houghton Mifflin, Boston, 1962) p. vii.
56. H. Blumer, 'Society as Symbolic Interaction' in *Symbolic Interactionism*, p. 78.
57. In fact one of the principal exponents of interactionism, Howard S. Becker, told me that he doubted whether it was possible to discuss symbolic interactionism as a unified entity at all.
58. It diverges markedly from another such reconstruction, for example. See the summary produced by a group whose affinity with the 'Iowa School' of interactionism is rather greater than mine. B. Meltzer *et al.*, *Symbolic Interactionism* (Routledge and Kegan Paul, London, 1975).

CHAPTER 2

1. Cf. A. Rose, preface to *Human Behavior and Social Processes*, p. viii.
2. J. Huber, 'Symbolic Interaction as a Pragmatic Perspective', op. cit., p. 275.
3. M. Kuhn, 'Major Trends in Symbolic Interaction . . .', in J. Manis and B. Meltzer (eds.), *Symbolic Interaction*, pp. 47, 48.
4. Indeed he argued that conversation was the best vehicle for the cultivation of thought. Cf. G. Lee, *George Herbert Mead* (King's Crown, New York, 1945) p. v. When he did publish, it was often in journals that were not routinely read by sociologists. Cf. M. Kuhn, 'Major Trends in Symbolic Interaction', p. 47.
5. Cf. C. Morris, introduction to *Mind, Self and Society* by George Herbert Mead (University of Chicago Press, Chicago, 1934).
6. H. Blumer, 'The Methodological Position of Symbolic Interactionism' in *Symbolic Interactionism*, p. 1n.
7. R. Faris, *Chicago Sociology*, p. 88.
8. Cf. 'Dialogue with Howard S. Becker', *Issues in Criminology*, p. 165.
9. Cf. J. Petras, 'George Herbert Mead's Theory of Self: A Study of the Origin and Convergence of Ideas', *Canadian Review of Sociology and Anthropology*, x 2 (May 1973); J. Petras, 'John Dewey and the Rise of Interactionism in American social theory', *Journal of the History of the Behavioral Sciences*, IV (1968); J. Petras, 'Psychological Antecedents of sociological theory in America: James Mark Baldwin and William James', *Journal of the History of the Behavioral Sciences*, IV (1968).
10. See for example, G. Allport, 'The Historical Background of Modern Social Psychology', in G. Lindzey (ed.), *Handbook of Social Psychology* (Addison-Wesley, Cambridge, Mass., 1954) vol. 1.
11. In the arguments of Heraclitus, Bishop Berkeley or David Hume, for instance.

12. Cf. G. Mead, *The Philosophy of the Act* (University of Chicago Press, Chicago, 1938) pp. 629–30.
13. Dewey and Mead, for instance, built critically on the works of Bergson and injected their influence into interactionism.
14. Thus Faris's *Chicago Sociology*, the principal history, does not refer to Kant or to Hegel. It mentions Simmel a mere seven times. Similarly, Meltzer *et al.* treat the early interactionists as if they had been almost entirely autodidacts (Cf. B. Meltzer *et al.*, *Symbolic Interactionism*, Ch. 1). Nevertheless, as I shall argue, that neglect is by no means universal. A number of symbolic interactionists are clearly aware of their roots. Denzin, Hughes and others make frequent allusions to Simmel. They are less inclined to pass back beyond Simmel, however.
15. Cf. D. Levine, introduction to *Georg Simmel on Individuality and Social Forms* (University of Chicago Press, Chicago, 1971); B. Meltzer *et al.*, *Symbolic Interactionism*, pp. 51–2; D. Ball, 'Sarcasm as Sociation,' *Canadian Review of Sociology and Anthropology*, II (Nov. 1965); N. Denzin, 'The Methodologies of Symbolic Interaction', in G. Stone and H. Farberman (eds.), *Social Psychology through Symbolic Interaction* (Xerox, Mass., 1970) esp. p. 456.
16. 'The Life Histories of W. I. Thomas and Robert E. Park', *American Journal of Sociology*, LXXIX 2 (Sept. 1973) p. 257.
17. Cf. L. Braude, '"Park and Burgess": An Appreciation', *American Journal of Sociology*, LXXVII (July 1970); R. Park; *The Crowd and the Public* (University of Chicago Press, Chicago, 1972).
18. E. Hughes, 'Robert E. Park', in *The Sociological Eye*, p. 544.
19. R. Park and E. Burgess, *Introduction to the Science of Sociology* (University of Chicago Press, Chicago, 1921).
20. Cf. S. Bruyn, *The Human Perspective in Sociology*, p. 10n. Arnold Rose claims that interactionism had an independent origin in the works of Max Weber and Georg Simmel: A. Rose, introduction to 'A Systematic Summary of Symbolic Interaction Theory', in A. Rose (ed.), *Human Behavior and Social Processes*, p. 3.
21. Instances are social marginality and the natural history of relations between groups. Cf. E. Hughes, 'Social Change and Status Protest: An Essay on the Marginal Man', *Phylon*, X (1st Quarter, 1949) p. 58, and E. Hughes, 'The Natural History of a Research Project: French Canada', in *The Sociological Eye*, p. 532.
22. That position has been partially undermined by the recent phenomenological invasion of symbolic interactionism. Some intellectual confusion has consequently arisen, and I shall discuss it at various points throughout the book.
23. Cf. H. Blumer, *Symbolic Interactionism*, passim; A. Cicourel, *Method and Measurement in Sociology* (Free Press, New York, 1964).
24. M. Janowitz, introduction to the 1969 edition of *Introduction to the Science of Sociology* (University of Chicago Press, Chicago, 1969) p. viii.
25. Cf. A. Reiss, introduction to *Louis Wirth on Cities and Social Life* (University of Chicago Press, 1964) p. xii.
26. Cf. E. Volkart, introduction to *Social Behavior and Personality* (Social Science Research Council, New York, 1951) p. 4.
27. Cf. H. Becker, 'The Career of the Chicago Public School Teacher', in *Sociological Work*.
28. Cf. J. Roth, *Timetables* (Bobbs-Merrill, Indianapolis, 1963).
29. Cf. P. Cressey, *The Taxi-Dance Hall* (University of Chicago Press, Chicago, 1932).
30. Cf. E. Goffman, *Asylums* (Anchor Books, New York, 1961).

31. Cf. C. Werthman and I. Piliavin, 'Gang Members and the Police', in D. Bordua (ed.), *The Police* (John Wiley, New York, 1967).
32. Cf. E. Goffman, *The Presentation of Self in Everyday Life* (Anchor Books, New York, 1959).
33. Cf. E. Goffman, *Relations in Public* (Allen Lane, London, 1971).
34. Cf. R. Park, 'Human Ecology', *American Journal of Sociology*, XLII (1936).
35. Cf. S. Messinger et al., 'Life as Theater', *Sociometry*, XXV (1962).
36. Cf. T. Scheff, *Being Mentally Ill*.
37. Cf. R. Park, 'Symbiosis and Socialization', *American Journal of Sociology*, XLV. (1939).
38. Cf. E. Hughes, *The Sociological Eye*, Part III.
39. Cf. H. Becker, 'Notes on the Concept of Commitment', in *Sociological Work*.
40. Cf. E. Goffman, *Encounters* (Bobbs-Merrill, Indianapolis, 1961).
41. Cf. H. Blumer, *Symbolic Interactionism, passim*.
42. Cf. D. Matza, *Becoming Deviant* (Prentice-Hall, N. J., 1969) Ch. 1.
43. Cf. B. Glaser and A. Strauss, *The Discovery of Grounded Theory, passim*.
44. Cf. A. Brittan, *Meanings and Situations* (Routledge and Kegan Paul, London, 1973).
45. R. Park and E. Burgess, *Introduction to the Science of Sociology* (1969 ed.) p. 15.
46. Cf. H. Blumer, *Symbolic Interactionism*, p. 34.
47. E. Hughes, 'Robert E. Park', in *The Sociological Eye*, p. 549.
48. N. Denzin, *The Research Act* (Aldine, Chicago, 1970) p. 15.
49. W. Thomas and F. Znaniecki, *The Polish Peasant in Europe and America* (Alfred Knopf, New York, 1927) vol. II, p. 1834.
50. L. Wirth, quoted in H. Odum, *American Sociology* (Longmans, New York, 1951) p. 230.
51. Cf. G. Psathas, *Phenomenological Sociology* (John Wiley, New York, 1973) p. 3.
52. Cf. F. Davis, *Passage Through Crisis* (Bobbs-Merrill, Indianapolis, 1963) p. 10.
53. H. Becker, 'Kinds of Deviance' in *Outsiders* (Free Press, New York, 1963) p. 23.
54. Cf. E. Goffman, 'The Moral Career of the Mental Patient', *Psychiatry*, XXII 2 (May 1959).
55. H. Becker, 'Marihuana Use and Social Control', in *Outsiders*, p. 60.
56. J. Auld, 'Transformations of Drug Use', in P. Rock (ed.), *Drugs and Politics*, (Transaction, N. J., forthcoming).
57. Cf. H. Becker and A. Strauss, 'Careers, Personality and Adult Socialization', *American Journal of Sociology*, LXII (Nov. 1956).
58. Cf. E. Goffman, *Stigma* (Penguin Books, Middlesex, 1968).
59. Cf. E. Hughes, 'Dilemmas and Contradictions of Status', *American Journal of Sociology*, L (Mar. 1945).
60. Cf. P. Rock and D. Downes, 'Social Reaction to Deviance', *British Journal of Sociology*, XXII 4 (Dec. 1971).
61. J. Lofland, *Deviance and Identity* (Prentice-Hall, N. J., 1969).
62. E. Lemert, *Social Pathology* (McGraw-Hill, New York, 1951).
63. T. Scheff, *Being Mentally Ill* (Aldine Press, Chicago, 1966).
64. Cf. E. Sagarin, *Deviants and Deviance* (Praeger, New York, 1975) p. 139.
65. Cf. J. Gibbs, 'Issues in Defining Deviant Behavior' in R. Scott and J. Douglas (eds), *Theoretical Perspectives on Deviance* (Basic Books, New York, 1972).
66. Cf. R. Akers, 'Problems in the Sociology of Deviance'.
67. Cf. A. Gouldner, 'The Sociologist as Partisan'.

68. Cf. I. Taylor, P. Walton and J. Young, *The New Criminology*.

CHAPTER 3

1. G. Hegel, *The Phenomenology of Mind* (Harper Torchbooks, New York, 1967) pp. 137−8.
2. Ibid., p. 808.
3. Ibid., p. 155.
4. For a fuller discussion of pragmatism and its diversity, see D. Rucker, *The Chicago Pragmatists* (University of Minnesota Press, Minneapolis, 1969) and C. Wright Mills, *Sociology and Pragmatism* (Paine-Whitman, New York, 1964).
5. Mine is not an entirely unjustified approach. Miller claimed, for instance, that Mead never voiced criticism of Dewey's work. Cf. D. Miller, *George Herbert Mead*, p. xx.
6. Cf. G. Mead, 'The Philosophy of John Dewey', *International Journal of Ethics*, XLVI 1, (Oct. 1935), p. 65; C. Wright Mills, *Sociology and Pragmatism, passim*.
7. Cf. R. Perry, *The Thought and Character of William James* (George Braziller, New York, 1954) esp. Ch. XVIII.
8. Cf. J. Nathanson, *John Dewey* (Scriber's, New York, 1951) p. 10.
9. Ibid., p. 18.
10. S. Hook, *John Dewey: An Intellectual Portrait* (John Day, New York, 1939) p. 13.
11. J. Dewey, quoted in M. White, *The Origins of Dewey's Instrumentalism* (Columbia University Press, New York, 1943) p. 36. See also D. Miller, *George Herbert Mead*, p. 4.
12. Cf. C. Morris, introduction to *Mind, Self and Society*, p. xiii.
13. G. Mead, 'Josiah Royce − A Personal Impression', *International Journal of Ethics*, XXVII 2 (Jan. 1917), p. 169.
14. Cf. C. Wright Mills, *Sociology and Pragmatism* (O.U.P., New York, 1966) p. 357; G. Mead, 'The Philosophy of John Dewey', *passim*.
15. C. Cooley, *Human Nature and the Social Order* (Free Press, Ill., 1956) pp. 36−7.
16. Cf. G. Mead, 'The Philosophy of John Dewey', p. 67.
17. Bergson and Renouvier formed the intellectual catalyst of much pragmatism. Cf. G. Mead, 'The Philosophies of Royce, James, and Dewey in their American Setting', *International Journal of Ethics*, XL 2 (Jan. 2 (Jan. 1930) p. 224.
18. Ibid., p. 227.
19. G. Mead, *Movements of Thought in the Nineteenth Century* (University of Chicago Press, Chicago, 1936) p. 351.
20. Cf. A. Strauss, introduction to *The Social Psychology of George Herbert Mead* (University of Chicago Press, 1962) p. ix.
21. Cf. C. Cooley, *Human Nature and the Social Order* p. 35.
22. J. Dewey, quoted in M. White, op. cit., p. 40.
23. Cf. R. Perry, op. cit., pp. 195−6.
24. G. Mead, 'The Philosophy of John Dewey', p. 70.
25. W. James, *Collected Essays and Reviews* (Longmans New York, 1920) p. 318.
26. J. Dewey, quoted in G. Geiger, *John Dewey in perspective* (O.U.P., New York, 1958) p. 13.
27. S. Hook, *John Dewey*, p. 14.
28. D. Rucker, *The Chicago Pragmatists*, p. 28.

29. J. Dewey, *Experience and Nature* (W. W. Norton, New York, 1929) p. 9.
30. J. Dewey, 'The Reflex Arc Concept in Social Psychology', *American Journal of Sociology*, vol. 2 (1896).
31. Cf. J. Angell, 'The Relations of Structural and Functional Psychology to Philosophy', in *Investigations Representing the Departments* (University of Chicago Press, Chicago, 1903).
32. J. Dewey, 'Perception and Organic Action', *The Journal of Philosophy, Psychology and Scientific Methods*, IX 24 (21 Nov. 1912) p. 648.
33. C. Morris, introduction to *The Philosophy of the Act* by George Herbert Mead, (University of Chicago Press, Chicago, 1938) p. xlvi.
34. Charles Peirce, quoted in C. Wright Mills, *Sociology and Pragmatism*, p. 158.
35. J. Dewey, *Logic* (Henry Holt, New York, 1938) p. 106.
36. Cf. J. Nathanson, *John Dewey*, p. 28; J. Petras, 'John Dewey and the Rise of Interactionism', p. 21; J. Dewey, 'Realism without Monism or Dualism – II', *The Journal of Philosophy*, XIX 13 (22 June 1922) p. 360.
37. G. mead, 'The Philosophy of John Dewey', p. 75.
38. J. Dewey 'Perception and Organic Action', *The Journal of Philosophy, Psychology, and Scientific Methods*, IX 24 (21 Nov. 1912) p. 649.
39. G. Mead, 'The Philosophy of John Dewey', p. 74.
40. J. Dewey, 'Perception and Organic Action', p. 646.
41. J. Roth, *John Dewey and Self-Realization* (Prentice-Hall, N.J., 1962) p. 24.
42. Cf. W. James, *A Pluralistic Universe* (Longmans, New York, 1920).
43. Cf. G. Geiger, op. cit., p. 10; G. Mead, 'The Philosophies of Royce, James, and Dewey in their American Setting', p. 229.
44. W. James, *Pragmatism*, (Longmans, New York, 1949) p. 30.
45. It requires some delicacy to maintain that analytic knowledge is itself unnatural. As I shall show, Mead argued that there is a contradiction in the pragmatists' anti-intellectualism. It is a contradiction which is exacerbated by the blurred distinction between the virtually essentialist account of immediate knowledge and the phenomenalist account of knowing as praxis. That latter contradiction is partially resolved, but it is a fragile resolution which gives rise to the ambiguities of interactionist ontology.
46. J. Dewey, *Logic*, p. 70.
47. J. Dewey, *Experience and Nature*, p. 8.
48. J. Dewey, *Logic*, p. 67.
49. Ibid., p. 104.
50. Ibid., p. 68.
51. W. James, *A Pluralistic Universe*, op. cit., 290.
52. Cf. J. Nathanson, *John Dewey*, p. 46.
53. Cf. A. Ayer, *The Central Questions of Philosophy* (Holt, Rinehart and Winston, New York, 1974).
54. W. James, *Pragmatism*, p. 67.
55. J. Dewey, *Reconstruction in Philosophy* (Beacon Press, Boston, 1948) p. 61.
56. W. James, *Pragmatism*, p. 51.
57. Cf. W. James, *Psychology*, (Henry Holt, New York, 1910).
58. Cf. M. White, *The Origins of Dewey's Instrumentalism*, p. 151.
59. Quoted in S. Hook, *John Dewey*, p. 20.
60. J. Nathanson, *John Dewey*, p. 52.
61. G. Mead, *Movements of Thought in the Nineteenth Century*, p. 385.

62. G. Mead, 'The Philosophies of Royce, James, and Dewey in their American Setting', p. 228.
63. C. Morris, introduction to *The Philosophy of the Act*, p. xii.
64. Cf. A. Gouldner, 'Romanticism and Classicism', p. 328ff.
65. W. James, quoted in C. Wright Mills, *Sociology and Pragmatism*, p. 268.
66. J. Dewey, quoted ibid., pp. 436, 430.
67. G. Stone and H. Farberman, *Social Psychology through Symbolic Interaction* (Xerox College Publishing, Mass., 1970) p. 7.
68. A. Gouldner, 'Romanticism and Classicism', p. 328.
69. W. I. Thomas, 'The Relation of Research to the Social Process', in W. Swann et al., *Essays on Research in the Social Sciences* (Brookings Institute, Washington, 1931) p. 190.
70. For an extended discussion of the use of the life history in interactionism, see N. Denzin, *The Research Act*, Ch. 10.
71. C. Shaw, *The Jackroller* (University of Chicago Press, Chicago, 1966).
72. E. Sutherland, *The Professional Thief* (University of Chicago Press, 1937).
73. C. Shaw, *The Natural History of a Delinquent Career* (University of Chicago Press, 1931).
74. H. Becker, 'The Life History and the Scientific Mosaic', in *Sociological Work*, p. 70.
75. Cf. L. Reynolds et al., 'The "Self" in Symbolic Interaction Theory', op. cit.
76. Cf. B. Glaser and A. Strauss, *Awareness of Dying* (Aldine, Chicago, 1965); A. Strauss, *Mirrors and Masks* (Free Press, Illinois, 1959); E. Goffman, *The Presentation of Self in Everyday Life* (Doubleday Anchor, New York, 1959).
77. N. Denzin, *The Research Act*, p. 185.
78. S. Bruyn, *The Human Perspective in Sociology*, p. 170.
79. Cf. E. Faris, 'The Nature of Human Nature', in E. Burgess (ed.), *The Urban Community* (University of Chicago Press, Chicago, 1926) p. 23.
80. C. Cooley quoted in N. Timasheff, *Sociological Theory* (Random House, New York, 1967) p. 146.
81. W. I. Thomas, *The Child in America* (Alfred Knopf, New York, 1932) p. 572.
82. N. Anderson, *The Hobo* (University of Chicago Press, Chicago, 1923).
83. H. Becker et al., *Making the Grade* (John Wiley, New York, 1968).
84. J. Douglas, *Research on Deviance* (Random House, New York, 1972) p. 4.
85. I am of course aware that Jack Douglas cannot be properly described as an interactionist, a pragmatist or a formalist. Yet he is concerned with parallel problems and his observations are often pertinent. It should not be taken that every sociologist cited in this book is necessarily a full proponent of symbolic interactionism.
86. J. Douglas, *Existential Sociology*, unpublished paper, 1973, p. 45.
87. Quotation from a letter to Kurt Wolff in K. Wolff, 'The Sociology of Knowledge and Sociological Theory', in L. Gross (ed.), *Symposium on Sociological Theory* (Harper and Row, New York, 1959) p. 571.
88. Ibid., p. 571.
89. In a sense, symbolic interactionism is itself unformulated because its nature is also treated as emergent.
90. A. Strauss, *Mirrors and Masks*, pp. 9–10.
91. H. Blumer, 'What is Wrong with Social Theory?', in *Symbolic Interactionism*, p. 148.
92. J. Dewey, 'An Analysis of Reflective Thought', *The Journal of Philosophy*, XIX 2 (19 Jan. 1922) p. 34.

93. H. Becker, preface to 'History, Culture and Subjective Experience', in H. Becker et al. (eds.), *Institutions and the Person* (Aldine, Chicago, 1968) p. 272.
94. J. Lofland, *Analyzing Social Settings* (Wadsworth, Calif., 1971) p. 2.
95. R. Kwant, *Phenomenology of Language* (Duquesne University Press, Penn., 1965) p. 144.
96. Cf. E. Hughes, 'The Study of Institutions', *Social Forces*, xx (Mar. 1942).
97. H. Becker, 'Field Work Evidence', in *Sociological Work*, p. 40.
98. Cf. R. Lichtman, 'Symbolic Interactionism and Social Reality: Some Marxist Queries', *Berkeley Journal of Sociology*, xv (1970).
99. Cf. H. Becker, 'The Life History and the Scientific Mosaic', in *Sociological Work*, pp. 65-6.
100. Cf. R. Park, *Race and Culture* (Free Press, Ill., 1950) pp. v-ix.
101. H. Becker, 'Labelling Theory Reconsidered', in *Outsiders* (1973 ed.), p. 190.
102. Ibid., pp. 189-90.
103. Cf. J. Ditton, *Part-time Crime* (Macmillan, London, 1973).
104. S. Bruyn, *The Human Perspective in Sociology*, p. xii.
105. A. Rose, preface to *Human Behavior and Social Processes*, p. vii.
106. Cf. R. Faris, *Chicago Sociology*, passim.
107. G. Mead, 'The Philosophies of Royce, James and Mead in their American Setting' p. 215.
108. Ibid., p. 215.
109. Cf. R. Park, 'The Urban Community as a Spacial Pattern and a Moral Order', in E. Burgess (ed.), *The Urban Community*.
110. Cf. S. Bruyn, *The Human Perspective in Sociology*, p. 10n.
111. Cf. C. Shaw and H. McKay, *Juvenile Delinquency and Urban Areas* (University of Chicago Press, Chicago, 1942).
112. Cf. S. Hook, *John Dewey*, p. 7.
113. D. Matza, *Becoming Deviant*, p. 26.
114. L. Shaskolsky, 'The Development of Sociological Theory in America', in L. Reynolds and J. Reynolds (eds.), *The Sociology of Sociology*, p. 18.
115. Ibid., p. 17.
116. Cf. P. Berger et al., *The Homeless Mind: Modernization and Consciousness* (Vintage, New York, 1973) Ch. 3.
117. Cf. J. Lincourt and P. Hare, 'Neglected American Philosophers in the History of Symbolic Interactionism', *Journal of the History of the Behavioral Sciences*, IX 4 (Oct. 1973) p. 333.
118. 'The Life Histories of W. I. Thomas and Robert E. Park', op. cit., p. 255.
119. B. Glaser and A. Strauss, The Discovery of Grounded Theory, p. 97.
120. Ibid., p. 154.
121. Ibid., p. 10.
122. It moot whether Park could be described as an interactionist. Evidently, there was no such developed school or perspective as interactionism when Park worked. His own work laid the foundations for interactionism: some was discarded, much was absorbed. He was an ur-interactionist in fact.
123. I have developed this argument more fully in 'Phenomenalism and Essentialism in the Sociology of Deviancy', *Sociology*, VII 1 (Jan. 1973).
124. R. Faris, *Chicago Sociology*, p. 62.
125. Cf. E. Lemert, *Human Deviance, Social Problems and Social Control*, (2nd ed., Prentice-Hall, N.J., 1972) Ch. 1.

126. Cf. G. Mead, *Mind, Self and Society*, p. 137.
127. Quoted in R. Perry, *The Thought and Character of William James*, p. 195.
128. 'The Life Histories of W. I. Thomas and Robert E. Park', op. cit., p. 249.
129. Cf. P. Baker, introduction, ibid., p. 244.
130. C. Cooley; 'Social Consciousness', *American Journal of Sociology*, XII 6 (Mar. 1907) p. 675.
131. Ibid., p. 677.
132. 'The Life Histories of W. I. Thomas and Robert E. Park', op. cit., p. 245.
133. E. Hughes, 'Tarde's *Psychologie Economique*: An Unknown Classic by a Forgotten Sociologist', *American Journal of Sociology*, LXVI 6 (May 1961).
134. 'The Histories of W. I. Thomas and Robert E. Park', op. cit., pp. 254–5.
135. G. Mead, 'Cooley's Contribution to American Social Thought', *American Journal of Sociology*, XXXV 5 (Mar. 1930) p. 702.
136. C. Cooley, *Human Nature and the Social Order*, p. 120.
137. D. Cressey, 'Role Theory, Differential Association and Compulsive Crimes', in A. Rose (ed.), *Human Behavior and Social Processes* (Houghton Mifflin, New York, 1962) p. 452.
138. Cf. C. Wright Mills; 'Situated Actions and Vocabularies of Motive', *American Sociological Review*, V (1940).
139. L. Taylor, 'The Significance and Interpretation of Replies to Motivational Questions', *Sociology*, VI 1 (Jan. 1972) p. 23.
140. T. Scheff, *Mental Illness and Social Processes* (Harper and Row, New York, 1967) p. 14.
141. H. Becker, 'Labelling Theory Reconsidered', in *Outsiders* (1973 ed.), p. 181.
142. Ibid., pp. 191–2.

CHAPTER 4

1. Cf. N. Denzin, 'The Genesis of Self in Early Childhood', *The Sociological Quarterly*, XIII (Summer 1972) p. 291.
2. W. James, *The Principles of Psychology* (Henry Holt, New York, 1890) vol. 1, ch. 10.
3. R. Perinbanayagam, 'The Significance of Others in the Thought of Alfred Schutz, G. H. Mead and C. H. Cooley', *The Sociological Quarterly*, XVI (Autumn 1975) p. 512.
4. Cf. C. Morris, introduction to *The Philosophy of the Act*, p. x.
5. G. Mead, 'The Philosophies of Royce, James, and Dewey . . .', p. 217.
6. Cf. W. James, *The Principles of Psychology*, vol. 1, ch. 3; G. Mead, *Mind, Self and Society*, pp. 136–7.
7. G. Mead, *Mind, Self and Society*, p. 184.
8. Cf. B. Meltzer et al., *Symbolic Interactionism*, p. 27.
9. G. Mead, 'Scientific Method and the Moral Sciences', *International Journal of Ethics*, XXXIII 3 (Apr. 1923) p. 247.
10. G. Mead, 'The Genesis of the Self and Social Control', *International Journal of Ethics*, XXXV 3 (Apr. 1925) p. 257.
11. Cf. G. Mead, *The Philosophy of the Act*, p. 361.
12. G. Mead, 'The Genesis of the Self and Social Control', p. 257.
13. Ibid., p. 256.
14. Cf. G. Mead, 'The Mechanism of Social Conduct', *Journal of Philosophy*,

Psychology and Scientific Methods, IX 13 (20 June 1912) p. 355.
15. G. Mead, *Mind, Self and Society*, p. 135.
16. It is this contention which must serve as the critical argument distinguishing interactionism from phenomenology and some styles of ethnomethodology. The argument has become increasingly obscured as interactionism itself has been advanced, but it still informs the bulk of the sociology. There remains a core phenomenalism despite the encroachments of phenomenology.
17. Cf. G. Mead, *Mind, Self and Society*, p. 148.
18. Cf. C. Cooley, *Human Nature and the Social Order*, p. 172.
19. Cf. G. Mead, 'A Behavioristic Account of the Significant Symbol', *The Journal of Philosophy*, XIX 6 (16 Mar. 1922) p. 159.
20. Cf. G. Mead, 'The Genesis of the Self and Social Control', p. 262.
21. G. Mead, 'A Behavioristic Account of the Significant Symbol', p. 161.
22. Cf. G. Mead, *Mind, Self and Society*, p. 192.
23. Cf. C. Cooley, *Human Nature and the Social Order*, p. 184.
24. Cf. F. Znaniecki, *The Laws of Social Psychology* (Russell and Russell, New York, 1967) ch. VII.
25. Cf. G. Mead, 'The Mechanism of Social Conduct', p. 355.
26. G. Mead, 'A Behavioristic Account of the Significant Symbol', p. 160.
27. Cf. G. Stone and H. Farberman, 'Further Comment on the Blumer-Bales Dialogue concerning the Implications of the Thought of George Herbert Mead', *American Journal of Sociology*, LXII 4 (Jan. 1967) pp. 409–10.
28. A. Strauss, *Mirrors and Masks*, p. 20.
29. C. Cooley, *Human Nature and the Social Order*, p. 179.
30. C. Peirce, *Collected Papers* (Harvard University Press, Cambridge, 1934–58) vol. V, p. 314.
31. Cf. A. Strauss, *Mirrors and Masks*, p. 33.
32. Ibid., p. 18.
33. Cf. H. Farberman, 'Mannheim, Cooley, and Mead: Toward a Social Theory of Mentality', *Sociological Quarterly*, 11 1 (Winter 1970) p. 11.
34. Cf. G. Mead, 'The Genesis of the Self and Social Control', p. 256.
35. G. Mead, *Mind, Self and Society*, p. 174.
36. Cf. H. Becker, 'Notes on the Concept of Commitment', *American Journal of Sociology*, 66 (July 1960).
37. Cf. O. Brim, 'Personality as Role-Learning', in I. Iscoe and H. Stevenson (eds.), *Personality Development in Children* (University of Texas Press, Austin, 1960).
38. Cf. J. Lincourt and P. Hare, 'Neglected American Philosophers in the History of Symbolic Interactionism', p. 336.
39. Cf. H. Farberman, 'Mannheim, Cooley, and Mead', p. 12.
40. Cf. A. Strauss, *Mirrors and Masks*, pp. 49–50.
41. W. James, 'The Self', in C. Gordon and K. Gergen (eds.), *The Self in Social Interaction* (John Wiley, New York, 1968), vol. I, p. 48.
42. Ibid., p. 46.
43. C. Cooley, *Human Nature and the Social Order*, p. 169.
44. B. Meltzer, 'Mead's Social Psychology', in J. Manis and B. Meltzer, *Symbolic Interaction*, p. 11.
45. Indeed, Kant offered a description of the 'I' and its 'me's' which anticipated the interactionist formulation. Cf. G. Hawthorn, *Enlightenment and Despair*, (Cambridge University Press, London, 1976), p. 32.

46. H. Becker, 'The Self and Adult Socialization', in *Sociological Work*, op. cit., p. 299.
47. Cf. O. Klapp, *Heroes, Villains and Fools* (Prentice-Hall, New Jersey, 1962).
48. Cf. O. Klapp, *Collective Search for Identity*, (Holt, Rinehart and Winston, New York, 1969).
49. T. Duster, *The Legislation of Morality* (Macmillan, London, 1970).
50. Cf. P. Rock, *Deviant Behaviour* (Hutchinson University Library, London, 1973) ch. 1.
51. Cf. H. Garfinkel, 'Conditions of Successful Degradation Ceremonies', *American Journal of Sociology*, 61 (1956).
52. C. Morris, introduction to G. Mead, *The Philosophy of the Act*, p. xv.
53. N. Foote, 'Identification as the Basis for a Theory of Motivation', *American Sociological Review*, XVI 1 (1951) p. 18.
54. A. Strauss, *Mirrors and Masks*, p. 59.
55. R. Turner, 'The Self-Conception in Interaction', in C. Gordon and K. Gergen (eds.), *The Self in Social Interaction*, p. 102.
56. R. Turner, 'Role-Taking: Process Versus Conformity', in A. Rose (ed.), *Human Behavior and Social Processes*, p. 22.
57. D. Cressey, 'Role Theory, Differential Association, and Compulsive Crimes', in A. Rose (ed.), *Human Behavior and Social Processes*, p. 452.
58. J. Baldwin, 'The Self-Conscious Person', in C. Gordon and K. Gergen (eds.), *The Self in Social Interaction*, p. 161.
59. Cf. R. Turner, 'Role-Taking: Process Versus Conformity', p. 30.
60. Cf. A. Strauss, *Mirrors and Masks*, p. 32.
61. G. Mead, *The Philosophy of the Act*, p. 616.
62. Cf. J. Kitsuse, 'Societal Reaction to Deviant Behavior', *Social Problems*, 9 (1962).
63. G. Mead, 'The Genesis of the Self and Social Control', p. 273.
64. A. Tonness, 'A Notation on the Problem of the Past – With Especial Reference to George Herbert Mead', *The Journal of Philosophy*, XXIX, 22 (27 Oct. 1932) p. 604.
65. Cf. J. Dewey, *Human Nature and Conduct* (The Modern Library, New York, 1930) pp. 216–17.
66. E. Goffman, *Interaction Ritual* (Doubleday Anchor, New York, 1967) p. 31.
67. Cf. E. Hughes, 'Dilemmas and Contradictions of Status', *The American Journal of Sociology*, L (Mar. 1945).
68. Cf. E. Weinstein and P. Deutschberger, 'Some Dimensions of Altercasting', *Sociometry*, 26 4 (Dec. 1963).
69. Cf. E. Hughes, 'Good People and Dirty Work', in *The Sociological Eye*.
70. Cf. E. Hughes, 'Dilemmas and Contradictions of Status'.
71. Cf. G. Simmel, *Conflict and the Web of Group Affiliations* (Free Press, New York, 1955); L. Coser, *The Functions of Social Conflict* (Routledge and Kegan Paul, London, 1965); T. Schelling, *The Strategy of Conflict* (O.U.P., London, 1973).
72. K. Wolff (ed.), *The Sociology of Georg Simmel* (Free Press, Ill., 1950), p. 350.
73. Cf. T. Scheff, *Being Mentally Ill*.
74. H. Blumer, 'Society as Symbolic Interaction', in *Symbolic Interactionism*, p. 88.
75. Cf. T. Burns and G. Stalker, *The Management of Innovation*, (Tavistock, London, 1961).
76. Cf. T. Scheff, 'Negotiating Reality: Notes on Power in the Assessment of

Responsibility', *Social Problems*, 16 1 (1968).

77. It is important to emphasise the strategic significance of the formalist conception of social structure. Those critics and advocates of interactionism who neglect it are constrained either to distort the sociology by borrowing intellectually alien ideas of structure or else to cast the world of symbolic interactionism as totally open and completely negotiable. One instance of that neglect is provided by Stokes and Hewitt. They claim that 'interactionist analysis is . . . weak in its failure to account for the locus, nature and persistence of culture . . . interactionists are left by their analysis with no real explanation of the massive fact that patterns of conduct persist over long periods of time . . . Culture . . . is at best residual in interactionist theory, which views conduct as relatively unconstrained improvisation in immediate situations.' (R. Stokes and J. Hewitt, 'Aligning Actions', *American Sociological Review*, 41, (Oct. 1976), pp. 839, 841, 847.) The remedy which they propose is that 'sociological theory reconceptualizes culture as a set of cognitive constraints – objects – to which people must relate as they form lines of conduct' (p. 847). If the idea of alienated synthetic *a priori* forms is accepted, as it is by many interactionists, not only does the Stokes and Hewitt characterisation of interactionism become untenable but their clumsier solution becomes unnecessary. There is a viable, albeit modest, theory of social structure and culture lodged in interactionism. It is a little curious that some interactionists themselves ignore it and turn elsewhere for ideas.

78. H. Becker, 'The Nature of a Profession', in *Sociological Work*, op. cit., p. 92.

79. Cf. M. Dalton, *Men Who Manage*; M. Crozier, *The Bureaucratic Phenomenon* (University of Chicago Press, Chicago, 1964).

80. A. Strauss, *Mirrors and Masks*, p. 73.

81. E. Goffman, 'Role-distance', in *Encounters*, (Bobbs-Merrill, Indianapolis, 1961).

82. Cf. E. Goffman, 'On Cooling the Mark Out: Some Aspects of Adaptation to Failure', *Psychiatry*, 15 4 (Nov. 1952).

83. An unflattering term for the attributes of the upper-middle and upper classes, derived from bourgeois travelling patterns on the P. and O. steamships. The comfortable sides of the boats to and from India were port outward, starboard home.

84. A. Strauss, *Mirrors and Masks*, p. 91.

85. H. Becker, 'The Career of the Chicago Public School Teacher', in *Sociological Work*, op. cit., p. 165.

86. A. Strauss, *Mirrors and Masks*, pp. 130, 131.

87. Cf. A. Niederhoffer, *Behind the Shield*, (Doubleday, Garden City, New York, 1967).

88. Cf. P. Maas, *Serpico*, (Fontana, London, 1973).

89. E. Hughes, 'Institutional Office and the Person', in *The Sociological Eye*, p. 137.

90. Nevertheless many adolescent girls do supposedly carve out careers in which they will become young and attractive widows.

91. E. Hughes, 'Dilemmas and Contradictions of Status', in *The Sociological Eye*, p. 144.

92. Cf. P. Berger, *The Sacred Canopy* (Doubleday, New York, 1967).

93. Cf. G. McCall, 'Symbiosis: The Case of Hoodoo and the Numbers Racket', *Social Problems*, 10 (1963).

94. Cf. E. Hughes, 'Good people and Dirty Work', in *The Sociological Eye*.

95. Cf. K. Erikson, *Wayward Puritans* (John Wiley, New York, 1966).

96. A. Rose, 'A Systematic Summary of Symbolic Interaction Theory', in *Human*

Behavior and Social Processes, p. 10.
97. Cf. H. Finestone, 'Cats, Kicks, and Color', *Social Problems*, 5 1 (1957).
98. Cf. R. Habenstein, 'Sociology of Occupations: The Case of the American Funeral Director', in A. Rose (ed.), *Human Behavior and Social Processes*.
99. Cf. M. Weinberg, 'Sexual Modesty, Social Meanings, and the Nudist Camp', *Social Problems*, 12 (1965).
100. Cf. J. Young, *The Drugtakers*, (MacGibbon and Kee, London, 1971).
101. T. Lafferty, 'Some Metaphysical Implications of the Pragmatic Theory of Knowledge', *The Journal of Philosophy*, 14th. April, 1932, XXIX 8 (14 Apr. 1932) p. 206.
102. Cf. H. Becker, 'The Self and Adult Socialization', in *Sociological Work*, p. 291.
103. Cf. A. Strauss, *Mirrors and Masks*, p. 34.
104. R. Perinbanayagam, 'The Significance of Others . . .', op. cit., p. 502.
105. E. Hughes, 'What Other?', in *The Sociological Eye*, op. cit., p. 351.
106. D. Miller, *George Herbert Mead*, p. 49.
107. G. Mead, quoted in D. Miller, *George Herbert Mead*, p. 50.
108. Cf. D. Miller, *George Herbert Mead*, esp. ch. 3.
109. T. Luckmann, *The Invisible Religion* (Macmillan, New York, 1967), p. 19. Indeed, Faris's review of Mead's posthumous work, *Mind, Self and Society*, maintained that the title belied the author's intention and argument. He suggested that *Society, Self and Mind* would have been more fitting (E. Faris, review of *Mind, Self and Society*, *Americal Journal of Sociology*, 41 6 (May 1936).
110. Cf. D. Miller, *George Herbert Mead*, p. 50.

CHAPTER 5

1. C. Morris, introduction to *Mind, Self and Society*, p. xv.
2. G. Mead, *Mind, Self and Society*, pp. 166–7.
3. Ibid., p. 169.
4. Ibid., p. 174.
5. Ibid., pp. 174–5n.
6. Ibid., p. 173.
7. Ibid., p. 187n.
8. A. Rose, 'A Systematic Summary of Symbolic Interaction Theory', in *Human Behavior and Social Processes*, pp. 14–15. In his own copy of the book, Peter Manning justly wrote 'silly' as a marginal comment to Rose's observation.
9. G. Mead, *The Philosophy of the Act*, p. 360.
10. R. Faris, *Chicago Sociology*, p. 95.
11. H. Blumer, 'The Methodological Position of Symbolic Interactionism', in *Symbolic Interactionism*, pp. 22–3.
12. Ibid., p. 49.
13. C. Cooley, *Human Nature and the Social Order*, p. 120.
14. Ibid., p. 120.
15. Ibid., p. 121.
16. Thus, in the case of the interactionist vision of deviancy, Young asserts 'the tendency was to ignore the fact that the human beings under discussion possessed a human body'. J. Young, 'Working-Class Criminology', in I. Taylor *et al.* (eds.), *Critical Criminology* (Routledge and Kegan Paul, London, 1975) p. 74.
17. Interestingly, Arnold Rose himself deplores the suppression of the organic and

cites it as one of the major criticisms of interactionism. Cf. A. Rose, preface to *Human Behavior and Social Processes*, p. x.
18. Matza has claimed that it is impermissible to describe him as an interactionist. He also admits that *Becoming Deviant* could be read as an interactionist thesis. Cf. 'Dialogue with David Matza', *Issues in Criminology*, 6 1 (Winter 1971). Yet the frontiers of interactionism are not strictly patrolled; Matza did base much of his argument on interactionist works (and on an essay by Howard Becker, in particular); and his impact on interactionism has been marked.
19. D. Matza, *Becoming Deviant*, p. 117.
20. C. Cooley, *Human Nature and the Social Order*, p. 119.
21. Cf. M. Kuhn, 'Major Trends in Symbolic Interaction . . .', op. cit., *passim*.
22. Cf. R. Perinbanayagam, 'The Definition of the Situation', *Sociological Quarterly*, 15 4 (Autumn 1974) p. 527.
23. W. Thomas, 'The Relation of Research to the Social Process', op. cit., pp. 189−90.
24. E. Goffman, *Asylums*, p. 168.
25. Ibid., p. 135.
26. Cf. H. Blumer, 'A Note on Symbolic Interactionism', *American Sociological Review*, 38 6 (Dec. 1973), p. 797.
27. Cf. J. Manis and B. Meltzer, *Symbolic Interaction*, p. 496.
28. I have discussed this focus in greater detail in Chapter 6.
29. G. Mead, *Mind, Self and Society*, p. 162.
30. G. Stone and H. Farberman, *Social Psychology through Symbolic Interaction*, p. 2.
31. H. Becker and B. Geer, 'Participant Observation and Interviewing: A Comparison' in J. Manis and B. Meltzer (eds.), *Symbolic Interaction*, pp. 110−11.
32. J. Dewey, 'An Analysis of Reflective Thought', *The Journal of Philosophy*, XIX 2 (19 Jan. 1922) pp. 29−30.
33. Cf. D. Miller, *George Herbert Mead*, *passim*.
34. There are idealist and phenomenological themes in the writing of a number of interactionists. Those who could be more explicitly associated with such Idealism are, as a forerunner, Cooley, and, more recently, Bruyn and Berger.
35. G. Psathas, introduction to *Phenomenological Sociology*, p. 13.
36. Ibid., pp. 13, 14.
37. See, for instance, his explicit rejection of analysing 'the essential core of the individual, the part that calls itself "I", the part that feels, thinks and originates action'. H. Becker; 'The Self and Adult Socialization', in . E. Norbeck *et al*. (eds.), *The Study of Personality* (Holt, Rinehart and Winston, New York, 1968).
38. That enlargement of scope has precipitated some methodological confusion and problems for the more phenomenologically bent interactionists. The return to the exploration of immediacy is particularly apparent in claims that are occasionally made for participant observation. Thus Norman Denzin is not an unorthodox symbolic interactionist, but it is clear that his definition of participant observation brings some difficulties in its train. He states: 'participant observation is a commitment to adopt the perspective of those studied by sharing in their day-to-day experiences' (N. Denzin, *The Research Act*, p. 185). Denzin does avoid the perils presented by marrying interactionism to phenomenology, yet there is an ambiguity in the terms 'sharing' and 'experiences' which is capable of generating some muddle. I shall pursue this general question in the next chapter.
39. Michael Phillipson has rather unkindly referred to interactionist methodology as

'verification by anecdote'.
40. Cf. H. and J. Schwendinger, 'Defenders of Order . . .', *Issues in Criminology*, 5 2 (Summer 1970).
41. J. Young, 'Working-Class Criminology', op. cit., p. 74.
42. G. Mead, *Mind, Self and Society*, p. 122.
43. Cf. L. Taylor, *Deviance and Society* (Michael Joseph, London, 1971).
44. R. Scott, *The Making of Blind Men* (Russell Sage Foundation, New York, 1969).
45. G. Mead, 'A Behavioristic Account of the Significant Symbol', op. cit., p. 163.
46. A. Rose, 'A Systematic Summary of Symbolic Interaction Theory', op. cit., pp. 16–17.
47. There are exceptions. One example is H. Becker, 'History, Culture and Subjective Experience', in *Sociological Work*, op. cit. Another is J. Carey, 'Problems of Access and Risk in Observing Drug Scenes', in J. Douglas (ed.), *Research on Deviance* (Random House, New York, 1972) p. 78ff.
48. Shibutani has however attempted to unite interactionism with psychoanalysis. In that union, he has tried to incorporate diverse layers of process. Cf. T. Shibutani; *Society and Personality* (Prentice-Hall, N.J., 1961) esp. p. 323.
49. Cf. A. Brittan, *Meanings and Situations*, pp. 190–204.
50. Cf. C. MacAndrew and R. Edgerton, 'The Everyday Life of Institutionalized "Idiots"', *Human Organization*, 23 (1964).
51. B. Meltzer *et al.* would claim Garfinkel as an interactionist, but there are fundamental cleavages between ethnomethodology and symbolic interactionism. Not the least of those differences is the interactionist commitment to a phenomenalism which ethnomethodologists depict as no more than epiphenomenalism. The rise of a phenomenological interactionism has clearly obscured the differences between the two styles of thought. Decisions about orthodoxy are complicated and often fruitless, but the major writings of the 1950s and 1960s, and those that preceded them, would share no affinity with ethnomethodology.
52. H. Garfinkel, *Studies in Ethnomethodology* (Prentice-Hall, N.J., 1967) pp. 1, 4.
53. G. Mead, *Mind, Self and Society*, p. 334.
54. Even the purer version poses vast problems. As Strauss remarks, 'little is actually known about these process [of role-taking] other than common sense observation.' A. Strauss, *Mirrors and Masks*, p. 60.
55. R. Zaner, 'The Theory of Intersubjectivity: Alfred Schutz', *Social Research*, 29 (Spring 1961) p. 76.
56. C. Cooley, *Sociological Theory and Social Research* (Holt, Rinehart and Winston, New York, 1930) p. 308.
57. N. Denzin, *The Research Act*, p. 8.
58. G. Mead, *Mind, Self and Society*, p. 178.
59. That is, some interactionists have restored the transcendental ego depicted by Kant: 'One may . . . say of the thinking I . . . that it *does not know itself through the categories*, but knows the *categories* only, and through them all objects, in the absolute unity of apperception, *that is through itself.*' I. Kant, *Critique of Pure Reason*, translated by M. Müller (Macmillan, London, 1881) p. 347.
60. Cf. R. Merton, 'Insiders and Outsiders: A Chapter in the Sociology of Knowledge', *American Journal of Sociology*, 78 1 (July 1972).
61. Cf. P. Rock, 'The Sociology of Deviancy and Conceptions of Moral Order', *British Journal of Criminology*, 14 2 (Apr. 1974).

62. E. Goffman, *Interaction Ritual* (Aldine, Chicago, 1967) pp. 44–5.
63. E. Goffman, *Frame Analysis*, p. 1.
64. A. Gouldner, *The Coming Crisis of Western Sociology* (Basic Books, New York, 1970), p. 385.
65. Cf. E. Schur, *Radical Non-Intervention* (Prentice-Hall, N.J., 1973) p. 169.
66. Cf. A. Rose, preface to *Human Behavior and Social Processes*, p. ix.
67. P. Manning, 'Deviance and Dogma: Some Comments on the Labelling Perspective', *British Journal of Criminology* 15 1 (Jan. 1975) p. 2.
68. The phenomenological interactionist attends to content, but his interest leads to other sources of levelling. I shall discuss such a focus below. Most symbolic interactionists are orthodox in their allegiance to Simmel and the pragmatists.
69. H. Becker in R. Hill and K. Crittenden, *Proceedings of the Purdue Symposium on Ethnomethodology* (Institute for the Study of Social Change, Purdue University, 1968) p. 200.
70. M. Truzzi (ed.), *Verstehen* (Addison-Wesley, Mass., 1974) p. 103.
71. Perversely, of course, the Idealist interactionists do not attempt to gain synthetic *a posteriori* knowledge but analytic *a posteriori* understanding.
72. S. Bruyn, *The Human Perspective in Sociology*, p. 104.
73. N. Denzin, *The Research Act*, p. 9.
74. Cf. M. Stein, *The Eclipse of Community* (Princeton University Press, N.J., 1960) p. 325.
75. H. Blumer, *Symbolic Interactionism*, p. 46.
76. E. Hughes, 'Mistakes at Work', in *The Sociological Eye*, op. cit., p. 316.
77. E. Hughes, 'Work and Self', in *The Sociological Eye*, op. cit., p. 342.
78. Cf. R. Perinbanayagam, 'The Significance of Others in the Thought of Alfred Schutz, G. H. Mead and C. H. Cooley', *The Sociological Quarterly*, 16 (Autumn 1975) *passim*.
79. S. Bruyn, 'The Methodology of Participant Observation', *Human Organization*, 22 3 (Fall 1963) p. 230.
80. See the comments on 'Role Conflicts in Social Studies', *Current Anthropology* (Dec. 1969) pp. 512–23.
81. E. Gellner, 'Concepts and Society', *Proceedings of the Fifth World Congress of Sociology* (Neualwaerts, Louvain, 1963).
82. Cf. E. Sagarin, *Deviants and Deviance*, p. 134ff.
83. E. Schur and H. Bedau, *Victimless Crimes: Two Sides of a Controversy* (Prentice-Hall, N.J., 1974) pp. 116–17.
84. E. Goffman, *Interaction Ritual*, p. 45.

CHAPTER 6

1. Cf. M. Zelditch, 'Some Methodological Problems of Field Studies', *American Journal of Sociology*, LXVII 5 (Mar. 1962).
2. For a complementary discussion of participant observation and its links with symbolic interactionism, see N. Denzin, *The Research Act*, esp. ch. 9.
3. Cf. C. Madge, *Britain by Mass Observation* (Penguin, Harmondsworth, 1939).
4. Cf. R. Lynd and H. Lynd, *Middletown* (Harcourt Brace, New York, 1929); R. Lynd and H. Lynd, *Middletown in Transition* (Harcourt Brace, New York, 1937); A. Hollingshead, *Elmtown's Youth* (John Wiley, New York, 1949); J. Dollard, *Caste and Class in a Southern Town* (Doubleday Anchor, New York, 1957).

5. Cf. H. Becker, 'On Methodology', in *Sociological Work*, op. cit., and G. Schwartz and D. Merten, 'Participant Observation and the Discovery of Meaning', *Philosophy of the Social Sciences*, 14 (Dec. 1971) p. 279.
6. Cf. D. Riesman, 'Observations on Social Science Research', in *Individualism Reconsidered* (Free Press, New York, 1954).
7. J. Douglas, *Investigative Social Research* (unpublished typescript, 1974) p. 1–5.
8. H. Blumer, 'The Methodological Position of Symbolic Interactionism' in *Symbolic Interactionism*, p. 33.
9. E. Borgatta, 'Prologue: The Current Status of Methodology in Sociology' in E. Borgatta (ed.), *Sociological Methodology 1969* (Jossey-Bass, San Francisco, 1969), p. xiv.
10. Cf. E. Borgatta and G. Bohrnstedt, prologue to *Sociological Methodoloy 1970* (Jossey-Bass, San Francisco, 1970) p. x.
11. Cf. R. Merton, *On Theoretical Sociology*, Free Press, New York, 1967) pp. 140–1.
12. L. Humphreys, *Tearoom Trade* (Duckworth, London, 1970) p. 22.
13. H. Becker, 'Inference and Proof in Participant Observation', *American Sociological Review*, 23 6 (Dec. 1958) p. 653.
14. N. Polsky, *Hustlers, Beats and Others* (Penguin, Harmondsworth, 1971) pp. 124–5.
15. F. Znaniecki, *The Method of Sociology* (Holt, Rinehart and Winston, New York, 1934) p. 49.
16. E. Goffman, *Frame Analysis*, p. 13.
17. S. Bruyn, 'The Methodology of Participant Observation', op. cit., p. 227.
18. S. Bruyn, *The Human Perspective in Sociology*, p. 33.
19. M. Daltón, 'Preconceptions and Methods in *Men who Manage*,' op. cit., p. 57.
20. Cf. H. Gans, 'The Participant-Observer as a Human Being' in H. Becker *et al.* (eds.), *Institutions and the Person*, p. 313.
21. *Social Forces*, 53 2 (Dec. 1974).
22. *Sociological Methodology 1969*, *Sociological Methodology 1970*, ... (Jossey-Bass, San Francisco).
23. T. Adorno, 'The Sociology of Knowledge and its Consciousness' in *Prisms* (Spearman, London, 1967) p. 43.
24. H. Blumer, 'The Methodological Position of Symbolic Interactionism' in *Symbolic Interactionism*, p. 53.
25. See, for example, F. Taylor, *The Principles of Scientific Management* (New York, 1913) and R. Barker and H. Wright, *Midwest and its Children* (Harper and Row, New York, 1955).
26. F. Kluckhohn, 'The Participant-Observer Technique in Small Communities', *American Journal of Sociology*, XLVI (Nov. 1940) p. 331.
27. S. Bruyn, 'The Methodology of Participant Observation', op. cit., p. 226.
28. G. Schwartz and D. Merten, 'Participant Observation and the Discovery of Meaning', op. cit., p. 282.
29. Cf. K. Wolff, 'Surrender and Community Study: The Study of Loma', in M. Stein *et al.* (eds.), *Reflections on Community Studies* (John Wiley, New York, 1964).
30. G. Hegel, *The Phenomenology of Mind*, p. 141.
31. G. Lichtheim, *Lukács* (Fontana, London, 1970) p. 71.
32. Cf. S. Bruyn, *The Human Perspective in Sociology*, p. 20.
33. Private communication.

34. A. Vidich, 'Participant Observation and the Collection and Interpretation of Data', *American Journal of Sociology*, LX 4 (Jan. 1955) p. 358.
35. A. Reiss, 'Systematic Observation of Natural Social Phenomena', in H. Costner (ed.), *Sociological Methodology 1971* (Jossey-Bass, San Francisco, 1971).
36. J. Douglas, *Investigative Social Research*, p. 2-2.
37. M. Schwarz and C. Schwarz, 'Problems in Participant Observation', *American Journal of Sociology*, LX 4 (Jan. 1955) p. 344.
38. Ibid., p. 346.
39. Ibid., p. 344.
40. H. Blumer, *Symbolic Interactionism*, p. 22.
41. Cf. B. Meltzer et al., *Symbolic Interactionism*, pp. 55-66.
42. Cooley, for instance, recommended the methodological practice of 'sympathetic introspection' which would devalue observational work: C. Cooley, *Social Organization: A Study of the Larger Mind* (Free Press, Ill., 1956) p. 7. (The sub-title is itself most significant.)
43. Thus Hall argues that the Marxist bifurcation of the ideal and the material must collapse in symbolic interactionism because the former mediates the latter. Cf. p. Hall, 'A Symbolic Interactionist Analysis of Politics', *Sociological Inquiry* 42 3-4, (1972) p. 75.
44. P. Berger, *A Rumor of Angels* (Doubleday Anchor, New York, 1970) p. 47.
45. Cf. P. Worsley, *The Trumpet Shall Sound* (MacGibbon, London, 1957).
46. In the case of the dramaturgical order, Messinger et al. have claimed that no more than analogy is intended. Goffman himself makes the same claim later. Cf. S. Messinger et al., 'Life as Theater: Some Notes on the Dramaturgical Approach to Social Reality', op. cit.
47. Cf. P. Berger, *A Rumour of Angels*, p. 8.
48. Cf. E. Webb et al., *Unobtrusive Measures* (Rand McNally, Chicago, 1966).
49. L. Reynolds and B. Meltzer, 'The Origins of Divergent Methodological Stances in Symbolic Interactionism', *Sociological Quarterly*, 14 (Spring 1973).
50. T. Lafferty, 'Some Metaphysical Implications of the Pragmatic Theory of Knowledge', op. cit., p. 205.
51. H. Blumer, 'The Methodological Position of Symbolic Interactionism', in *Symbolic Interactionism*, p. 3.
52. Ibid., p. 44.
53. J. Dewey, 'Realism without Monism or Dualism – II', *The Journal of Philosophy*, XIX, 13 (22 June 1922) p. 353.
54. A. Rose, preface to *Human Behavior and Social Processes*, p. ix.
55. J. Douglas, *Investigative Social Research*, op. cit., pp. 1-8.
56. It is again apparent that my description of the claims made for participant observation is selective and borrows rather heavily from the phenomenologically-sympathetic strand of interactionism. Yet I believe that most participant work is necessarily entangled with some phenomenological assumptions. It would not otherwise be participant.
57. Cf. B. Junker, *Fieldwork: An Introduction to the Social Sciences* (University of Chicago Press, Chicago, 1960).
58. Cf. J. Lofland, *Analyzing Social Settings*, pp. 94, 99; and M. Sullivan et al., 'Participant Observation in a Military Program', *American Sociological Review*, 23 6 (Dec. 1958) p. 663.
59. R. Gold, 'Roles in Sociological Field Observations', *Social Forces*, 36 3 (Mar.

1958) p. 220.
60. M. Dalton, 'Preconceptions and Methods in *Men Who Manage*', op. cit., p. 54.
61. J. Douglas, *Investigative Social Research*, op. cit., p. 1–12.
62. Cf. The elaborate description of front-management in J. Irwin, 'Participant-Observation of Criminals', in J. Douglas (ed.), *Research on Deviance*.
63. Cf. R. Beck and J. Adams, 'Establishing Rapport with Deviant Groups', *Social Problems*, 18 1 (Summer 1970) p. 108.
64. W. Foote Whyte, *Street Corner Society* (University of Chicago Press, Chicago, 1943) p. 304.
65. M. Sullivan *et al.*, 'Disguised Observation in a Military Program', op. cit.
66. K. Erikson, 'Disguised Observation in Sociology', *Social Problems*, 14, (Spring 1967) p. 340.
67. M. Weinberg and C. Williams, 'Fieldwork Among Deviants: Social Relations with Subjects and Others', in J. Douglas (ed.), *Research on Deviance*, p. 166.
68. Ibid., p. 167.
69. Cf. W. Foote Whyte, 'Observational Field-Work Methods', in M. Jahoda *et al.* (eds.), *Research Methods in Social Relations* (Dryden Press, New York, 1951), vol. 2, p. 497; N. Polsky, *Hustlers, Beats and Others*, pp. 126–7; J. Lofland, *Analyzing Social Settings*, pp. 100–1.
70. K. Lang and G. Lang, 'Decisions for Christ: Billy Graham in New York City', in M. Stein *et al.* (eds.), *Identity and Anxiety* (Free Press, Ill. 1960).
71. A. Reiss, cited in P. Manning, 'Observing the Police', in J. Douglas (ed.), *Research on Deviance*, p. 246.
72. A. Vidich, 'Participant Observation and the Collection and Interpretation of Data, op. cit., p. 357.
73. P. Manning 'Observing the Police', op. cit., p. 248.
74. H. Becker, 'Field Methods and Techniques: A Note on Interviewing Tactics', *Human Organization*, 12 4 (Winter 1954) p. 32.
75. H. Gans; 'The Participant-Observer as a Human Being', op. cit., p. 304.
76. S. Miller; 'The Participant Observer and "Over-Rapport"', *American Sociological Review*, Sociological Review 17 1 (Feb. 1952).
77. P. Berger, *A Rumor of Angels*, p. 8.
78. Cf. M. Sullivan *et al.*, 'Participant Observation in a Military Program', op. cit., *passim*.
79. Georg Simmel, quoted in P. Manning, 'Police Lying', *Urban Life and Culture*, 3 3 (Oct. 1974) p. 284.
80. Cf. K. Erikson, 'Disguised Observation in Sociology', op. cit.
81. Cf. E. Hughes, 'The Place of Field Work in Social Science', in *The Sociological Eye*, p. 505.
82. D. Douglas, 'Managing Fronts in Observing Deviance', in J. Douglas (ed.), *Research on Deviance*, p. 113.
83. Ibid., p. 113.
84. Ibid., p. 111.
85. J. Skolnick, *Justice Without Trial* (John Wiley, New York, 1966).
86. P. Rock, *Making People Pay* (Routledge and Kegan Paul, London, 1973).
87. F. Davis, 'Comment on "Initial Interaction of Newcomers in Alcoholics Anonymous"', *Social Problems*, 8 (Spring 1961) p. 365.
88. Some subjects subsequently appear to have wished that they had never given consent. See, for instance, the reported reactions of Middletowners to the book

Middletown: R. Lynd and H. Lynd, *Middletown in Transition*, pp. xi—xiii.
89. D. Douglas, 'Managing Fronts in Observing Deviance', op. cit., p. 111.
90. No sociologist I know would himself agree to become a subject of observational research.
91. P. Berger, *A Rumor of Angels*, p. 38.
92. It would be interesting, for example, to explore some of the effects wrought by particular community studies. *Middletown* is one example, so is the unflattering portrait of a middle-class suburb contained in J. Seeley et al., *Crestwood Heights* (Basic Books, New York, 1956).
93. R. Gold 'Roles in Sociological Field Observations', op. cit., p. 220.
94. W. Scott, 'Field Work in a Formal Organization', op. cit., p. 163.
95. R. Janes, 'A Note on Phases of the Community Role of the Participant-Observer', *American Sociological Review*, 26 3 (June 1961) p. 449.
96. Cf. R. Janes, 'A Note on Phases of the Community Role of the Participant-Observer', op. cit., p. 448.
97. Cf. H. Becker and B. Geer, 'Participant Observation and Interviewing: A Comparison', *Human Organisation*, 16 3 (Fall 1957).
98. M. Weinberg and C. Williams, 'Fieldwork among Deviants', op. cit., p. 166.
99. T. Lafferty, 'Some Metaphysical Implications of the Pragmatic Theory of Knowledge', op. cit., p. 207.
100. J. Dewey, 'Realism without Monism or Dualism – II', op. cit., p. 356.
101. G. Stone and H. Farberman, *Social Psychology through Symbolic Interaction*, p. 7.
102. Cf. H. Blumer, *Symbolic Interactionism*, p. 32
103. T. Lafferty, 'Some Metaphysical Implications of the Pragmatic Theory of Knowledge', op. cit., p. 204.
104. Cf. A. Tonness, 'A Notation on the Problem of the Past', op. cit., p. 600.
105. Cf. H. Blumer, 'A Note on Symbolic Interactionism', op. cit.
106. Cf. B. Geer, 'First Days in the Field', in P. Hammond (ed.), *Sociologists at Work*.
107. Private communication.
108. S. Bruyn, *The Human Perspective in Sociology*, p. 49.
109. Cf. A. Rose, 'A Research Note on Experimentation in Interviewing', *American Journal of Sociology*, LI 2 (Sept. 1945) p. 143.
110. Private communication.
111. H. Becker, 'Inference and Proof in Participant Observation', op. cit., p. 653.
112. M. Schwarz and C. Schwarz, 'Problems in Participant Observation', op. cit., p. 345.
113. E. Hughes, 'Introduction: The Place of Field Work in Social Science', in B. Junker, *Field Work*, p. xi.
114. W. Foote Whyte, 'Observational Field-Work Methods', op. cit., p. 510.
115. Cf. J. Lofland, *Analyzing Social Settings*, pp. 105—6.
116. Cf. S. Bruyn, *The Human Perspective in Sociology*, p. 38.
117. Cf. P. Rock, *Deviant Behaviour*, ch. 1.
118. H. Blumer, *Symbolic Interactionism*, p. 35.
119. A. Gouldner, 'Romanticism and Classicism: Deep Structures in Social Science', op. cit., p. 347.
120. W. Foote Whyte, 'Observational Field-Work Methods', op. cit., pp. 510—11.
121. J. Poincaré, *The Foundations of Science* (Science Press, New York, 1913).
122. J. Watson, *The Double Helix: A Personal Account of the Discovery of the Structure of DNA* (Atheneum, New York, 1968).

123. Ibid., p. 511.
124. H. Becker, 'The Culture of a Deviant Group', *American Journal of Sociology*, LVII (Sept. 1951).
125. J. Roth, *Timetables*.
126. N. Polsky, *Hustlers, Beats and Others*.
127. W. Foote Whyte, 'Observational Field-Work Methods', op. cit., p. 504.
128. H. Gans, *The Levittowners* (Pantheon Books, New York, 1967).
129. F. Kluckhohn, 'The Participant-Observer Technique in Small Communities', op. cit.
130. H. Farberman, 'A Criminogenic Market Structure: The Automobile Industry', *The Sociological Quarterly*, 16 (Autumn 1975) p. 440.
131. E. Liebow, *Tally's Corner*, (Little Brown, Boston, 1966) p. 233.
132. Cf. E. Goffman, 'Alienation from Interaction', in *Interaction Ritual* (Doubleday, Garden City, 1967).
133. Cf. R. Scott, 'Field Work in a Formal Organization', op. cit.
134. Friedrich indeed claimed that Weber also solved the problems of *Verstehen* by fiat. Cf. C. Friedrich, 'Some Observations on Weber's Analysis of Bureaucracy', in R. Merton *et al.* (eds), *Reader in Bureaucracy* (Free Press, Ill., 1952).
135. Private communication.
136. Thus Douglas stated 'the first thing a sociologist must do is be able to *do* social life.' J. Douglas, *Investigative Social Research*, p. 6–20.
137. E. Hughes, 'The Place of Field Work in Social Science', in *The Sociological Eye*, p. 498.
138. H. Gans, 'The Participant-Observer as a Human Being', op. cit., p. 301.

CHAPTER 7

1. R. Lichtman, 'Symbolic Interactionism and Social Reality: Some Marxist Queries', op. cit., p. 77.
2. A. Gouldner, *The Coming Crisis in Western Sociology*, p. 382.
3. D. Smith, 'Symbolic Interactionism: Definitions of the Situation from H. Becker and J. Lofland', *Catalyst*, (Winter 1973 7) p. 74.
4. B. Meltzer *et al.*, *Symbolic Interactionism*, p. 116.
5. H. Farberman; 'Symposium on Symbolic Interaction: An Introduction', *The Sociological Quarterly* (Autumn 1975 16) p. 435.
6. Cf. R. Aron, *Main Currents in Sociological Thought*, vol. 1 (Penguin Books, London, 1967).
7. Cf. E. Durkheim and M. Mauss, *Primitive Classification* (University of Chicago Press, Chicago, 1972).
8. Cf. K. Mannheim, *Ideology and Utopia*, (Harcourt, Brace, New York, 1936).
9. Cf. T. Adorno, 'The Sociology of Knowledge and its Consciousness', in *Prisms*.
10. Cf. B. Meltzer *et al.*, *Symbolic Interactionism*, p. 100ff.
11. Cf. J. Young, 'Working-Class Criminology', op. cit.
12. Cf. A. Gouldner, *The Coming Crisis in Western Sociology*.
13. Cf. R. Lichtman, 'Symbolic Interactionism and Social Reality', op. cit.
14. Cf. B. Meltzer *et al.*, *Symbolic Interactionism*, ch. 3.
15. Cf. A. Gouldner, *The Coming Crisis in Western Sociology*, p. 379.
16. Cf. J. Young, 'Working-Class Criminology', op. cit.
17. Cf. A. Gouldner, 'The Sociologist as Partisan', op. cit.

18. This is best illustrated in H. Becker and I. Horowitz, 'The Culture of Civility', *Transaction* (12–19 Apr. 1970).
19. B. Meltzer *et al.*, *Symbolic Interactionism*, p. 117.
20. Chauncey Wright, quoted in C. Wright Mills, *Sociology and Pragmatism*, p. 103.
21. Cf. E. Freidson, *Profession of Medicine*'(Dodd, Mead, New York, 1970) p. 211.
22. Thus Farberman mapped the pressures which forced the occupants of different social worlds to engage in law-breaking. Used car sales were affected by policies adopted by the sellers of new cars and by the willingness of purchasers to collude in tax evasion. Those sellers, in turn, were constrained to engage in deviant practices because of the measures taken by the large manufacturers. A chain of processes is thus charted in a way that locks four groups together. It is a chain which has structural properties, but it would be a little inflated to call it a social structure in the sense usually intended by the sociologist. Cf. H. Farberman, 'A Criminogenic Market Structure: The Automobile Industry', op. cit.
23. For a complementary argument, Cf. R. Dahrendorf, 'Out of Utopia: Towards a Re-Orientation of Sociological Analysis', *American Journal of Sociology*, 64 (1958).
24. Cf. G. Hawthorn, *Enlightenment and Despair*, p. 112.
25. B. Meltzer *et al.*, *Symbolic Interactionism*, p. 120.
26. J. Huber, 'Symbolic Interactionism as a Pragmatic Perspective', op. cit., p. 282.
27. H. Zinsser, *Rats, Lice and History* (Bantam, New York, 1971) p. 25.
28. Cf. M. Davis, 'That's Interesting! Towards a Phenomenology of Sociology and a Sociology of Phenomenology', *Philosophy of the Social Sciences*, 14 (Dec. 1971).

Index

absolutes, 31, 153
acts, 69
ad hominem criticisms, 217, 223
Adorno, T., 29, 185, 222
alienation, 31, 219
  and formalism, 42
  and interactionism, 56–7
  and Idealism, 61, 63
  and pragmatism, 67, 69, 104
  and analysis, 71
  and the self, 126
Althusser, L., 234
analytic induction, 91
Anderson, N., 83, 94
anti-intellectualism, 53, 59, 75, 79
Aron, R., 220
artlessness, 198, 214
Auld, J., 56

Baldwin, J., 123
Becker, H., 3, 4, 6, 11, 27, 51, 56, 80, 81, 83, 88, 90–1, 101, 117, 134, 157, 172, 183, 190, 201, 209, 214, 215, 223
Berger, P., 141, 193, 204
Bergson, H., 42, 159
biography, 125
biological matrix, 66
Blumer, H., 6, 9, 20, 23, 26, 51, 131, 152, 174, 182, 186, 192, 194, 212
Borgatta, E., 182
Broom, L., 6
Bruyn, S., 21, 82, 92, 173, 176, 184, 187, 209, 212
Burgess, E., 6, 47, 53
Burke, K., 52, 212

career, 56, 136, 155, 205
causality, 55, 153
character, 119–20
Cicourel, A., 48
Cohen, S., 17
common sense, 89, 226, 232
comparative analysis, 175
conflict, 142

conjunctive thought, 11, 26–7, 108
constitutive analysis, 158
contingency, 155
Cooley, C., 65, 66, 82, 99, 100, 107, 111, 114, 118, 152, 153, 167, 191, 227
Cressey, D., 79, 100
Cressey, P., 79
Crick, F., 214

Dalton, M., 22, 184, 197
Darwin, C., 59, 65, 66
Davis, F., 27, 203
Davis, M., 231
definition of the situation, 83
Denzin, N., 54, 82, 174
deviance, 57
Dewey, J., 5, 48, 60, 64, 93, 100, 148, 158, 194, 231
  and evolutionism, 66
  and experience, 67–8
  and spectator theory, 69
  and praxis, 70
  and formal logic, 73
  and definition of society, 77
  and deductive logic, 88
  disowned by W. Thomas, 99
dialectics, 57, 63, 104, 210
dirty work, 141
Douglas, D., 203
Douglas, J., 84, 182, 191, 197
dramaturgy, 50, 170
drug-taking, 164
durée, 42
Durkheim, E., 29, 47, 141, 220, 234
Duster, T., 120

ecology, 7, 50, 93
eidetic reduction, 160
emergence, 8, 55, 199
  and pragmatism, 66
  and practical knowledge, 70, 194
  and interactionism, 86, 183
empiricism, 62
Erikson, K., 17, 141, 198

Index

ethnography, 53, 79, 92
ethnomethodology, 17, 173
ethology, 17, 50
evolutionism, 66, 75
exchange theory, 17

face-work, 127
Farberman, H., 78, 157, 208, 215, 219
Faris, E., 26, 97, 152
feedback, 209
Finestone, H., 142
Foote, N., 121
formalism, 24, 28, 36, 44, 48, 55, 85, 93, 96
forms,
  and content, 39
  and synthetic *a priori*, 40, 51
  as system, 42, 50
  and autonomisation, 42
  in ecology, 93
  reified by Park, 97
Freidson, E., 7

Gans, H., 201, 214, 215
Garfinkel, H., 165, 171
Geer, B., 157
Gellner, E., 176
generalised other, 143
Glaser, B., and Strauss, A., 20, 51, 96
Goffman, E., 7, 17, 27, 50, 51, 56, 127, 135, 155, 164, 170, 172, 177, 184, 211
going native, 196, 200
Gold, D., 7
Gold, R., 196, 204
Goldmann, L., 29, 189
Gouldner, A., 15, 77, 78, 171, 212, 219, 223

Habenstein, R., 142
Hegel, G., 28, 59, 60, 62, 64, 188
Hook, S., 67
Huber, J., 12, 25, 230
Hughes, E., 6, 20, 47, 51, 53, 90, 99, 139, 141, 175, 211, 216
Hume, D., 32
Humphreys, L., 183, 203, 214

'I', 103, 104, 116–18, 149
ideal forms, 134
idealism, 61, 151, 167, 187, 192
immediacy, 69, 75, 81, 106, 107, 196
immigration, 95
incompetence, 199
indeterminacy, 70, 154, 190, 193
institutions, 131
invidious labelling, 171, 176

'Iowa School', 192

James, W., 48, 60, 64, 67, 96
  and evolutionism, 66
  and immediacy, 70, 72
  and Absolutism, 77
  and knowledge, 88
  and mind, 98
  and the self, 103, 118
Janowitz, M., 49

Kant, I., 24, 28, 31, 59
Klapp, O., 120
Kluckhohn, F., 187, 214
knowledge,
  as practice, 8, 67, 69
  'spectator theory', 65, 67
  as process, 69, 70, 105
  as stratified, 70
  and ineffability, 70
  bifurcated, 73, 88
  as self, 74
Kornhauser, W., 7
Kuhn, M., 25
Kuhn, T., 11
Kwant, R., 89

Lafferty, T., 142, 193, 208
language,
  and self, 75, 111, 113
  and emancipation, 111
  and objectification, 112
  as autonomous form, 115
Lemert, E., 27, 57, 155
Levi-Strauss, C., 220
Lichtheim, G., 61, 189
Lichtman, R., 219
Liebow, E., 215
life history, 80
Lofland, J., 16, 57, 89
'looking-glass self', 111
Luckmann, T., 146
Lukács, G., 19, 29, 63, 189

macrosociology, 221
Mannheim, K., 11, 29, 63, 86, 185, 222, 229
Manning, P., 171, 201
marginality, 200, 211
Marx, K., 29, 47, 187, 220, 229
Matza, D., 22, 51, 57, 79, 94, 153, 159, 172
Mayhew, H., 94
'me', 120, 124, 125
Mead, G., 5, 26, 60, 65, 92, 103, 148, 149, 150, 156, 163, 166

and pragmatism, 66, 75
and thought, 75, 104, 107
and anti-intellectualism, 75
and Cooley, 99
and significant gesture, 109, 118
and language, 111
and the 'I', 119
and time, 125
meaning, 157
Meltzer, B., 193, 219, 220, 225, 230
memory, 163
Merten, D., 187
Merton, R., 19
methodology, 20, 181, 193
'Middletown', 204
Miller, D., 144
Miller, S., 201
mind,
    as dualistic, 103
    as dialectical, 104
    and nature, 104
    as objective, 104
    and ineffability, 107
    as ideal-type, 152
    as disembodied, 168
'more-life' and 'more-than-life', 42, 55, 56
Morris, C., 68, 76, 103, 120
motives, 122

natural areas, 92
natural history, 80
nature, 76, 191
Niederhoffer, A., 138
normal science, 4, 11
noumenon, 33, 61, 160

Ogburn, W., 6
oral tradition, 5, 25, 45
organism, 149, 162

paradox, 22, 88, 211
Park, R., 5, 47, 53, 56, 91, 92, 96, 97, 99, 235
participant-observation, 76, 81, 84, 178
Peirce, C., xii, 68, 114, 117
Perinbanayagam, R., 103
Petras, J., 28
phenomena, 33, 37, 41
phenomenalism, 57, 60, 181, 186–7, 189, 192, 197, 209, 218, 219
phenomenology, 35, 160
Plummer, K., xiii, 8
pluralistic realism, 70, 106, 208, 232
Poincaré, H., 213, 229
politics, 10, 224

Polsky, N., 183, 214
positivism, 35
Poulantzas, N., 234
power, 133
pragmatism, 28, 59
    and Hegel, 64
    and Idealism, 65
    and logic, 72
    as provisional, 74
    and the self, 74
    and interactionism, 77
    and self-repudiation, 79, 96
    limitations, 85
    reversed, 96
praxis, 178
prereflexive experience, 107, 194, 213
presuppositionless stance, 16
Psathas, G., 160

radical criminology, 18
rationality, 161, 164, 166, 197, 223
reflex arc, 67
reflexivity, 75
Reiss, A., 191, 200
residual rule-breaking, 131
Reynolds, L., 6, 193
role-distance, 135
romanticism, 15, 213
Rose, A., 92, 142, 150, 195
Roth, J., 214
Royce, J., 65

Sapir, E., 5
Scheff, T., 17, 57, 100, 131
Schmitt, R., 12
Schur, E., 177
Schutz, A., 35, 85, 154, 159
Schwartz, G., 187
Schwarz, C., 191
Schwarz, M., 191
Scott, R., 162
Scott, W., 205
self,
    as organic unity, 69
    as knowledge, 74
    as problematic, 74
    and language, 75, 111, 114
    as analytic centre, 79, 81, 102
    and participant observation, 81
    discussed, 102ff.
    as thought, 103
    and prereflexive knowledge, 106
    its ambiguity, 116, 148
    as a form, 117

self (contd)
  as inference, 117
  as cartoon, 122
  as imitative creation, 123
  and affirmation, 127
  as undifferentiated, 147
  disembodied, 151
sensitising concepts, 9, 87
Shaskolsky, L., 95
Shibutani, T., 17
Short, J., 7
significant gestures, 109, 118
Simmel, G., 24, 27, 85, 96, 117, 130, 131, 169, 202, 218
situations, 71, 82
Skolnick, J., 203
Small, A., xii, 46
Smith, A., 180
Smith, D., 219
social class, 140, 228
social statics, 49
social structure, 48, 78, 90, 93, 95, 131, 171, 219, 228
society, 78
sociology of deviance, 15, 57, 58, 97, 156, 212, 223
sociology of knowledge, 222
Spencer, H., 47
Stark, W., 223
status passage, 137
stigma, 163
Stone, G., 19, 78, 157, 208
Strauss, A., 21, 27, 87, 114, 135, 138
subjective experience, 148
subject-object, 61, 63, 68, 80, 82, 103, 187, 191, 194, 200
Sutherland, E., 79
symbiosis, 141
symbolic coalescence, 141
symbolic interactionism,
  in Britain, x
  and praxis, 3
  difficulties of exposition, 3
  and normal science, 4
  and teaching, 8

  and vulgarisation, 9
  as a craft, 10, 99
  and orthodoxy, 17
  named, 26
  and formalism, 44
  and 'authenticity', 51
  as emergent sociology, 86
  and disorderliness, 87
  and orthodox sociology, 91
  and ethnography, 92
symbolic interactionists, 6, 98
synthetic *a priori*, 33, 62

Taylor, L., 100, 162
Thomas, W., 5, 50, 80, 83, 99, 154
Thomas W., and Znaniecki, F., 54, 56
timetables, 137
Tonnes, A., 126
Tönnies, F., 47
trust in fieldwork, 202
Truzzi, M., 173
Turner, R., 122

Uniqueness, 83
University of Chicago, 5, 92

verstehen, 148, 156, 165, 215
Vidich, A., 190, 200
Von Wiese, L., 44

Warming, E., 95
Warner, L., 6
Weber, M., 30, 47, 218
Weinberg, K., 17
Weinberg, M., 199, 206
Whyte, W., 198, 211, 213, 214
Williams, C., 199, 206
Wirth, L., 50, 54
withdrawal and return, 202, 212

Young, J., 142, 162

Zaner, R., 166
Zinsser, H., 231
Znaniecki, F., 48, 111, 183